Marketing and Client Relations

FOR INTERIOR DESIGNERS

Marketing and Client Relations

FOR INTERIOR DESIGNERS

Mary V. Knackstedt, FASID, FIIDA

WILEY

John Wiley & Sons, Inc.

For general information about our other products and services, please contact our
Customer Care Department within the United States at (800) 762-2974, outside the
United States at (317) 572-3993 or fax (317) 572-4002.

Wiley also publishes its books in a variety of electronic formats. Some content that appears
in print may not be available in electronic books. For more information about Wiley
products, visit our web site at www.wiley.com.

Library of Congress Cataloging-in-Publication Data:

ISBN: 978-0470-26048-7

Printed in the United States of America

10 9 8 7 6 5 4 3 2 1

This book is dedicated to the many designers I've had the privilege of working with who have seen through their actions that these systems do work and have great power. Designers keep coming to me and saying: We want a certain type of work from a quality client; how do we develop our practices?

Their comments are the reason for this book. I thank the many designers who have worked with me to raise the quality of the interior design profession. We know that together we can do exceptional work for our clients. We can offer them both lifestyles and work styles that are incredibly enhanced through the profession of interior design.

Contents

Preface

There is no easy way, no quick fix, for building and maintaining a quality relationship. Designer-client relationships are the same. However, there are procedures and systems that have been tried and proved effective.

This book presents many of them.

They are all formulated with the position of the designer as the key.

After all, we are not the same as our clients. We don't want to be, and they don't want us to be. But we do need to realize that we have the ability and the need to build strong relationships with people of many different orientations.

Psychologists have shown us many methods for directing our communication efforts so they are understood by people who think differently from ourselves. This book is based on simple, easy processes that are constantly at work building and enriching that relationship that bonds a "best" client with a "best" designer.

This kind of relationship is based on teamwork with clients sitting on their side of the table, working with them. They buy—we don't sell. The relationship is cooperative, helpful, sensitive. It has many variables. We must keep the structure for this freedom so that we can accomplish our objectives. Every form or process is created to keep us on track so that we are constantly aware of mutual goals.

This book will give you pointers and details that will help to develop your expertise and help you to relate to the client—the essence of any design practice. It addresses the particular needs of the design discipline, calling on the talents, abilities, and tools available to a design firm.

The marketing and communication procedures and processes described here are designed to complement the practice of interior design. They call on talents and abilities you already have. They take a proactive approach, which turns everyday issues into marketing and sales development opportunities.

As you review and plan your company's strategy, consider and concentrate on:

- Responding to clients—their needs, desires, and wants. They are our partners—they come first.
- Using your resources, staff, and sources with respect and care.

- Creating opportunities that use the best products in the correct places.
- Giving talented staff the opportunity to grow and develop; creativity grows and blossoms with success.
- Completing projects as efficiently as you can. We must respect both our own and our clients' time. Have new and exciting items, and use good-quality procedures and skilled craftspeople to execute your design efforts. Be sure schedules fit the clients.

This book is important for large firms. The best-functioning large firms today operate as if they're small firms. They're very personally involved with their clients and have the same type of designer-client relationship that a small, very personal company would have.

This book is important for small firms. Small companies are now functioning like large firms. Technology and virtual relationships allow an individual to operate in any location in the world today and service clients very directly and efficiently.

From their perspective, clients want both small and large firms to operate identically.

Acknowledgments

To the many designers who have encouraged or "forced" me to find systems that work.

To Amanda Miller and John Czarnecki at John Wiley & Sons, who have encouraged me to write this and the other books I've written.

Most of all, to my staff and immediate group: Allison Stewart—who has typed and typed and typed. With her fresh design attitude, Allison has questioned and commented on many issues in the book. Barbara Trainin Blank—for her excellent editing and her contribution in the News Release section, since this is her profession.

And to the many others whose comments are throughout this book.

Effective Marketing Strategies

CHAPTER 1

Positioning Your Firm

Design firms constantly need to think about how they present themselves. Presentation is the basis for business development. We talk about this in the form of marketing and selling design services. Marketing comprises all the activities that build the relationship between the designer and client, including product development, research, and promotion. Selling is a process of educating and communicating directly with potential buyers. It begins when you attract their attention and continues through developing their interest and giving them the information that helps them evaluate the decision. It ends with the commitment.

Just as McDonald's learned to sell hamburgers and hospitals learned to sell medicine, interior designers need to learn to market and present design services. Many designers have a built-in aversion to selling. The word has so many negative connotations. I don't want to sell or to persuade. I want to educate and communicate with clients to help them make informed choices.

Designers need to develop techniques of communicating effectively with the particular client group they seek. The firm that knows both how to market and how to communicate is most likely to get the business. Clients sometimes call us about a project for purely emotional reasons. They may want a more inspiring environment, or they may have specific design problems to solve. Either way, they consider their issues critical.

3

A designer's business is to solve problems that the client cannot or does not want to solve alone. It is the designer's job to identify the problem, and through technical skill and expertise, demonstrate an ability to solve problems. To sell their services, interior designers must show that they are businesspeople who understand construction, scheduling, and budgets.

It is up to the designer to educate the consumer through marketing. Only an informed consumer can differentiate between partial service and full service, unqualified and qualified designers. Designers like to believe that they can rely on referrals as their major marketing tool. But any informed firm knows that this is no longer enough. Established firms can lose jobs to inexperienced newcomers to the field who have sophisticated techniques to market their design skills.

In order to be effective, market development must be a highly systematized, structured process, with exact schedules, measurements, and reviews of each part of the process—from defining your market and making the first contact, through writing proposals into production and follow-up.

The purpose of the marketing plan is to help your firm focus directly on the type of work that is most appropriate and profitable for it. The marketing plan is also designed to help you understand who you are, what you really want, and how to attain your goals. After all, as a designer, you want to create your own destiny. You don't want to sit there and wait for something to happen; chances are that what happens won't be right. You want to design your firm to enhance your chances for success. Obtaining the wrong business doesn't really develop a design studio; it can only destroy it.

What does it really take to devise a program that is profitable and directly related to securing the appropriate business for your firm?

First, what projects are appropriate? A big part of marketing is defining what type of work is best for your firm and refining that definition as your market changes. You need to think about who you are. You need to analyze your values, systems, mission, and exactly where you want to be.

You must look at who your clients are. Any good program is a partnership or marriage between a client and a firm with capabilities that complement the client's needs. It is a mistake to place your entire emphasis on existing or prospective clients and overlook in-house capabilities.

Building Your Definition

In the design field, each of us comes from a different background, a different school, a different part of the country. We have aptitudes in many varied areas. Some of us are involved with very technical work and very detailed contract specifications. Others are doing highly inventive work. Each of these different design disciplines has its own management requirements. Each specialty has its own vocabulary, so the process must be designed to meet its requirements.

Your marketing plan helps you set a direction. It is essential to approaching the right kind of client. It also helps you to minimize day-to-day problems. If you are going in 74 directions, you cannot be effective or achieve professional results. You—and everyone who works with you—need to understand your goals and where you are going, in order to work in the same direction. Mutual understanding will eliminate a good deal of confusion. Directed firms don't waste as much time with crisis management.

With a proactive, progressive approach, you spend time directing and staying on track, and therefore you achieve greater results. You are also able to maximize your own potential. In some instances, this progressive approach may require a firm to alter its qualifications and, to some extent, retrain the staff or team with other specialists. You know what the needs are. You've explored them with your clients and reviewed the current market. You've looked at what other design firms and specialists are doing. You really have an understanding of the demands of today's market.

The most effective way to achieve your goals is to create a MAP (Multiple Action Plan). Figure out where you want to be and decide on the best ways to get there. As you work on your marketing plan, it is important to focus on your abilities and resources, to consider how you can relate to your clients, and to offer the best possible product. Today our clients want exceptional design. Having the ability to do exceptional work efficiently with appropriate prices is the key to building a client base.

For a marketing plan to be valuable, dedication and a regular schedule are required. You must act consistently, not just when business is poor, to obtain the results you want. This is the benefit of a good marketing plan: It provides your firm with opportunities—opportunities that would not exist otherwise. It gives you the chance to create your future.

A marketing plan takes both management and leadership. Every person in the firm, starting with the CEO, must be dedicated to this plan. In addition, someone must manage the plan's direction to make sure that every phone call, networking system, meeting, and whatever bridging systems you use are accomplished. Each person in the firm must be involved, but someone must be responsible for managing the process.

You need a specific structure to ensure that your firm operates productively. Building a client base requires consistency. Be sure you are able to fulfill any commitments you make; otherwise, you will neither be able to build your clients' trust nor make these marketing systems work. Select your actors, and direct their roles with flair.

BASED ON WHAT THE CLIENTS NEED & WANT TO PURCHASE

Successful Design Firms

Today's successful firms are very heavily market driven. They are based on what the clients need and want to purchase. Those firms understand exactly how their clients perceive them and how the firms, in turn, perceive their needs. Design firms that spend time researching and developing clients find it easier to obtain, produce, and complete projects. A great deal of time is invested in this process, and it pays off a hundredfold.

Take into account that it costs you nine times as much to attract a new client as it does to retain an existing one. A client who has worked with you before knows your firm, knows your strengths, and knows exactly how to work with you. You stand a greater chance of winning a good, profitable job from an existing client than from a new one.

Very few firms can operate up to capacity without a marketing program. You need an ongoing program, most likely led by the chief executive officer, especially in the smaller firms. The leader must see this as his or her most important job and be ready to dedicate whatever it takes to make the program work. If you work alone, and many of us do, you need to dedicate a portion of your time each week to marketing. For example, you may simply set aside two hours each morning for working on the marketing program before attending to anything else. If your firm is large enough, you may be able to assign the day-to-day management of the program to someone else.

Consider the current trends. We are in a very competitive period, a period when even the best-known design firms must invest in sales development to maintain their shares of the market. Projects are awarded to firms that have something exceptional to offer. They must also have the ability to handle the needs of the client. They must understand their clients' needs and be willing to be part of their teams.

The goal is to build long-term relationships with clients who appreciate our work. This requires a special type of staff that understands it is strategic to be client-oriented. Every staff member, vendor, and craftsperson working on a client's project must realize that maintaining a good relationship is critical. We expect to be with these clients as long as they have any type of design needs. We become part of their company or family. This type of relationship leads to great opportunities for high-level work, as well as a profitable practice. It's less expensive to keep our clients happy than to get new ones.

Let's look at who needs what we are able to provide. Not everyone needs or wants our services, in which case we'd better find another client. Who is looking for what we have? Who is making changes? What are the geographic limitations for managing the type of work we do best? What production methods and details should be considered? You must answer these questions before defining the "best" client.

Success in this marketplace calls for ability, understanding, planning, and maintenance.

1. who is looking for what we have
2. who is making changes
3. geographic limitations
4. what production methods need to be considered

Interior designers need basic technical ability, backed up by good resources and staff who know how to complete a job successfully without too many problems.

We must understand our market, our clients. What are they all about? What are their particular likes, desires, and interests? What do they want from us?

We must have a method of bridging, of building a link between our firm and our clients. Once built, the link needs constant maintenance. We must adhere to a consistent schedule for client contact so that we see them eye to eye, person to person as often as possible. Clients don't want distant design experts today; they want designers who understand their special needs and are ready to respond.

The reasons for buying architecture, engineering, and all areas of design services have changed considerably. Today's clients look for a firm that can produce a creative job. It is of utmost importance that the firm has the ability to complete the job using great craftspeople and artistry, within the expected budget and time. Budgets on large projects can often be based on a percentage of business completed. There are many different financial ways of coming up with these numbers. The designer selected may be the one who is able to perform best within that budget. At other times, projects have unlimited budgets. Design professionals may be asked to team up with other contractors to provide the owner with a single contract for a complete project.

Our success as designers isn't simply based on how creative we are, but on how well we understand our clients' professional or personal requirements and whether we can deliver this highly technical knowledge. It isn't just the beauty of the design that matters, but how efficiently and economically we can deliver it.

Most clients like to hire someone that they feel they know and trust; the investment is heavy, and the project is important to them. Building that rapport and developing that communication system with the client is very important; it must start long before that job is awarded.

You have to understand your abilities as a design team, including the production abilities of your sources. You must research and define the best client group for your firm, then specifically select that target group and develop a bridging system. Many of these systems are presented in the section on bridging techniques—including advertising and promotion, networking, and other ways of acquainting yourself with these people and creating a bridge between the right firm and the right client.

I think you can see that building your marketing program doesn't stop when you win the project. It continues throughout the job in the way you present yourself, the way staff members relate to clients, and how well they do their jobs. The paper hanger out on your project is either enhancing your firm's reputation or destroying your job.

There are many ways to develop your lifestyle to complement your marketing program. Everything you do, from where and how you live, to your hobbies and where you do your grocery shopping, affects your position as a designer.

Focus Your Market

Focusing on a particular segment of the overall market improves a firm's chances for positioning and success; this way the firm can concentrate on identifying and acquiring the best clients and using its talents to the greatest potential. For instance, have you thought about what your firm will need in terms of outside human and material resources, consultants, other professionals, and products?

Focusing increases efficiency: Once you know where you're going, you can direct your energies accordingly, making your firm better able to compete for work that might not have been attainable previously. The commitment to competitiveness is stimulating—the staff reaps greater rewards.

Marketing efforts are expensive, both in time invested and money spent. To limit the costs of your marketing efforts, confine your market area to those individuals or organizations that need what your firm can provide.

Success

Success in business is based on:

1. The client. Today's clients come first. They want what they want. If you can't do it, there are plenty of others out there who will. Today's clients are also very knowledgeable. They have extensive and global resources, often reaching information sources faster than the designer. On the whole we're dealing with a very educated and interested group of people. They want what we offer, but they also expect us to consider their input as well. Our field is ever so transparent.
2. Communication ability. Most of the ability to develop your position in a company depends on your ability to communicate. Often it is the simple, everyday issues such as a lack of clear communication that build or destroy a job. Sometimes we forget or just don't think these small things are noticed. They, like housework, are most noticeable in their absence.
3. Teamwork. We cannot work alone and accomplish the masterful level of design work we all desire. We must be able to build an appropriate team to complete the job. This takes many levels of experience. It also requires consideration and an understanding of the team's various crafts and disciplines. The interior designer is

the design coordinator. Like an orchestra leader, we must be sure everyone is playing the same music.

4. Speed. Today most clients expect results fast. They see things delivered within several hours; therefore, they expect us to be able to do the same. This is possible in many situations. But if a project is going to take an extensive period of time, we must be able to explain to the clients why this time investment is required, so they'll be willing to wait.

5. Change. This is the only thing you can count on. Fortunately, interior design is based on change. Each part of your work and career will be constantly in the process of redesign. Fortunately, we were trained for this. This is part of the character of interior design.

Before you begin your marketing plan, it's important to define carefully what you want your company to be and what its demands are (Figure 1-1). An independent practitioner with very low overhead can accept quite-different jobs than a large firm with a considerable overhead. Designers often select their work systems not by choice but by the type of jobs they want to acquire. In some instances, designers are working alone, teaming virtually with other high-level professionals, so they have the flexibility to take on very creative jobs at a high level in a practical fashion. They can have the flexibility to be creative and move on to other more unusual projects. In other cases, companies establish a structure that permits them to service particular types of clients quickly and efficiently. Before you begin your marketing plan, look at what you want your business to be. What is the basis of your income? What type of services do you produce? Define your type of clients and projects, the staff needed, other professionals required, and the income expected. What do you consider success?

What I Want Our Business to Be

1. Our income is accomplished by providing these services
2. Type of projects
3. Our clients are
4. Staff, consultants, vendors, craftspeople
5. Income expected
6. Success is

Figure 1-1

A marketing plan begins with the aim of our practice, exactly what we do. What are our past accomplishments? What makes our firm different from other firms? What do we really do with excellence?

What do we want to do within the next three years? It's almost impossible to plan for a longer period of time, but in order to keep challenged and excited, we need a projected design goal. We need to know what our company aims to do and can accomplish in the next few years.

The next issue is geographic. In a very detailed residential practice, it's often desirable to work with a team. Therefore, it's more practical to work within a certain distance. The distance may vary depending on your location and type of services.

The next consideration is the size and type of projects. In this situation, you will want to consider the projects that are most profitable. Sometimes a large project can take so long it can prove too expensive to manage. More medium-sized projects can turn over more quickly and be easier to manage; therefore, they may be more financially profitable.

Last of all, if we reach our goals in three years, what will we be doing? How do you visualize your firm? What do you hope to accomplish?

You can use the following example as a reference (Figure 1-2).

AIM OF OUR PRACTICE	Hospitality	Health/Medical	Residential
WHAT WE DO	Design and specify only; design and supply parts	Turnkey (complete job)	Research, design, specify detail, secure items needs, supervise the process
OUR ACCOMPLISHMENTS	Leader in hospitality	Great experience in nursing homes	Historic restoration
WORK THAT IS APPROPRIATE TO OUR FIRM WITHIN THE NEXT 3 YEARS	Expand to other countries; hotel chains	Retirement centers with rehabilitation, assisted living	Work with finer artists and master craftspeople
PRACTICAL GEOGRAPHIC RANGE TO WORK	Worldwide	Within 200 miles	Within 100 miles
TYPICAL-SIZED PROJECTS	$5 million to $1 billion	$100 million to $500 million	$1 million+
IF WE REACH OUR GOALS IN NEXT 3 YEARS, WE WILL BE DOING	Exceptional high levels, varied hotel owners	Projects for resort-type residences for aging	High budget with antiques of special quality; publishable work

Figure 1-2 Examples of three different types of firms.

CHAPTER 2

The Marketing Plan

The question always is: Where do we start? We start with looking at a firm's abilities and at what a designer sees as the firm's best accomplishments. The interior design profession is very broad; we can't do everything, nor do we want to. We need to select our best qualities so we can contribute the most to the present-day market.

This chapter will help you understand better who you are and where you are going. This is definitely the starting point. You will find as you go through the book that you'll want to incorporate many of the other techniques and processes as part of your marketing plan. But this is where you start.

Goals

- Have the kind of work we do best.
- Have the right clients.
- Have consistent work throughout the year, or at least fewer highs and lows.
- Increase our market shares.
- Increase profits so we can properly compensate our staff and acquire the tools we need to develop and expand.

Aim

To accomplish your goals, *yours*, and not someone else's; own your career.

- Learn from others. They know how they want to be treated.
- Demonstrate sincere caring. This is worth more than anything you can buy.
- Help your clients realize their great potential through appropriate interior design. Make them look great.
- Realize the excitement of knowledge. Study and learn. Improvement and success start with ability. Today this takes constant training.
- Take the time necessary to build the proper relationships with clients. Only the right relationships will give you the basis for doing the right job.

Our consultants, sources, and craftspeople are what make us. Without them, we cannot do interior design.

Fortunately, you learned enough in school to get a job in design. Keeping that job depends on what you continue to learn from your present teachers, clients, consultants, sources, and craftspeople.

Commit to what it takes to create and carry out a successful marketing plan. You will need to define, on paper:

1. Your mission
2. Objectives
3. Values statement
4. Company's goals—results you want
5. Budget
6. Company profile—internal
   a. Staff experience and background
   b. Specialty
   c. Experience: past projects
   d. Past revenue sources
   e. Product: Define what it is that you have to sell.
   f. Strengths and weaknesses
   g. Sales force
   h. Income profile—past revenues and current expenses compared to the current market
7. The Marketplace—external
   a. Client profiles, current and potential
   b. Geographic limits
   c. Prospect list
   d. Resources: suppliers, crafts, and trades
   e. Competition
   f. Economic conditions
   g. Social and cultural trends
   h. Legal, governmental, and regulatory forces
   i. Technological issues
8. Market research
9. Compare your company profile and the market of potential clients. Define your best client.

10. Create a bridge between your firm and the best client.
11. Select a leader and a manager.
12. Create a map, a plan to make this happen.
13. Prepare needed materials.
14. Make it happen.
15. Measure results; make changes as needed.

Budget

Good market development requires that you invest in promotional tools. How much should a public relations and marketing program cost? A minimum of three to five percent of your gross income, not gross sales.

If you're employed by a large practice that has its own budget for promotion, you should still dedicate five to ten percent of your gross income to promoting your career. There may be projects you have done that demonstrate your abilities. For instance, you may have done an outstanding dental office project. The firm may choose not to photograph this project even though the work was excellent, because its interests are not in attracting more dental office business. You need to put money aside so that you can photograph your own work.

You may see an area of specialization you're interested in. An investment in specialized education in that area would add to your abilities and give you the opportunity to lead a project in the future.

Your Mission Statement

A mission statement is basically a goal with a deadline. It's the foundation of your marketing plan.

Designers are often told they are dreamers. As designers we know that dreaming is the first part of any accomplishment. The question is, how does this dream become a realizable mission, an achievable goal? As designers we can continue to survive, but surviving is not the highest level of creativity. The goal is to put your firm in a position that allows you to do truly creative work, and to take some of that creative passion and put it into practice.

To figure out where you want to be, decide who your heroes are. What can you learn from them? What are you aiming for? There are many really beautifully designed interior spaces—some that we admire. How were these accomplished?

Build on what you admire, set yourself a goal, write your mission statement, and take steps to accomplish it. This mission must coordinate the demands of your lifestyle with those of your business.

Your mission very strongly directs how you conduct yourself through-out your business career. As you write and develop your mission statement, consider how it will affect the way you live, both as a designer and personally.

The mission directs the activities of your firm's efforts. By clearly defining the objectives of your practice, you establish what is needed to accomplish your mission. The mission states the aim of our practices— our basic orientation. This must be specifically defined in order to know how and where to position the firm within the market.

Your mission statement must be written down, and you will most likely change it many times until you get it just right. Your mission statement is not that you simply want to earn a living.

Define your business and its unique position in the design field. How are you different and superior? What are your competitive advantages?

You need to develop a focus. A major problem of many interior design firms is a lack of focus. Too many firms are willing to take any type of work that comes along because it's interesting. That does not lead to a profitable business. Review the work you have done, consider your abilities, and then decide what is worth focusing on. What can you do that will retain your interest for a long time? What are you excited about doing?

The answer to these questions should be your specialty. And, if you are willing to take the energy to specialize, you will also become an expert in your field. You will be working with it every single day; soon you will know where all the problems are long before they occur, because this is your interest; this is your focus. Many designers refuse to do projects in which they don't have some jurisdiction over the standards of the products and the craftspeople working on them. They want to be sure all of the standards they have created in their design are carried through in the final project.

Values

The next statement you need is your value statement. For example, most designers will not undertake any work that does not adhere to the building codes of the state in which they live and work. Although certain International Code Council (ICC) codes may not be required in the area, the design firms may believe that they are important and will be required eventually. Therefore, these firms designs must meet those additional codes; they feel morally responsible to meet those standards.

Values change throughout the years. At this time, there are many designers who are interested in green design and will not consider doing a project that doesn't meet environmental standards. We have been looking at buildings that are aiming to be zero energy buildings (ZEBs), which makes sense at a time when we're so concerned about the cost of utilities. Other designers love to use fine antiques and don't want to use any reproductions, because their standard is only a certain level of antiquity. Our values come from so many parts of our lives, not just our profession. They're often personal. Some people refuse to work with anyone who doesn't have certain ethical and moral standards, even though the income may be tremendous. You need to consider your values and see how they fit into your work. We're never happy if we're working under circumstances that don't meet our basic standards.

Do What You Love

It's important to be excited about a project. We feel so much better when we're working on a project that's very creative in which clients and everyone involved share the excitement. A spirit of excitement also generates a much better project. Review what it takes to do the job, and be sure you've covered all the requirements. Be sure this job is something you can handle—at least eighty percent of it—with great skill. It's easy to bring in consultants and others to share the other twenty percent, but it's almost impossible to do something just because it's exciting when we don't really understand the parameters of the project.

What do you really care about? After years in the field, you may be tired of certain kinds of projects. Regardless of who the client is, you won't be able to do your best because you can't put in the effort the project requires and deserves. So review the project carefully to see whether you really care about it.

> Do you like the client?
> Are you interested in improving his or her situation?
> Does the project have a purpose?
> What is the most important part of the project?
> Does the subject interest you? Are you excited to learn more about it?
> Do you want to invest time in this particular specialty?
> Don't underestimate the importance of being excited about your work.
> Creativity is exciting, stimulating, and keeps you healthy.

How Great Do You Want Your Practice to Be?

A great firm is developed; it doesn't just happen. It's developed by people who are looking at ordinary, everyday issues and trying to find just one small way of making them better. You can't make one item a hundred percent better, but you can improve a hundred different items by just one to three percent.

Look at your practice every day and ask yourself what you can do to improve it. If you can afford to improve it, make it happen. Giving your clients the best possible service is how you build and maintain a practice.

If you give your best daily, your practice won't require major changes or revamping. It will gradually grow and progress with the need and direction of the field.

The clients will see you're great. They'll keep coming back to you because they are attracted to what you do. There's some special aura about your practice. This is a practice that enhances their work or private lives. They really enjoy being around you; they're comfortable in investing with you. This gives them the confidence to invest in the better-quality products that your work requires.

CHAPTER 3

Objectives

What are your objectives? Do you want to produce a high-quality project at a reasonable price? Perhaps your objective is to give the best quality of design within a particular specialty. A designer who specializes in penal institutions or public spaces has different objectives from one whose work appeals to personally emotional spaces, such as residential work or some types of marketing and executive spaces.

The basic objective is to practice the discipline of interior design while earning an appropriate income to support yourself and to meet the expenses of staff and office. Beyond that, you may believe that your design work can improve the quality of people's lives. Is your objective to present a specific design style? To enrich people's lives? To brand their firm? To solve space problems?

One of your key objectives should be a deep commitment to communicating the opportunities of design through the process of marketing and to build a relationship with a potential buyer.

There are usually two major reasons for any marketing program. One is to develop a higher profit within your projects. Second, you want to gain more of the market share—not necessarily a larger share of the market, but a better share of the market, one that is more appropriate to your firm.

If volume is your objective, you need to determine how much and where. You don't want to add confusion; instead, you want to add specific, defined growth. To do so, you must be able to take on and manage this larger volume successfully.

Quality

One marketing goal is improved quality. All of our clients like to hear that effort is made to improve work or products. The design world is one of constant change, and our clients enjoy seeing these improvements.

Quality is very often totally independent of cost. The fact that something is good doesn't necessarily mean that it's expensive. The quality of an item can depend on its suitability for the particular project.

Quality isn't always a question of giving a client a good product; it's a question of our ability to produce a quality design at an effective price. This most often relates to the way we produce the job. Is there a way to improve the quality of the design and to simultaneously achieve a product that will be good for a long period? For instance, one firm has chosen "less is less" as its motto. This means the firm has chosen to work for fewer clients, and to do it right the first time. There will be less waste of time, materials, and energy—all in all, a more exacting art.

To achieve quality work and produce it at effective prices, designers need to acquire and keep the very best possible people for their studios. We need first to determine the components of good performance and what results are expected on the job, and then to let our staff do it. Let them be creative. Create an atmosphere in which your staff can work with excellence and efficiency.

Specialization and repetition can teach you the shortcuts that allow you to achieve higher quality with less effort and aggravation. Increased volume in purchasing certain products often means quantity discounts that can be passed along to the client. Is there a way to design your practice so that it's oriented to both quality and production—so that you can give your client a better product at an economical price?

Profit

One goal of a marketing plan is to increase profits. There are two primary ways to do this.

1. Increase the total sales or amount of income secured by the design firm.
2. Increase the amount of profit or markup. It isn't enough to simply increase sales; you need to keep track of the percentage of profit on each particular job.

This is as much the basis of marketing as it is any other financial program. Growth is really the key to profit for many business endeavors. The future of a company depends on its flexibility and willingness to grow. Decide whether you should become larger or smaller, or stay the same size. Decide which is the most appropriate and profitable direction for your company.

Consideration

Let's look at how designers make money. We expect designers who secure multimillion-dollar projects to have formidable incomes and wonderful opportunities. Some practices that you'd expect to be the most profitable are actually among the least profitable.

Why? On these multimillion-dollar projects, there are large numbers of people involved. Yet today, the average budget for office space is roughly $250 per square foot—of which only five dollars is allotted to cover all design services. These include architecture, engineering, all the specialists and consultants called in on a project, and, of course, the interior designer.

Think of the amount of liability and control and management that is purchased for five dollars a square foot and you will see the problem. There's a problem whenever you have a lot of responsibility for a low amount of money. Interior designers are responsible for the entire multimillion-dollar project, yet the total budget for all design services is one-fiftieth of the project budget.

At one time, budgets for design services were much higher, but the current competitive market limits what we can charge. Unless you offer a service or product that is unique or different, you can charge only what other people are charging. Clients know the charge per square foot on a given project. You must bid with caution to be sure that your amounts fall within the accepted range.

This means that the only way to achieve higher income levels is to make your firm's services unique. One way is to become a specialist, to develop your practice in such a way that no one else can install that type of job as well, and as easily, as you can. Being a specialist makes your services price effective.

Some of our ability to produce quality design work at an effective price depends on our resources. In seminars, when I asked design professionals to rate the products and services in our industry, I was shocked at the level of dissatisfaction. Often designers didn't feel that they had the appropriate products available. They didn't feel resource companies were ready or willing to stand behind them in the event of a problem with the merchandise.

Interior designers need to be able to control situations. We need to know that our resources will ship the quality products we order, when we need them. Especially when we have projects that stretch our abilities, we need to know that the factory is behind us and ready to meet the requirements of the design.

When design professionals create something truly unusual, it almost always succeeds best in a design-build situation, where the factory is close at hand and works intimately with the designer. If there is a problem, it can be solved on the spot immediately.

On projects in which everything is specified in detail and must be bid, it's often necessary to use more standard items. Too much creativity can cause problems, since the designer may not have control of the sources of the products used. (Hospitality design, for instance, demands a certain amount of creativity to provide that signature look.) The dealership that is awarded the bid may decide to substitute, or the factory may say the work can't be done as specified. The end product may not be what you planned, and items don't properly coordinate.

I asked hospitality design specialists what percentage of the job was actually produced exactly as they had specified. They said that if they hit sixty percent, they were delighted.

In many situations, sixty percent accuracy is not enough. You want and need more precision, but if sixty percent accuracy is all that is expected, can you design your projects to allow for this?

When you're specifying million-dollar projects, you need to consider the contractors, craftspeople, artisans purchasing system and delivery process. Will that project be completed within the time allotted and within the specifications if you add a creative features? A designer needs to know the capabilities of his or her vendors. The results are usually based on the constitution of the production team and process, not necessarily the size of the job.

These aspects of design are important when you design your company profile. You must decide how creative you are able to be within the limitations of the types of work you do. What are you realistically able to offer your clients considering, their needs and ability to invest in the project?

Create your program using the methods and suggestions in this book. Choose techniques that fit your chosen clientele, and use the ones that are most comfortable for your firm. To keep your commitment high, you and your staff must be able to accomplish and succeed and feel good about yourselves. So map out a schedule that's possible within the realm of your company's capabilities.

CHAPTER 4

Company Profile/Internal

- Aware of the skills and abilities of my practice.
- understand exactly who we are
- what makes up different?
- how can we differentiate ourselves from other designers

Each of us comes from a different background, a different school, a different part of the country. We have aptitudes in many areas. Some of us deal with very technical work and very detailed contract specifications. Others are doing highly inventive work. Before you begin your marketing program, you need to be aware of the skills and abilities of your firm. These are what distinguish your firm. You have to communicate this distinction through your marketing plan.

In establishing our right position in the marketplace, one of the most important things we can do is understand exactly who we are. Who we are is not just the building we own or the place we're located in, but all of our staff and the people who work with us. What makes us different? How can we differentiate ourselves from the other designers who are part of our market? Today's market is made up of many designers with many different backgrounds. What makes your firm different? At this point, let's look at what you're about and exactly what your best skills are.

What Do You Do Best?

Look at yourself. What is the best thing you do, and what are your personal limitations? Design your career around these two factors. If you're a person who loves details, fine; make sure that you do the detail work. If this is something you prefer to skip over, remember that it is still a necessary part of the interior design profession, and hire someone else to take over this responsibility.

Review past projects in terms of accomplishment and satisfaction. Make a list of what you do best, and keep it beside you as you consider new projects. When you hit a client situation that is really not within the range of what you or your firm should be doing, either bring in a consultant or possibly refer the project to someone else. Accepting a project that is too far beyond your range can destroy your company, seriously affect your profits, and jeopardize the entire project. We can't do everything well; do what you do best.

Best Type of Staff for Your Firm

Interior designers so often hire the person with similar training and abilities; this may not be the best person to hire. You need someone who is talented in skills you lack. Some of the most successful organizations are based on teams—with one person who works best as a designer, highly creative and focused on all the details of design; another team member who is good at communicating and presenting projects; and a third who enjoys managing the business.

Is your current staff oriented toward your firm's direction? You may have to replace staff members to achieve your goals.

Each person on your staff represents your firm in his or her every action. Build your staff and your group of consultants with the best people you can find. Strong people complement other strong people. If they're not qualified, they only pull the rest of the group down.

You want people who are reasonably bright and intelligent. It's much easier to work with them, and if you're a very bright person you may find it difficult to get along with people who aren't reasonably smart. Also, find people who are well educated, both as a result of schooling and of learning by doing.

Anyone you hire should have a good basic character. In addition to reviewing potential employees' professional abilities, do a credit check as well as a character check. Find out as much as you can about prospective staff, because the way they manage their lives affects their ability to do well in your firm.

Are they compatible with the people in your firm, and with your clients? Sometimes people who perform well don't fit your style of working. In a small firm, you'll be working together constantly. There must be some camaraderie; you have to be able to get along.

Finally, because the field of interior design requires a lot of effort and at times, long hours, it's important to find someone who has the energy to put into the field. Energy is the single most important characteristic of a successful person. If staff members have too many outside interests, they may not have the time or the energy to dedicate to the design practice. Are they willing to exert the kind of energy it takes to make it happen?

Design Staff Questionnaire

Now let's look at your staff and the professionals you work with outside your firm. Exactly what type of designers or specialists are they? You need to know as much about them as possible. What do they bring to your firm? How can you best present them as professionals? Ask each of them to fill out a Design Staff Questionnaire (Figure 4-1).

Using the Design Staff Questionnaire, ask each employee for an update every six months, and keep the completed forms in your business development file. Don't forget to fill one out yourself! The questionnaire asks each staff member to look at his or her education and experience in terms

DESIGN STAFF QUESTIONNAIRE			
Name:	Address:	Phone No.:	
		Date:	
Design School or College:			
Degree Received:			
Courses Studied:		From:	To:
Awards Received:			
Other Education: (workshops, seminars, etc.)			
Subject:		Dates Attended:	

Source © Design Business Monthly

Figure 4-1

Employment Experience:

Company:	From:	To:
Your Title:		
Job Experience:		

Company:	From:	To:
Your Title:		
Job Experience:		

Company:	From:	To:
Your Title:		
Job Experience:		

Company:	From:	To:
Your Title:		
Job Experience:		

Professional organizations to which you belong and offices, committees, or posts that you have held in these organizations:

Any special abilities or knowledge that you feel would benefit the firm, i.e., certain social acquaintances, fluency in foreign languages, knowledge within other disciplines, list of prospective clients with whom you are familiar or have had experience:

Source © Design Business Monthly

Figure 4-1 (*continued*)

Design Project Experience:

Type: Date:

Client or Owner:

Cost of Total Project:

Cost of Work Done by Design Firm:

Services Rendered by Design Firm:

Your Responsibilities:

Accomplishments on This Project:

Type: Date:

Client or Owner:

Cost of Total Project:

Cost of Work Done by Design Firm:

Services Rendered by Design Firm:

Your Responsibilities:

Accomplishments on This Project:

Other Relative Information:

Source © Design Business Monthly

Figure 4-1 (*continued*)

of what was accomplished or learned. You need specific information, so the more precise a staffer is, the more useful the form will be in your assessment of the capabilities of your firm. Once the profiles are completed, go over them and determine what the staff people have done in their past work experience.

Where was the person educated, and what degree did he or she earn? Was the school in the East or the West; was it a specialized school with a particular emphasis, such as historical preservation, contemporary design, or barrier-free environments? What is his or her particular emphasis?

What courses were studied, when, and what was learned or accomplished? Sometimes we take a particular course for a reason, perhaps because of an outstanding professor. The course may have been misnamed; you thought it was going to be dedicated to one issue but it turned out to emphasize another. Outline what special things were learned from those courses.

If the staff person received awards, what are they, and how did he or she earn them? Was it a solo project or done as part of a group?

What other education has he or she received? This can include seminars, lectures, and workshops. Again, you want to know the subject and dates attended, and what was learned or accomplished. Has the staff person served as an apprentice, or participated in volunteer programs?

The second page of the questionnaire details employment experience. In addition to the names of the companies, positions held, and the dates, what was the staff person's on-the-job experience? In conducting this type of interview or review, I find there is often a great deal of difference between the title of a job and what it actually entails. I think we need to look at the person not only in terms of where he or she worked but exactly what he or she did and learned in doing it. For example, an interior designer may have gone into a firm as an assistant designer but was involved principally in project management. That experience may have involved contact with certain types of contractors or clients, and that may be very beneficial to a future project.

Is there experience in lighting? In acoustics? In any other type of specific design? What was really done on those jobs, and what were the accomplishments?

Consider the extra work an employee has done, perhaps within a professional organization such as the American Society of Interior Designers (ASID), International Interior Design Association (IIDA), or the International Furnishings and Design Association (IFDA). Did the employee gain experience there? Did he or she hold an office, help run a convention, or organize an event? Has he or she done volunteer work that would develop certain talents or skills?

What special abilities does this person have that contribute to the firm? It could be educational, such as knowing a foreign language or another discipline. It could be social: acquaintance with prospective clients. Or it could be a hobby.

For example, a designer I profiled in *Career Options for Designers* had learned stage design through his interest in the theater. He worked on two plays a year and learned about lighting and stage presentation—skills he wouldn't have picked up in a traditional interior design practice. This background gave him an edge in creating outstanding lighting for many of his corporate jobs.

The third page of the questionnaire asks for details of project experience: the type of projects and when; the client or owner; the budget for the entire project. What was the budget for specific services rendered? What specific responsibilities did the staff person have, and what did he or she learn or accomplish on this project? After reviewing your staff, analyze the size of your firm and its general qualifications based on the staff members and all of their past experiences—as noted in the individual projects reviews.

A similar history is necessary for all consultants, associates, or special craftspeople who are part of your team. This will help you define what makes your firm unique.

Specialties

Among the more successful design firms of the seventies and eighties were those with high technical knowledge; they were able to say, "Here is a need and we are able to fill it." The market demands specialties, and this is part of the excitement of being in interior design today.

Many of the most successful firms have specialties. They have found ways of differentiating themselves from other firms because of their particular knowledge, staff, or the teams they've put together. They, therefore, can provide certain services other firms wouldn't be able to with as much expertise and efficiency.

The key today is being different. What separates you from the other firms competing in your market? How can you show that you have the ability to do things other firms aren't able to do with as great a skill?

Often specialties are based on demand or market presentation. There are ways of putting things together with a different phrasing or schedule that helps complete something quickly, because the people involved are ready to move immediately. Or, there are ways of approaching a subject from a slightly different angle. We've seen specialties developing in many types of practices—from the office-furnishing project that could be completed within a few weeks to the projects that involve special branding skills incorporating the design firm's total package. Whether the project is residential or belongs to any of the specialties, there are many ways a firm can enhance individual service packages so that they become more desirable to the potential client.

Then consider the market needs, and find a way of incorporating a package that fits that particular market. Design firms are forced to change their "packages" based on the needs of the market and the offerings of competitors. That is why we need to know not just what we have but the market and our competition as well.

Each specialty has so many demands that our educational structures are changing to accommodate this. For example, there's now a two-year specialty program that has been promoted and developed in conjunction with the National Kitchen and Bath Association (NKBA) as an add-on to interior design programs at educational institutions so designers can qualify as kitchen designers.

You have the opportunity to develop a creative specialty no one else has considered. This makes me think it's really wrong to take only one test to become an interior designer. I feel that you really need to be tested in each of the specialties. Obviously, if you specialized in law offices, you would need to understand their library and technical requirements. If you're doing medical facilities, you must understand the complete process of the medical procedures done there, the codes, and the equipment that is required.

The specialty of residential design usually pays far better than any of the other design specialties. However, it takes a certain type of personality. You must be seen as a professional designer by your clients, who are, therefore, willing to give you the respect and freedom necessary to invest in a high level of creativity and products. Another area that pays very well is any specialty with a high degree of originality—something no one else knows how to do, something very special.

In the past, residential design was looked down on as too common and undistinguished. The feeling was that anyone with minimal training could do it. In reality, some of the most creative aspects of our discipline are in residential design. You can be more creative in a residential project because usually there's more freedom. You also don't have to meet all the codes and technical requirements that commercial projects may require.

The next most profitable specialty is any project that demands a high level of creativity. When you offer goods or services that people have never seen before, the perceived value is higher. Can you do something unexpected, something highly inventive? When you design a project using only items from standard production lines, anyone can buy those items. Clients can go to the Internet, visit a design center, or go to High Point. When you specify an unusual finish or other change that makes the product unique, the clients will want to purchase the items through your company. They're unlikely to question your pricing because it has been done in a special manner just for them. So use your design ability to create that "something special."

You can choose from an extensive range of specialties. There are hundreds of specialties today, and every time I visit a new group I hear of a new specialty. Right now the list descriptions are almost twenty-three pages long in the *Interior Design Business Handbook*. To date, they are:

Acoustic design
Adaptive reuse
Administrative headquarters design
Airplane design
Amusement park design
Apartment/condominium/co-op design
Aquarium design
Art consultant
Art dealing
Audiovisual center design
Auditorium design
Barrier-free design
Bathroom design

Beauty and barber shop design
CAD specialist
Carpet and rug design
Ceramic tile design
Closet design
Code safety design law specialist
Color consultation
Commercial design
Computer office design
Construction supervision
Corporate campus design
Corporate in-house design
Cosmetic dentistry
Country club design
Dental office design
Design coordinator
Design for children
Design for in-home medical care
Design for vision or hearing impairments
Display/exhibit design
Energy conservation design
Ergonomic design
Estate manager
Facility management
Factory/production consulting
Faux finishes and stenciling
Feng shui
Forensic consulting
Funeral home design
Furniture design
Furniture manager
Geriatric design
Graphic design/signage
Greenhouse design
Hard surface flooring design
Hardware design
Health club design
Historic preservation and adaptive reuse
Home office design
Home theater design
Hospital design
Hospitality design
Houseboat design
Human factors
Interior landscaping
Journalism

Kennel design
Kitchen design
Law office design
Leadership in Energy and Environmental Design (LEED)
Library design
Licensing
Lighting design
Lighting fixture design
Liturgical design
Manufacturer in-house design
Manufacturer's representative
Marine design
Mausoleum design
Marketing specialist
Medical center design
Medical office design
Medical spa specialist
Model home furnishing
Modular prefabricated design
Mural painting
Museum design
Nursing home design
Office design
Park design
Party and ball design
Passenger train and bus design
Patio and outdoor room design
Photographic set design
Photography styling
Plumbing fixture design
Prison design
Privacy design
Product design, evaluation, and marketing
Product display
Professional or promotional organizations
Project management
Proxemics
Psychiatric care facility design
Public relations
Purchasing
Real estate development
Real estate upgrading
Rendering
Residential design
Resort design
Restaurant design

Restaurant kitchen design
Retail and specialty selling
Retail store design
Security systems design
Set design
Shop-at-home services
Shopping mall design
Showroom design
Solar design
Spa and skin clinic design
Spaceship and rocket design
Stadium and arena design
Storage design
Tabletop display design
Teleconference center design
Television design
Tenant development services
Textile design
Training center design
Transit center design
Transportation center design
Turnkey services
Underground habitation design
Universal design
Vacation home design
Vastu
Wallcovering design
Wall finishes
Wayfinding
Window treatment design

You are a designer; use your talent and training to gain the competitive edge. You need to present a creatively different product—something different from what everyone else is offering within your community, but not too different, because it's very difficult to make a profit being a missionary.

Experience

Keeping a design project analysis on each and every job you do will give you a yardstick of past accomplishments to evaluate which potential projects are right for your firm. The sample Design Project Analysis form will simplify the task (Figure 4-2). Reviewing your last three years of work will tell you what's easiest and most profitable for you. It also will help you pinpoint the type of work your firm has done, as well as the work experience of your staff. These are important factors, since,

DESIGN PROJECT ANALYSIS		
Client:	Project:	Staff:
Address:	Contact:	Date: Started:
	Phone:	Completed:
Type of Construction: (new, renovations, etc.)	Size of Project:	
	Construction Budget:	
	Furnishings Budget:	
Type of Services the Firm Provided:	Design Accomplishments:	
Size of the Fee:	Source of the Job:	
Method of Charging:	Expected Referrals:	
Profit of the Project:	Percentage of Profit on Total Project:	

Source © Design Business Monthly

Figure 4-2

principally, you're offering service. The abilities of your team—you, your staff, and your consultants—are your product. Anyone can buy furnishings. It's the way you use them that makes your firm different from the others.

This background is necessary to establish your marketing program, as well as to price your projects. The effort you spend reviewing these project analyses will be useful throughout your practice. Analyze projects done four, five, six, and even ten years ago. Projects performed more than ten years ago have limited use for today's market, although they should be considered. Compare the abilities and skills of your staff then with those of your present staff; compare past sources with those available today.

Determine which types of jobs have been most suitable to your firm's abilities and most profitable during the past five years. A marketing structure must be based on work yet to be done, while building on the experience of past efforts. Of course, it's best to analyze the projects when they're under way; trying to remember all the details three or four years later doesn't work. You can use our form, or depending on the software package you have, a great many of these numbers can be pulled from that information. The important part is to put the information aside in a simple form for future reference so when you look at your future market investment, you have this for easy reference.

Whether you use our form or not, your design project analysis should contain this basic information: client, size of project, whether you purchased or reused furniture, the profit, and how you won the job.

Design Project Analysis Form

First, identify the client, address and phone number, and the name of the contact person. What did you commonly call the project? Was it the name of the site, the building, the corporation, or the client? Who worked on the project? What date did it begin, and when did it end?

How large was the project? The analysis should tell you whether it was a new project or remodeling; whether you were responsible for any interior architectural changes or recommendations; and whether other architects, engineers, and designers were involved. First, consider the fees you obtained for perhaps space planning, finishes, or other areas in which no product was involved. Then you may want to define specific types of purchases, such as carpeting, wall surface materials, and drapery and window covering. Outline all the services your firm provided, from feasibility studies and basic design drawings to follow-through with project management and construction inspectors.

Did you reuse pieces the client already owned, or were all new furnishings, equipment, and finishes used? How much restoration was carried out on the building; what were the other changes? Was any of the furniture purchased through your company or your suggested vehicles, or did the client handle purchasing?

At the end of the project, when you evaluated the hours versus the income base, and your hourly fees versus the amount of profit, what was the profit? What was the final billing for professional service fees and purchases? How did that job look from an accountant's viewpoint, and how did it look from a design viewpoint? Did you accomplish what you wanted, or was it a project in which, for any number of reasons, things didn't turn out quite the way you had expected?

What did the clients think of the project when it was finally installed? Check to see what they think of it in three months, six months, a year, and perhaps two years. Also, check how the project has retained its quality over that period of time.

What was the source of the project? Was the client a referral from an existing client, or a prospect brought in by your advertisements or public relations efforts? It is important to identify the source of the job so that additional marketing information can evolve. Include any factors you feel contributed to your firm's being awarded the job.

Can you expect future referrals from this project?

Finally, is there a potential for publicity on this job? After the project is complete, you may want to ask whether the client would enjoy or consider exposure in a magazine or publication.

When you have answered these questions concerning your projects of the past five years, analyze the projects by years. How many projects did you undertake in a year? What types were they, and how successful were they? Consider the time invested and other management and business effects. What were the costs and percentages of profit for each job? This analysis should help you understand the trends of your company.

Obviously, you want to identify which jobs have been profitable. However, even experience gained on projects that were unprofitable can be helpful in giving your firm the new direction that is often necessary to make it competitive in the present market.

Although your revenue base may change, it is advisable when reviewing past projects to evaluate the income resources as they compare to the investments made in terms of time expended, marketing costs, and wear-and-tear on your firm.

Product

What is your product? With your firm's particular capabilities, what can you produce? There is no better way to ruin a design firm than by offering something you cannot produce, a project that calls for abilities your firm lacks.

What is your best product? What can you do that's different from anyone else? In this instance, you want to look at not just the product but the quality of the product and services you offer as well. Do you specify for hospitals and institutions, or does your work entail very fine decorative detailing that is appropriate for only executive offices or fine residences? Do you design and specify or provide turnkey projects?

Identify the type of business most appropriate and most profitable for your firm. That is your best product. The clients who need this work are your primary market.

A good product is one that can meet the wants and needs of clients, your capabilities, and the resources available. Does your service or product have a purpose that is viable today? Can you produce it within the confines of available human and material resources? Can you produce it within the time constraints and financial restrictions of the prospective client?

What size is your firm? Are you a one-, two, or three-person firm, or are you a hundred-person firm? Obviously, the types of projects you want to pursue are different in each situation. It's common for small firms to team or undertake a joint venture with other groups to accomplish large projects. Many firms find this type of joint venture very attractive. With the right structure, small firms are able to compete with large firms.

Can you define your product, and do so in a sentence? If someone at a party asks what type of work you do, you want to be able to set yourself apart from every other designer in the field. Are you able to explain your work in simple terms to someone who doesn't know our field, so that he or she could explain it to a friend or associate?

That's is a big question, and one most of us can't answer without preparation.

How do you work? What is your preferred method? In the past, our professional associations suggested that designers do design; this is what we have been trained to do. Today, they suggest designers should work only on a professional fee basis. These associations don't believe we should be in the business of selling merchandise, because it's not truly professional. They also warn of the responsibilities and liabilities involved in selling merchandise; it is a specialized business that requires a completely different structure. It would be a great world if we could do only design.

But design only will not work for all projects, because you'll never be able to achieve the quality level you need with a design-only operation. Projects involving standard products can be specified and installed by any successful bidder. It would cost more to write the specifications for some specialized, creative, one-of-a-kind projects than to build the job. In some highly creative areas of design, there are special techniques, even secret proprietary processes, that may be essential to the design. Most fabric design can be printed by almost any firm as long as it has the right ground cloth and screens. However, the printing processes of Fortuny fabrics are so unusual that this proprietary process has kept the company in a strong position for generations.

If your work is highly creative and calls for a design-build situation, do you have what you need to complete this project? You may need to structure your own workroom, or create an exclusive joint venture or partnership with the appropriate craftspeople. Remember, ten percent of any project is design; the other ninety percent is making it happen. How is the project going to happen? Are you going to control it, or will someone else take control?

Our clients want the extraordinary. There is an opportunity for a better income—if a designer knows how to execute a project success-fully. Therefore, special control is necessary. There are many special design processes that cannot be specified for mass production. They are handcrafted processes, tricks of the trade.

Sales Force

Sales is a highly skilled and organized profession, dedicated to bringing a needed product to a buyer—an interested person who can afford to buy our product. The design product can vary substantially, depending on the firm's specialty and the extent of services offered. The history and definition formulated in the designer profile will help determine the best method and salespeople to make up the force.

Today, the people able to bring in sales are *most* often the highest earners within *most* firms; they often dictate the direction of the job. Many firms will not employ anyone who does not bring in work, and even the lowest level of support staff are expected to be out generating business.

The position of a salesperson in a design firm has not always been respected. In fact, the marketing or sales department often occupied the last office down the hall. Today, the CEO or other top executive of most leading firms is a marketing person or salesperson. Very often a sales or marketing position is the highest paid position within a design firm. The salesperson determines the direction and the success of the firm. After all, if we don't have work, we can't design.

Some designers don't like to sell. If this is the case, then team up with a partner who *lives* to sell. To succeed at selling, you must enjoy the process, or you won't be willing to go the extra mile necessary to win the job.

To determine who should be handling the sales, first define exactly what product you are presenting and to which types of clients. Reexamine your past projects to enable you to pin down your product, a past client profile, and a profile of potential clients before you decide on the appropriate sales force. You may have to define other parts of your marketing plan and then come back to this section.

Consider what is most comfortable for you, but be aware that your marketing plan requires a sales force. Once you find the contacts and know where you're going, you will need to consider who will carry out the next part of your marketing effort.

Make a list of everyone within your firm. Each person should play some position on your sales force or marketing team. Review the individual abilities of all your employees and the areas in which they would have some outside involvement.

Do you work with another company or design professional whose product or service complements yours? Perhaps you can create a specialized market together that you could not have accomplished alone. Often two small offices can team together or engage in a joint venture in order to compete successfully with much larger firms. Look for a simple way to merge with the goal of supplying the extraordinary, that unique service that can put you in a noncompetitive market.

Income Profile

Using information from the Design Project Analysis form you filled out for projects of the past three years, review your methods of charging, profit, and percentage of profit on each project. This should provide you with a clear understanding of where your past revenues came from.

Compare the project profiles to the profit results. What kinds of projects were most profitable for you? Designers tend to think of the project or client they liked the best as the most profitable, but you may find that "ordinary" projects earned you the greatest profit.

Profit bases change. The moneymaker of yesterday or today may not be viable tomorrow, so compare your history with the current market.

That specialty of yours that brought in higher revenues may now be a common practice everyone else provides at lower fees.

At one time, space planning was a highly paid specialty. Today, there are computer programs designed for space planning. Every client knows the cost per square foot for a specific type of plan. Design firms must develop new services on which to base their incomes.

(There is more information on selling in Part 2 of this book.)

CHAPTER 5

The Marketplace

In the 21st century, if you're putting all of your time into new business development every month, you're in trouble. You'll be spending too much time and money to build a successful practice. Now is the time to develop existing clients and keep them happy, while creating a bank of prospective clients. People purchase design services because of need or because they're enticed to want or need. That need may not be specific or concrete; it may be psychological. Identifying the needs and aspirations of our clients is market research.

Some of this is part of day-to-day practice in which we collect client responses to various interactions and general trends. The more time you spend up front listening to what clients want, defining their needs and their projects, the easier it is to design and produce the projects. Good research increases your chances of a successful project, one that is based on understanding and good rapport and will bring you referrals for new clients.

The marketplace of today demands that we be proactive—that we entice, excite, and stimulate the clients who are most appropriate to our practice. We cannot simply wait for people to express needs; we must create them. We must present our firms in a way that clients are so excited about what we do that they demand our services.

Successful design firms find ways to meet potential clients. They don't wait for a formal request for a proposal to be issued. They don't wait to be put in the position of competing with other design companies. Instead, they establish relationships with potential clients. Keeping in touch and having great rapport with their past clients often leads to developing referrals with new clients. But more than that, as designers we need to find ways to share experiences with potential clients so they get to know us and see us as part of their teams.

To succeed, we must investigate and seize any opportunity to become part of a client's team. As design professionals, we cannot afford to be seen as marketers and sellers. We need to be regarded as people who understand the clients' needs and who will function as teammates to solve their problems.

Service

We are living in a service period. Design firms—in fact, almost all industries—are dedicated to servicing clients. This can also be a cause for concern: Our clients think of the furnishings field as providing a tremendous amount of service, based on its past tradition. Years ago, it was traditional for furniture stores to take care of your parents' furniture for years on end. If there was a problem with the furniture, even five years after it was purchased, your parents called the store and they sent a person to repair it. Furniture stores then worked on a keystone markup. They had a profit range that allowed them to provide these services.

Today, design firms work on a very small spread. Providing continuing care is expensive and not possible on this margin. This is something we need to consider before positioning ourselves with our clients.

Although clients today expect and demand customer service, the basics of customer service are not part of the standard design curriculum. Many design firms are ill-prepared to meet the ongoing demands of clients.

Today we have many types of clients. We have clients who need and want to be serviced for as long as a piece of furniture is in place. Some design firms offer a service contract similar to the one you buy for an automobile or appliance. These firms are paid a certain fee to inspect the furniture each year or season to determine how to keep it in perfect form as long as it's in use.

Many clients today don't want just a beautiful design, great presentation, and beautiful boards: They expect a job to be completed for a certain budget within a specified time. Why? In many past instances, clients paid a tremendous amount of money for design, and the bids they received for the project were for three or four times the amount of money available. As a result, we now see managers of community projects and corporate projects going out on bids with cost ceilings, saying, "We have 35 million dollars to do this project; please give us a proposal to design, to build, and to complete the project within this range." This is what the client wants to buy.

How do interior design firms fit in? In order to be considered for this type of project, a firm must form a partnership or a joint venture with all the necessary design specialists, architects, engineers, landscape architects, vendors, and contractors. We must design the project so that it can be completed within the restrictions of the job.

Talk to your clients. Some of them just want a beautiful and wonderful project, and they're willing to pay for it. Other clients need a product that works. We must be willing to consider clients' financial positions to determine if it's appropriate for them to spend only a certain amount of money on their offices during this period. Then you have to decide what can be done within that budget to meet the client's needs and whether you can work within that range.

Design is often part of a business, so a designer becomes part of a client's corporation, a member of the team. We can't just sit across the table advising clients; we have to develop a program that fits with their business plan.

Client Profile

Who are your current clients? What do they have in common, and what are the differences among them? Look through your Design Project Analysis forms to refresh your memory and develop a profile of them.

Consider common attitudes about buying interior design services: what your clients liked best about the experience and what they liked least.

What Are Customers Looking For?

1. They are looking for professional assistance. They come to a designer because they want to accomplish their projects at a higher skill level than they are capable of doing.
2. They want you to see them as a very special and important person. They believe that they should be first in your practice, and it is up to your firm to treat them this way.
3. They want to reduce their doubt. They don't know much about this field, and they know there will be many decisions to make. With your input, they're more confident in their decisions.
4. They want a designer who they believe respects them, listens to them, and understands them. If you're not willing to exert the energy to really listen to your clients and take the trouble to be sure you understand what they want as well as their reasons for wanting it, find yourself another client. Some personalities just don't work well together.
5. They come to you because they have a project that's beyond their capabilities, and they want you to assist them in making it happen. They want you to take some of their problems away and show them that these problems can be solved with professionalism.

The Mature Market

America today is called "the graying society." This means there will soon be more people over sixty years of age than there are under twenty years of age—something our country has never seen before. This group has discretionary income and is psychologically prepared for and interested in it's interior environments.

The major thing we must remember is older people don't want to be treated as if they're older. Today, people who are sixty act like they're thirty, people who are seventy act like they're forty. They're very young in attitude, and they also want what they want.

People from their sixties to one-hundred-plus form a discriminating market. They know what they want, and they know exactly what they want to buy. They are well educated, not just in terms of where they went to school but in terms of life experience as well. They've invested time in reading about and studying the design items they want to add to their living environments.

They may have physical limitations brought on by aging, so the interiors must be easy to use. They want comfortable, workable, attractive spaces.

Older people expect active customer service. They want things done for them and need a design practice that is staffed to service their needs now, not next week or next month.

The mature market is a growth market, but study it to determine whether it's the right one for your combination of skills, goals, and experience. This market demands special attention to communication. There are marketing specialists who dedicate their careers to these issues.

If you're presenting anything to older people, be it a printed document or any form of advertising, make sure it's easy for them to read. People in their forties may not be wearing glasses—though maybe they should be—but they expect to see everything. Be careful that you have the proper size type.

Developing Your List of Potential Clients

Who wants what we have to offer? Not everyone needs or wants it. If a client doesn't want it, we'd better find another client. So the question is, who is looking for our services? Who's making major changes?

What is the potential? You may find that if your firm's direction has changed, you need to add different clients. Based on your company's abilities, who should you be looking for? When considering your prospective client list, first look at the kind of client you've been serving. Start with your Design Project Analysis forms. We can learn so much from them. It's often a question of how well we match with these prospective clients.

Existing market trends also must be considered. Even if your past projects aren't exactly the types of projects available and in demand at present, reviewing them will give us some basis for building a preferred group of prospects.

This is where research comes in. You must narrow the field of potential clients to those you can reasonably expect to reach. For example, not everyone in your city wants or can afford design services. Of those who want design services, some want skills outside your experience. Can those who want design services afford them? There are many ways to find the answers. Run credit reports. Talk to other professionals who have worked for them. Identify the potential clients and their needs. Refining your definition of potential clients gives you a better chance of reaching them.

Then build a sales program around that particular type of client. From that point on, your program may consist of Webpages, video, a series of letters, phone calls, or invitations to various seminars or programs, or an ongoing list of activities that build the program.

Referrals

Prospects are often based on referrals. Since interior design is a sizable investment, most prospective clients are wary of hiring a designer they don't know. If a firm is doing exceptional work, usually a large percentage of its work will come in through referrals. A great project creates demand among the client's friends and acquaintances for your design work.

Obtaining work through referrals should not be a random process. Many companies whose work comes mostly through referrals have an organized program. Set aside a regular contact time for talking to past clients to learn about potential jobs. You're unlikely to get referrals just by waiting for them. You'll have to dig, move, and work with your referrals to develop them into paying clients. Everything is subject to change: the economy, your practice, your clients' practices. Does their new direction fit with what you're doing?

Our referral list can begin with friends, even though some people are happy with this type of relationship and others are not. You alone can decide whether you want to work with friends. Still, many designers began their careers by working for friends or people they know.

Ask your staff members if they know people who might be influential in buying or directing a building or an interior project. Ask them to consider college roommates, friends, neighbors, relatives, landlords, past employers, or people who serve on the board of directors of a firm or organization. Hold regular meetings to update this list. Keep your staff thinking about who they know, and ask them to gather as much information as they can about these people. Your staff members need to see that they play a part in finding and developing clients.

Other good sources of referrals are other professionals—architects, engineers, or other designers. Check into what they're doing.

Interview both general contractors and subcontractors to learn the types of projects in which they're involved and if there's a need for a design professional. Your contractors can be one of your most important marketing tools. They're often able to develop and direct work to your firm. The closer you work with a contractor and the more rapport you develop, the better chance you stand of getting good referrals.

Interior designers and architects who form a very close relationship with their contractors are often able to work at a higher level with greater efficiency. The contractors might suggest cost-cutting measures and let the designers decide whether these measures would compromise design. This interaction has proved beneficial in so many ways that design firms have incorporated it into their working styles. Including your contractors on your team and using them as consultants before detailing the final job can ensure that you both understand all the construction parameters of the project.

When there's a wide range of costs in a project that's put out to bid, it invariably means that the prints or specifications are not well documented. This usually suggests future problems and changes in orders. If your prints and documents are so well detailed that all the contractors understand them, the potential for problems is much less.

Manufacturers, wholesalers, suppliers, and distributors all have salespeople in the field, and they're often aware of future projects. They know the type of furnishings and products you buy as well as the type of work you do. They've seen many of your finished projects. When they feel they're a part of your team, they're an excellent source of referrals. People will often ask reps who they recommend. When a rep recommends your firm, it's considered an excellent referral.

I know several designers who have started good businesses with the families that they met at their children's schools. Consider every type of activity you're involved in, from the tennis court to the people you meet while playing soccer mom or dad. It's amazing where you can meet people who can become part of your referral system, which is why it's often said we're always seen as designers. We need to consider how we dress and conduct ourselves in all forms of social interaction.

Potential Referrals

Make an ongoing file of potential referrals:

> Childhood Friends
>> Neighborhood
>> Elementary School
>> High School
>> College

Educational Seminars
Other Causes
Family Friends
Yours
Your Parents'
Your Sisters' and Brothers'
Spouse's
Children's
Community Activities
Clubs, Country or Social
Special Interests
Houses of Worship
Charities
Past Employment
Business Associates
Other Professionals
Vendors
Contractors
Theater and Sporting Events

Learn as much as you can about all your past clients, friends, and associates. Keep some form of filing system, whether on your computer or in a simple card file, whatever works for you. Keep notes of special events and ways you can keep in touch with them. This will pay off in so many different ways. Develop a system of organizing your contacts so that when you have a particular need or reference, you know which card to pull.

Our Resources

Consider what suppliers, trades, and craftspeople are available to you. There are times when certain products are readily available. Then we go through periods when they're very expensive or difficult to procure. Before you determine your marketing direction, make sure you have the resources you need. If your specialty demands that everything be individually crafted, you must control or at least be very close to an excellent shop.

To produce good design, we must use great products. We also need to know the resource firms and their abilities. These firms change often. Many that were prominent a few years ago aren't around any longer; many new companies are springing up.

A close relationship between vendors and designers would make our access to new technical information more timely. Our vendors are a great source of technical information. Timely information means the right product will be specified for the right places.

Build a close relationship with consultants and suppliers, and learn to know them. Also, we must let them know when products don't perform appropriately. How else will they know if the products have problems? We are part of their quality control system.

This way we can deliver the highest quality finished product at the most effective price. In this tight economy, we have neither the time nor the financial resources to build new relationships for each new project. We need to have our working teams ready at all times.

Competition

Look at the movers and shakers in your field. What jobs are they doing? Do you think your firm could do these projects even better? How do they handle their marketing? You may be doing things better than they are, but perhaps they have a different method of presenting their abilities.

Questions to answer about your competition:

1. Who are they?
2. Who are the most important?
3. What kind of staff do they have?
4. Who are their clients?
5. What is their marketing plan?
6. What services do they provide?
7. What is their direction?
8. How do they charge?
9. What are their successes?
10. What are their problems?
11. What can we learn from them?

Interior designers face stiff competition. Interior design services and products can be purchased from many sources—not only locally but nationally and internationally. The Internet and "800" numbers have also brought us sources from different parts of the world. Many other types of business, such as office supplies and medical suppliers, have now added a design division. They have regular contracts with their clients and therefore know them better.

Architects, engineering firms, and other design professionals offer interior design services because they want to control the entire package. They know they can often charge a higher fee for interior design than for some of their other services. In many states, there is legislation in place, which is also pending in other states, that would permit architects to do the same work as interior designers. In fact, in some instances, legislation prohibits interior designers from doing some of the work that was traditionally within their specialty.

What many people do not realize is that interior design as practiced by interior designers is more detailed than interior design by architects.

A lot more effort is put into architectural projects for the amount of dollars per square foot invested. Architecture has much larger budgets; therefore, the fee structure needs to be considerably different.

The reason it's so important we know about our competition is that design firms have limited amounts of money to spend either in marketing or on sales overhead. It's important to be able to spend that money effectively. Consider the cost of running your firm; how much markup do you need to cover your expenses? Example: If your firm requires a thirty to thirty-five percent markup, there's no point in competing with firms who are doing similar work, or work our clients may see as similar, using only a five or ten percent markup. Such an approach will be generally fruitless. Therefore, if we must compete with them, we should offer a different service and a different way of presenting a project—or we must go to different clients. Now you can see why time spent learning as much as you can about your competitors is extremely beneficial and necessary: it saves you a lot of effort. Sometimes the highly publicized jobs everyone is competing for prove to be the least profitable, because if so much competition is involved, there is almost no profit left for anyone. Very often the little jobs will pay so much better because they are unknown and offer you an opportunity to do the specialized work at which you excel, and to use your design creativity—rather than simply bidding on a job that's based purely on the lowest bidder.

Location

What geographic limitations are appropriate for the type of work you want to attract? For example: Some types of work, such as residential or detailed contract work, are better located close to the projects so that you can visit the site often in order to avoid problems. Because the project is small, it could cost more to write the specifications than to build the project, so close contact with the craftspeople is essential.

Larger projects usually are based on documentation and specifications, and the project management is carried out by others. If a firm has refined its specialty and all its requirements, it may be able to work globally with great success.

Consider the type of design work you are doing. Then establish your geographic limitations.

We found in our own practice that with highly creative work, we perform better when projects are closer to home. When a project is long distance, we need to partner with another team in that location so they can handle the day-to-day project management. Fortunately, with today's tools and the ability to communicate visually with technology, we can see the detail on a project many states away. This technology permits us to do a lot of work that would not have previously been possible. However, there is still the question of rapport with craftspeople—having them feel we're in partnership with them on the project and instilling them with pride. That's very difficult to do long distance. One of our major tasks is to help craftspeople feel that this is one of the best projects they have ever worked on, so we get the best work for our clients. There's nothing that can compare with eye-to-eye communication.

Factors That Affect Our Marketplace

A tight economy is a red flag warning that change may be needed in the way interior designers market their services. There are many potential clients who want our services, but are they able and willing to pay? As you select your specialty and develop a marketing approach, keep in mind that you need to be sure that those who want your services can afford to pay for them.

Business and economic conditions cause change. Change is part of interior design. It is necessary for designers to keep track of changing business trends; otherwise we might be doing business as usual while the market disappears. Keep track of business changes, and incorporate them into the way you practice design. You'll find a list of sources for information on trends in the section on market research.

Social and Cultural

For many years, we've been dealing with the Americans with Disabilities Act. It has become part of every project we work on, but we are now more conscious of how the design field affects the environment and the health of everyone who uses spaces.

Christine Barber, director of research at Genslers, points out the trends in design innovation—including globalization and the opportunities it has created for designers. Another trend is the growing importance of female clients. Barber cites Marti Barletta, author of *Prime Time Women*, who states that women in their fifties and sixties are the healthiest, wealthiest, most educated, and engaged in history. They handle eighty to eighty-five percent of the spending decisions in their households. Women, for example, are forging a strong connection between their environment and their sense of satisfaction. So we should direct many of our efforts toward women.

A survey of 385 marketing sales service managers by the Stravety Corporation revealed that eighty-five percent said there's an extreme demand for fast interaction. Customers *want it now*. They expect their solutions to come almost immediately. Managers also stated that companies able to offer high quality, along with quick delivery, will lead the way in the future. Speed is the new competitive advantage.

Regulatory Forces

Government, legal, and regulatory forces affect our ability to work. Sometimes the number of laws and liabilities is so great that I'm afraid to work in a certain market. Look at these issues. Understand what it will cost you to do business and what laws affect your practice. For instance, in some states, many of the practices that had been part of interior design now require stamping by a registered architect. We need to know the requirements for both interior design and various other specialties, as well as the contracting requirements in the states we work in, so we can be sure to meet them.

Technology

Technology has not only changed how we work, but what we are able to do. It's incredible what we can do today that would have been impossible in the past. We can be reached anywhere in the world. I had a very interesting experience not long ago. Expecting that a client was in town, I called him on his cell phone so I could verify an issue. I asked him, "By the way, where are you?" He said, "I'm sitting on top of a volcano in Hawaii." He sounded as if he was next door. It's just amazing.

We realize we're available to people all the time. That can be a positive or a negative, depending on the situation. The important thing is that we use the opportunities of today's technology appropriately. At one point we had many great draftspeople who did beautiful work. Now we're finding that because we communicate via the Internet, everything needs to be done accurately using computer-assisted drawing (CAD) programs. We were so happy when we had a fax machine. We no longer use faxes as much because electronic communication is much more accurate. Computers have changed our work in every respect, whether in the "smart house" or our office.

The way we communicate with clients and everything we do is affected by technology. The Web becomes a constant tool for our portfolios. Many designers no longer have a hard copy of their portfolio; it is all on the Internet. We're doing much more purchasing through Websites. In many cases, they've become our catalogs. We also find our clients going online to research interior designers. Certain specialists are finding that the Web is one of their main sources of client referrals. Others find it's not as effective.

ASID has just done a study of how interior designers are using Websites. Surprisingly, although many designers are using their Websites as a marketing tool, the majority of them view it more for resources than for marketing. But this may change in the near future. We could write several books on how technology has changed our projects. Even in residential spaces, the amount of computer technology is extensive. We thought it was really futuristic when, in 1987, the book *Future Perfect* talked about the Japanese building industry. We now see this process being incorporated in almost every part of our building industry. The factory-built industry brings us great quality and incredible opportunities we aren't able to accomplish on-site.

Using modern technology in every step of the design and building process—from the computer catalog of parts, to the drafting of the plan, to the controlled production line for building—housing manufacturers can provide extensively customized detail at an effective price.

The major manufacturer of prefab manufactured homes in Japan makes 110,000 units per year. In the United States, the largest manufacturer of similar units produces only 2000 per year.

Mass customizing on a different scale is practiced by almost every paint company, which deliver true colors that precisely match the samples for an extensive color line. Paint companies provide dealers with computers that measure light frequencies of color samples. This computerized control permits a perfect color match every time the store mixes a batch of paint. Even an amateur can produce perfectly matched colors.

We need to be ten steps ahead of our clients, not just two. Amateurs can do some things perfectly, so we have to be able to use technology at its very best to stay ahead of our clients.

CHAPTER 6

Current Issues Influencing Our Market

Today we can't pick up a publication or anything relating to our field without seeing either "luxury" or "green" featured. These are the topics of the day.

"Green," "organic," "environmentally friendly"—these terms are part of our clients' vocabulary. Environmental issues strongly affect our market today. They have become central in our practices, whether luxury or functional. It's not left up to the specialist for green concepts to be part of every practice.

Designers have produced both environmentally healthy and luxurious interiors as long as our profession has existed. But today, people are looking at both these elements with a much more serious eye. They want something special. They also want something healthy. You'll find that this attitude is becoming imbedded in every part of our profession. It's important that we talk about luxury and green issues. It's also important that we recognize that these issues need to be part of our work and incorporated appropriately into our presentations.

> The style of luxury is blending functional needs with self-expressions. Clients want their interior spaces to express who they are.

Luxury Today

Luxury today means something very different than it once did. It's a question of personal pleasure and self-expression and not as much about status. At one time, we bought our clothing and dressed according to our social status. One could very quickly distinguish a blue-collar worker from a professional. This is not true today. A person may mix a very expensive pair of jeans with an inexpensive blouse, or carry a handbag that cost several thousand dollars with clothing that is in no way comparable in price.

The same thing has happened in our homes and in our furnishings, whether they're for residential or commercial spaces. The question is: What is the client's personal style? How are clients expressing themselves? Are they showing that they are connoisseurs of art rather than people who have status furniture? Status furniture today is not necessarily a roomful of Louis the 16th; it may be an expression of contemporary abstract art made out of primitive materials, mixed with a luxuriously comfortable piece of upholstery.

Luxury can mean many things to different people. At one time, the term "luxury" related specifically to one's station in life. Now it's very different. Often luxury is considered something tranquil and meditative. Others see luxury as something formal, in silk and satin. Still other people have the image of something informal and comfortable. When we consider spa designs in many homes, we realize the investment has been made for strictly private use.

Luxury for some people may mean the ability to restore and reupholster furniture that has been part of their heritage. They believe they never need to buy something new. This indicates that luxury today is an emotional thing.

Michael Love, ASID, a New York designer, says that luxury is that special something, which may or may not equate with "expensive."

Living in comfortable, easy, workable, and beautiful surroundings is often considered luxury. A client will come to a designer saying he or she wants luxury, but it often means a very different thing than in the past. Luxury may be having the ease and time to enjoy a space.

The Luxury Market Council, a thirteen-year-old worldwide network of luxury manufacturers, sees the luxury market growing at the rate of fifteen percent per year.

Sometimes luxury is associated with quality. As a Rolls Royce advertisement states, "Because they have learned to distinguish and appreciate the difference between the merely very good and the truly great."

Pamela Danzinger of Unity Marketing says, "Luxury goods must have superior quality, outstanding style and design, and the right price/value relationship to be called 'luxury'. As an example of luxury that fits her definition, a set of Léron bed linens takes a year to make in Italy and costs $60,000.

Years ago, the dream house was delivered via the mail in the Sears, Roebuck & Co. catalog. Some of these dream houses still exist. They were considered a wonderful product at the time. Today, we may see a $65 million to $100 million house with twenty-four bathrooms and all sorts of entertainment and social spaces, as well as areas designed purely for indulgence. One of the designers in our Designer's Business Forum was doing a house 75,000 square feet in size.

Today people are more label-conscious, especially with all the questions about quality in products coming from China. Our clients are currently very conscious of whether something is made in America. Often this consciousness leads to the opportunity for more creative as well as better quality products.

Luxury has created a demand for many services. Most people either don't have the time or don't want to invest the time in what designers do. There are many personal shoppers and lifestyle coaches. They help people develop and maintain their lifestyle by helping them with all the little issues that contribute to the quality of life they want. This in turn has created many specialties for people in the interior design profession. But you have to look at your own individual market. What is considered luxury in the forests of Maine is not the same as luxury in New York, California, or Texas. Each area has its own style. Look around and see what the demands of your area are. How can you take something that reflects a somewhat common need and develop it into a demand and also a luxury?

The big question in luxury today is: Why are people willing to spend ten times the price of a typical item just because it's luxury? It's amazing to see the cost of items today. For example, the price of mattresses and other standard items once considered common are now incredibly expensive. We all see mattresses advertised in our publications today that cost $50,000. In the past, mattresses were thought to be of good quality if they cost $1000. An Aga stove, for example, costs $26,000. I have a client, a single woman, who had to have one of these stoves. She does some entertaining, but on the whole, it's difficult to understand why she needs an Aga stove for one person.

GE Monogram has a walk-in wine vault that looks like an enormous safe. It's made of stainless steel, with a touch-screen console. The vault has a label scanner and includes software inventories of your collection. It's temperature-controlled—and holds more than 1000 bottles of wine. The cost of the wine vault is $25,000.

As Dan Heath and Chip Heath, authors of *Made to Stick: Why Some Ideas Survive and Others Die*, point out in an article in *Fast Company*, "products make the leap from pedestrian to premium" when the products' creators think of them as ideas. That's why people are willing to pay $300 for a pair of jeans. "Luxury has become more about personal pleasure and self-expression and less about status," they say.

Luxury Purses

Handbags have become an extreme-luxury item. It's not unusual to see someone working for a modest salary who has a $3000 to $5000 handbag. If it isn't the Kelly bag, it's the Birkin. People are acquiring collections. I know clients who have done a full wall showing their collection of handbags. It's a feature in their home. Others keep the handbags in a safe and carefully boxed for security.

There's a *Washington Post* article on the front page of the business section that describes a $52,500 purse entitled "the Tribute Patchwork." Brigit Andrews, regional vice president of Louis Vuitton, says the hand-bags are something special; they're being made for clients who want the handbags for their collections. A limited number of these luxury handbags are being made—five of which will be offered for sale in the United States, and the others worldwide.

Milton Padraza, chief executive in the marketing research firm Luxury Institute, says, "The ultra-wealthy are those who are worth at least ten million dollars. They demand services and products that set them apart from those who are merely wealthy."

A study of the meaning of luxury indicates that luxury is based on branding and personal desires. For example, a gentleman standing at a hotel lobby desk commented that he has a home in Palm Springs and had just bought a Bentley station wagon. He bought the car because it had throw pillows in the back seat as well as a refrigerator in which to keep his Hershey Kisses.

Wealth Versus Luxury

Early in my career, I was told by one of my very wealthy clients that wealth means having everything and never needing to buy anything.

I remember visiting the exhibit of Jacqueline Kennedy's clothing at the Metropolitan Museum in New York City. Kennedy wore her mother's riding attire and was very proud to do so; she didn't need her own because she had her mother's. Many of the young women I went to school with were given a pair of riding boots when they were teenagers and continued to wear them throughout college and into their adult lives. They never thought of buying a new pair. They had the boots restored and resoled many times but not replaced. This is quite a different attitude from that of the consumer audience today.

Which brings up the questions: Who is buying luxury? Who is spending the money for many of the great marvels of today's market?

Most people today are starved for creative expression. Our clients believe that through interior design, they're buying a lifestyle as well as opportunities for that creative expression.

Luxury Turned Common

These days, luxury products are no longer relegated to the specialty shops of New York, Paris, or Milan. High-end products can now be found in the nearest mall. In her book *Deluxe: How Luxury Lost Its Luster*, culture and fashion writer Dana Thomas documents the evolution of the luxury industry from an array of family-owned houses into a $157 billion a year mass market whose products lack the exclusivity on which their cachet was based. "Luxury wasn't simply a product," Thomas writes. "It denoted a history of tradition, superior quality, and often a pampered buying experience."

Thomas senses a consumer backlash growing in response to the "tarnished" quality of luxury today. She quotes a French shoe designer, Christian Louboutin, who says, "Luxury is the possibility to stay close to your customers, and do things that you know they will love. Luxury is not consumerism."

Green

Designers today don't just want to do beautiful work; they want to do buildings that are both healthy and environmentally supportive. Our designs are affected by the way energy resources are generated, as well as by concerns about the materials we use that might affect air quality within the building.

We now hear that very large homes are out of vogue because clients realize slightly smaller homes are more efficient. I'm not sure we'll go back to the very small houses we once had, but people are looking at the economics as well as environmental issues that prove smaller spaces are more efficient and appropriate.

Green issues are not just for the home in the country; they're becoming part of every type of environment, including our major cities. "Green building" refers to everything we practice—from energy to water, and to all the resources used as part of the building.

Designers are now looking at reusing materials when appropriate. They have to consider whether reusing materials is efficient and how these products can be substituted for new ones. Both professional designer publications and general publications are filled with articles regarding environmental and green design. This has become a key part of many design practices.

In my practice, I've been concerned about contaminants and, there-fore, have refused to put any products into my projects that contain them. Most of my clients were not concerned, but I was. I knew how harmful contaminants can be to our environment. Therefore, we just didn't use them in our practice. We don't necessarily talk about it, but we're careful to make sure the products used in our projects are environmentally appropriate.

Fortunately, we now have an awareness program coming at us from all directions. We're far more aware of these issues; they've become part of our practice. Because our clients are talking and asking about green issues, we are changing the types and quality of the products we use.

In Tiffany & Co.'s beautiful brochure entitled "Sustainability—Our Most Important Design," Michael J. Kowalski, chairman and CEO, says: "Tiffany & Co. is committed to obtaining precious metals and gemstones in ways that are socially and environmentally responsible. It is simply the right thing to do, and our customers expect no less." The brochure goes on to explain that since the store's opening in 1837, it has looked to nature for designs. The brochure also explains Tiffany & Co.'s system of mining; the way the company monitors suppliers, including paper and packaging; and its energy-conservation directions—especially the solar-electric project at the store's New Jersey distribution center. Tiffany & Co. wants to be seen as one of the leaders in responsibility for our environment.

Now we're seeing a great emphasis on things like green mansions. "Eco-Friendly Luxury," an article in *Absolute* Magazine, talks about Manhattan's sustainable design revolution. The important part is we're now concerned about Leadership in Energy and Environmental Design (LEED) quality.

"Green" features are many of the items mentioned in the LEED program. LEED is looking at everything from internal sewage treatments to plant-covered roofs, from banks of photovoltaic cells that reduce water usage and conserve energy to pollutant-free paints and finishes. Our green world is quite different today than it had been. We're looking not just at conservation and healthy materials but at every single item going into a project. Our clients are aware of green issues, and we must be certain we understand all the details of the products considered green.

In some instances, the wood itself may be a green item, but it doesn't come from a managed forest. Even if it is from a managed forest, the wood could have a finish on it containing a contaminant. There are so many details that need to be reviewed. Fortunately, we have the ability to review them today—and the mandate. Our clients are demanding that we be up to date on these issues and that everything we do in a space will be environmentally appropriate.

Today we want our homes comfortable as well as healthy.

Recycled materials are featured in new environments as well as in restoration projects. We can find many building resources directories on the Internet that include companies specializing in all forms of recycled material. This has also become a specialty for many design firms that prefer to incorporate reused materials in their projects.

Green is a holistic process. It begins when we start a design, and it carries through the use of that design and all its maintenance issues.

Green Organizations

Most everyone in the field believes that green is here to stay as clients become more aware of what green means to the environment. It's not just LEED that is establishing standards for green design.

The Forestry Stewardship Council (FSC) aims to develop forest management standards that represent a well-managed sustainable forest. The FSC provides certification for approved managed forests and the products that come from them. Clients look for this certification to determine whether the products used in their projects comply with sustainable forestry practices.

There is also an organization called the Sustainable Furniture Council (SFC) that promotes sustainable practices within the home furnishings business.

We are seeing many more of these organizations becoming part of our practices.

Organic Leather and Fabrics

Organic is everywhere. It's fascinating to see how strongly organic issues have gone from the food industry into our textiles and other furniture products. We now have organic leather. "Green" leather comes from free-range cattle treated with vegetable dyes rather than processed with heavy metals.

Organic Leather, a company in California, sells organic leather made from the hides of wild animals or those raised to produce organic meat. This leather is often used in furniture, particularly in headboards and other items we're exposed to for long periods. There is also an Organic Trade Association, which has established standards for processing textiles. These standards exclude all heavy metals and components such as formaldehyde, but they do allow the use of synthetic sewing threads.

CHAPTER 7

Market Research

M arket research can help interior design businesses stay successful during a downturn in the economy. *A Survival Report*, a study issued a number of years ago by the International Interior Design Association (IIDA) (and funded by Polsky/Fixtures Furniture Endowment), examined a terrible decline in business in Texas due to a petrochemical crisis. The crisis resulted in economic disaster for the state.

The design businesses observed for the report found that the first issue was how much work needed to be done; cost was second; then came design. It wasn't a question of whether the design was beautiful. Interior designers had to research very heavily the reasons for purchasing design. They learned that you can never know too much about your potential clients. A period of crisis or economic disaster brought the designers much closer to their existing clients and made them realize that as designers, they must offer a very-high-quality, well-priced project.

Many firms, especially in the contract field, have learned that there is not much loyalty from clients. Selecting a design firm is often done on a single-project basis. This means the cost of developing the project is an important factor. If there's going to be continuous work, it may be worthwhile to work on a limited profit or lose money. If there isn't going to be repeat business, there's nothing to justify this kind of investment.

Most studies show that designers need to spend a considerable amount of time and effort developing their potential clients. Leaders of successful firms have stated that they spend as much as sixty percent of their time on business development.

The important point is that every change, whether social or economic, means the design field will also change. This may result in firms changing their specialties or working in different ways or in different geographic areas.

For the design firms examined in *A Survival Report*, the final decision for the majority of new jobs depended on the facilities manager. Here was a different kind of client, more sophisticated and closely involved in controlling the design process from the financial viewpoint. Time and budget issues became a major part of the reason one firm was selected over another. The design firms that won the projects offered a high level of service and were responsible for controlling the projects' finances.

Some firms decided to diversify geographically, extending their services to parts of the country that were hit less hard. (At this point, many of the surviving firms are not just national, but international.) Most of the design firms covered by the report reviewed their client base to identify specific design needs and how these could be met. They also looked for joint ventures with other companies, developing the kinds of relationships that allowed them to apply their expertise on preexisting projects outside their normal geographic area for marketing.

They realized that specialization was important, but that it had to be on a national basis; their market areas had to grow much wider. To maintain their specialties, rather than taking any project that came along, many of them opened new offices in other market areas. This entailed extensive traveling, which could be exhausting and expensive. It also meant investing in electronic linkages via computer, fax, and telephone to enable them to contact their vendors and consultants all around the country more quickly. Fortunately, the technology existed to meet their needs.

Design firms have learned that to stay profitable in slow times, they must focus on clients' needs and wants. This is not a time to entice or educate, but to expend effort to find out what potential clients believe they need and design our presentations accordingly. This effort builds rapport, putting the design team in the position of friend or team member. Responding to a perceived need is part of an understanding relationship built on mutual respect. Do everything you can to encourage your clients to see your relationship as dedicated to their best interests.

Keeping in touch with your clients is still one of the most important things you do. Whether it's a busy time or a slow time, it is critical that clients understand you are a part of their team. We must remember there is a great deal of competition out there vying for the same projects. If we want to keep our clients, we need to understand their directions and keep in touch with them on a regular basis.

Time is a major issue today. So often the people who have the money and can afford it don't have the time to buy it. Many of those who have the time don't have the money or interest in buying what we have to sell.

The Basics

In our research, we look for change and for trends. Change is what brings us business. As we look at the opportunities for research, the key is to find what's different and then determine whether that difference is better. Market research is an important tool for the design firm, as we are dealing with such a specific market. Market research identifies the clients, their backgrounds, and their needs. It gives you your market segment, a subgroup of the entire population. Positioning, the image a company projects with respect to its customers and competition, is one step of a marketing plan.

In the past, there has been a strong emphasis on focus group research. Marketers would bring a group of people together to get their response to a specific product or offering. The response then became the basis for approaching other clients. Focus group research has been valuable in determining just how a product is accepted by a specific group.

Marketers coined the term "psychographics," which in essence means that people with similar lifestyles and similar habits respond in similar ways. Today, everything we purchase can be reviewed. Chips inserted by barcodes on the products we buy can determine how many times a person sits on a certain chair or applies lipstick and how hard a fabric is. Marketing researchers can learn so much about us that it's scary. There's no such thing as privacy.

This means that everyone expects that we, as interior designers, also have similar knowledge. Some of it is available to us, but on the whole, designers don't have the sophisticated barcode systems and technology to be able to collect this type of information.

You can hire someone to do this for you, but few design firms are large enough to afford the luxury. If you can afford it and want a professional market researcher, a good place to start is with *Bradford's Directory of Marketing Research Agencies*, 7720 Wisconsin Avenue, Bethesda, Md. 20814. It lists firms, their principals, number of employees, and the types of marketing research they undertake.

A good market research professional, someone who dedicates his or her energies to the field, has a proven track record. A person who does nothing but market research may be more skilled at it than an advertising agency or public relations firm would be.

Is it expensive? Yes it is, but sometimes this investment could save you time and money. A firm that spent $50,000 on a research project saved $2 million: it had allotted that amount to a new program but found it would not be well received, and ultimately did not undertake the program. Even if you're doing small programs, test small market groups, talk to your clients, stay in touch, and keep a record of the results. Don't collect information for its own sake; collect information you can use.

Tools of Market Research

Where can we obtain information, what type of information do we need, and where are we to go for this information?

When we think of market research tools, we first and foremost think of the Internet. We believe we can find anything on the Internet. There is a mass of information there. We must be very cautious, however, because a lot of this information isn't verifiable. It does give us a good basis to begin researching, however.

Newspapers, business publications, magazines and state-wide organizations are source materials for the research marketer. Special-interest publications such as *Wall Street Journal, Barron's, BusinessWeek, Forbes, Time, The New York Times, Fast Company,* and others help you spot the trends. They report on what companies are doing and the changes they are making.

The U.S. government is the largest publisher in the world; you can make good use of government publications if you know how to find them. A popular guide is available by writing to the U.S. Superintendent of Documents, U.S. Government Printing Office, Washington, DC 20401. You can request catalogs and specific recommendations for publications in this way or contact the Small Business Administration Office or the Department of Commerce field offices.

McGraw-Hill publishes the *Dodge Reports*, which lists buildings under construction by geographic areas. Other data included are design firms and other professionals involved, and details of the contracts.

Standard & Poor's *Industrial Surveys* analyzes trends in construction utilities and transportation.

Local papers published by the Chamber of Commerce and statewide business organizations and local business journals can be valuable. Don't underestimate the value of local newspapers and magazines!

Which section should you check first in your local newspaper? You may want to look at the sections on companies on the move, and on changes within the community. On a daily basis, look at firms that are hiring or are looking for new types of personnel. If they're changing their personnel, they are likely to be changing their interior spaces, and they will need design services.

Sources for Trends

Learn to look for and recognize the trends. Before you can create a marketing plan, you need to investigate what is happening in the interior design field now and in the next twelve months. We are still in a dramatically service-oriented period. Service must be part of every design practice, whether it's very small or a superstar. This is a requirement. Nordstrom department stores, for example, have been a service model for many years because they go just a bit further to ensure customer satisfaction. We realize service is an important part of our professions and every member of our team must contribute.

Another top trend today is that people want excitement and unusual experiences. They don't just want an average interior; it has to say something.

Some of our greatest competitors right now are clients who are doing their own work. Whether these are co-workers or family members, these individuals think they can do it. It's true: they can do many things that they couldn't in the past. Technology has permitted them to find sources that only designers had access to before. This has taken away most of the mystique of interior design.

However, once these individuals have some actual experience in design, they may realize they can't do the exceptional. This is what our market looks for. They search for the exceptional. They look for people who really want something different, who themselves are doing something outstanding. Those are the people who want and need the professionals.

Real estate agents and building owners know when companies are on the move or purchasing properties. Cultivate a source in the real estate field. Some firms have developed great practices just because they know one or two strong people in the real estate field. Owners of any large project, such as an apartment building or office building, are a good source of information. Usually these owners want to set and maintain a design standard and tone for their building, and are therefore happy to share this information. Every region has several organizations dedicated to business development. The Chamber of Commerce is one of many. Some organizations handle business development for very specialized groups, such as minority-owned firms.

Often community government officials are aware of new building projects and industries coming into your area. Keeping in touch with your local officials gives you an early warning of local trends.

The government is a major purchaser of design services and products today. It is a special type of client with specific communication requirements, both in qualifying a project and in documenting the job. To formulate the appropriate approach, you may want to attend a course on the subject. The Small Business Administration and other local business development organizations offer courses, as well as up-to-date guides and contact lists.

CHAPTER 8

Targeting the Right Clients

N
ow that you have defined your company through a company profile and examined the marketplace needs, compare your findings. How well do the skills and abilities your company has to offer fit the demands of the marketplace?

You have a general profile of potential clients. Now is the time to narrow it down to a definition of the best client you would like to attract. Do this by defining "good" and "bad" clients.

Good Clients

1. Good clients see your firm as a partner and an asset.
2. They ask your firm to do work that is within the realm of what you do best.
3. They are demanding in a way that stimulates your staff to perform at its highest level.
4. They respect and follow the directions you present as a result of mutual project development by your team and theirs.
5. Finally, good clients are willing to pay you appropriately for the energies and commitment you dedicate to their projects.

Bad Clients

1. Bad clients don't value your firm and are unwilling to develop or continue a relationship. They don't give you the time and information you need to develop the job.

2. Bad clients ask you to perform work that is outside your experience or specialty. They make demands for types of work that may be your weak points—you are not prepared to handle their day-to-day support or extensive paper flow, for example. Their style of management is drastically different from yours.
3. Bad clients don't follow your professional direction. After much design effort has been invested, the bad client will change the design and do it his or her own way without considering the problems such a change will cause elsewhere.
4. Bad clients weaken you and your staff by decreasing your enjoyment in your work.
5. Finally, bad clients don't want to pay appropriately for the efforts you extend on their behalf.

Profitable firms build on the common denominator. Know who your best clients are. Many designers believe their best clients are those whose projects they enjoyed working on, or those who are easy to get along with. But there are other factors to consider, such as the time invested, the project budget, the profit, and any referrals you derived from the work.

In any good project, the client has to make demands. He or she must want to live and work in appropriate and well-designed spaces. Some clients may communicate these demands by calling you forty times a day, but being demanding doesn't necessarily mean being a pest. Good clients must feel that their spaces are important, or they wouldn't be willing to invest the money, time, and effort it takes to produce a good project.

A project can only be as good as the client. You relate better to clients when you understand their behavior—what they want or will do, when, and how. Learn about this best client's behavior. Is the client's profession one that is steeped in tradition or one that is known for swift action?

Are clients willing and able to invest what is appropriate to their situations? The client's firms must show a profit, so there is a limit on what he or she can appropriately spend. If the client underspends, the project won't meet the required standards for his or her need. If he or she overspends, it will overtax the client's finances. To mortgage the client for the rest of his or her life to do design work on an office or an apartment is foolish. There must be a balance between the cost, the use, and the funds available.

What attitudes do the best clients have? They may be able to afford anything, but they don't just spend the money. How do they value design? Education and exposure are part of that best client's background. If the client has never seen it, he or she probably doesn't want it.

What services must you provide? How much effort and expense will you incur to win the project? We can afford many things, but not everything.

We all like to think we are individuals, but we do fall into patterns. The more precisely a design firm can define its best clients, the better it can serve them.

Choosing the Right Jobs

You must determine which clients are worth approaching and how much seems wise to invest in each individual project.

Large projects and continuing commissions are the most financially desirable projects, but keep in mind that there is a great deal of competition for those jobs. Sometimes the most lucrative projects come from smaller clients with whom your firm has a rapport. Review your success in getting jobs. If you are trying for projects in a certain geographic area and you've lost the last six or eight, you are either going after the wrong jobs or your marketing presentation needs to be rethought.

What kind of project do you do best? What do you do so well you can do it without even thinking? There's usually one type of project you know how to handle almost completely without any point of reference, any reviewing, any studying, or talking to anyone else. It is something that you know inside and out.

Define your best work. It should be the cornerstone of your marketing plan. There is no point in spending time, money, and effort to win projects that are hard to produce and unprofitable.

When I look at a project, I estimate how much of it is familiar and easy for our firm to accomplish. If we are familiar with at least seventy or eighty percent of the project, I know that we can produce it with no problem. The minute you find this drops below seventy percent I suggest that you run from the job! Stay as far away from it as possible because there is far too much risk involved. Yes, I like to be creative ... but keep that creativity at no more than thirty percent to safeguard your ability to manage and profit on the project.

A little challenge is great, but don't let the challenges get too high. Sometimes a project seems too exciting to pass up. If you want a project that really doesn't relate to your past experiences, there are ways to team up and work with other people to develop the job. Still, you must take risk into account. If you involve other professionals, will the job then be profitable? How can you manage this project, keep your client happy and come home with a bit of profit at the end of the job?

The fastest way to ruin a company is to allow it to grow too fast or take the wrong projects. What jobs are right for your firm? What jobs are most profitable? A project can involve dollar amounts and seem prestigious, yet still be less profitable than most other work.

My firm worked on a country club project a few years ago, a highly visible project with active committees. At the same time, we had another project that was simply replacing textiles. The two projects produced just about the same dollar volume. The textile replacement project was with a client with whom we had worked two or three times. It was completed very quickly—in a matter of hours. We worked on the country club project for weeks and months on end, from six in the morning until eleven at night on many days. Obviously, it was less profitable than the textile replacement project.

As you look at the profit on your projects versus the time you've spent, you come to realize which jobs are right for your firm. It's best to look for jobs within that range. Some jobs may be financially beyond your abilities. Other projects may simply take too long. Or a fast-track job may come in at the wrong time for you.

Each time you consider a project, take into account these issues.

1. Is this the right job for your firm? Is it an area of design with which you are familiar?
2. Is it the right size?
3. Is there an opportunity for professional growth? Does the job offer new challenges? Otherwise, it's not stimulating.
4. Can your client make decisions? Some people can't. One corporate firm that I know of has been working on a decision for nearly seven years, and the firm has yet to assign the project. It just can't seem to make a decision within this area of work. So try to learn how well a firm makes decisions, or the job may never get off the ground.
5. Have you had experience in working with the firm? Is there an established relationship?
6. What experience does the client have in working with designers?
7. Will you be working with reasonable people? Or are they overly demanding and impossible? If they have been unreasonable with the contractors and other designers on the project, they're probably going to be the same with you.
8. Is the timing right? Will you have to rush to prepare your proposal? Usually, a poor proposal is worse than no proposal. Can you complete the job within the expected schedule? Does it fit into your current schedule? Has the client allowed adequate time to do the job properly?
9. Does the client pay his or her bills? Before you decide to take on a new client, obtain credit reports and check with other people the client has worked with. If it will be impossible to collect your fees, it's better to stop right now!

10. Is the potential client connected to a competitor? Does the client have a relative or a very close friend in the field who is also a designer, or has a furniture business or dealership? If so, it is probably not worth any great effort to pursue this client.
11. What is the competition? How many other firms are vying for the job?
12. What will it cost you to develop this client? We can go after almost any type of project, but some projects are more expensive than they are worth. Look at your cost in time and money, and decide if it's worth it.
13. Will this job be profitable?

Now that you have looked at what makes a good client and what such clients mean to you, we need to consider whether our branding process is appropriate to attract them; whether we have the right relationships; and whether we're representing ourselves in an appropriate way to the right clients. The rest of the book will help you explore these issues further to determine whether you are presenting yourself in the right way to the right clients.

CHAPTER 9

Partnering with Technology

There was a time when the computer was more of a production tool. Today, it's a key communication tool. I remember when we had people in our office who did wonderful computer-assisted drawing (CAD), while someone else did great drafting. There were times we used regular drafting because it looked nice and was great. We went back and forth for thirty years. Now, there's no question, everything is done by CAD. There's no choice, because we're sending plans to all types of vendors, contractors, and architects.

It's said that when Alexander Graham Bell invented the telephone, people asked, "What will I do with that?" I think we felt the same way about the computer. Today, it is a major communication tool, as key as the telephone is.

When using the computer, though, we must be very cautious about how people receive it. Some people check their email twenty times a day. With others, we're lucky if they check it once a week. We find that a fax is noticed much more than something that's mailed. But in some offices, an email is more noticed than a fax. In others, a fax is far more noticed than an email. The point is to know your receiver.

The accuracy and detail of email are incredible. We can send beautiful pictures in color; we can do wonderful script and beautiful graphics that couldn't be received via fax. But we have to ask: Does the person at the other end have the equipment to receive what we send? Keep a file on each of your clients and the other people you communicate with.

Speak with them occasionally, and find out their best technological tool. Gear your communication accordingly. Fortunately, we can mass-email quickly—such as a press announcement about completing a new building with environmental considerations the media might want to see or perhaps include in their publications. We can send a release to thirty publications as quickly as we can send it to one. Yet, in some instances, a publication may want to be treated with discrimination. The editor may want to know he or she has first rights to publication. Again, we need to know to whom we're sending something and how we're sending it. How we handle sending information can make or destroy the whole process.

Also remember that not everyone whose email address or phone number you have wants to hear from you. Decide which people are really interested in hearing from you. Do you have the email address of the top twenty percent of your clients who are really interested in what you do, so you can keep in touch with them on a regular basis?

INTERNET IMPROVES BUSINESS

Americans spent over $100 billion on products and services over the Internet in 2006. To put this into perspective: In 2006, $83 billion worth of residential furniture and bedding was sold at retail in our country, with about $800 million of that sold on the Internet.

Jerry Epperson, "Internet could help improve your business," *Home Furnishings Daily*, 2006.

Another use of the Internet is for "virtual events," or "webinars." These combine an Internet feed displaying images of a speaker and other materials—such as a PowerPoint presentation—with a telephone connection for live question-and-answer sessions. Virtual events are a wonderful vehicle for designers, especially specialists, can use to present what interior design can do for a particular group. One of the advantages of virtual events is that audiences can "attend" wherever they happen to be, in their home or office.

While the Internet gives us wonderful opportunities, it's also an arena for piracy and fraud. We're seeing more items being taken and used illegally for other purposes. Recently a designer had one of the photographs pulled from her Website and put into the publication of a competitor. You can expect to see more of this type of piracy and fraud, and we need to keep guarding against it. There are legal responses available, but these are difficult and expensive.

Designer Use

ASID recently released a research report about the way designers use the Web. The finding was that designers principally use the Web for resourcing and not as strongly for marketing. My experience with the Designers' Business Forum has indicated something very different. Designers are using Websites more extensively than in the past. They see Websites becoming an important marketing tool. In most instances, except for some specialties, designers aren't generating jobs directly from the Web. However, they're referring people to the Web to see their portfolios. Some of the specific specialties, especially the more commercial ones, find Web resourcing very effective for their marketing.

More designers are looking critically at the quality of their Websites, realizing they must keep them simple and specific, with good photography and graphic presentation. At first many designers used photographs they took themselves. They're good photographs, but not good enough. People looking at the Internet are very critical. Webpages must be laid out with style and have good-quality photography to ensure that the Internet is the most valuable communication technique possible.

If you're going to use voice-over, use a professional voice. It's best to have someone speaking about you and your firm objectively rather than doing it yourself.

Email Etiquette

Just as there is etiquette for other forms of personal communication, such as the telephone, there's a proper etiquette for email.

Be professional. Use appropriate language that respects the professionalism of your firm.

Be efficient. State your subject and get directly to the point. Make sure your message isn't overly long.

Protect your firm from liability. Both liability and lawsuits can arise from inappropriate emails. This is becoming more of an issue, so be cautious and remember that your email is a permanent record. Add disclaimers as appropriate.

Answer emails as quickly as you can, but give accurate information. If you don't have the correct answers, don't say anything.

Emails should look attractive and professional. Use the proper structure and layout. After all, you're a design firm.

Read your emails carefully before sending them to be sure you've said exactly what you want to say—keeping in mind that this is a professional, and can be a legal, document.

Obtain permission for copying a message or an attachment. Don't use email when discussing confidential information, since it can be handled inappropriately.

Put the subject matter in the beginning of the email on in the "subject line" so that the recipient will know immediately who the email is from and can decide to accept or reject it.

At the end of your emails, state the response or reply needed.

Guidelines
- Be precise. Avoid using long sentences.
- Answer all questions directly and specifically.

- Use proper spelling, grammar, and punctuation.
- Make the message personal, but still professional.
- Use standardized templates if you're sending repetitive emails to contractors or vendors, so they'll know exactly where in the email to look for the information they need.
- Make sure your emails are legible. Use a font and type size that are large enough and easy to read.
- Don't write in capital letters. It'll appear as if you're shouting at the recipient. This is something many people find offensive.
- Add the recipient's address last to avoid an accidental "send" before you complete and read over your message.

Websites

The Website can be one of our best promotional tools. It's not necessarily a selling tool, although a few Websites have done well with a limited number of specially designed products. But on the whole, the Website is a great introductory and support tool for most design firms.

Websites provide an excellent way for potential clients to get to know a design firm. Clients today are not necessarily buying off the Web, although some firms do feature certain products they've created on their Websites and claim it's a viable business. But mostly, a Website is a reference tool for clients who want to decide which firms to use and to learn more about a firm before making an appointment.

Design firms keep their portfolios online and find this practice is an excellent source for references. When a client calls a firm regarding a project, the designer can refer him or her to the firm's Website so the client can look at the portfolio. You can also customize what you want to show a client and email it.

When presenting your design portfolio online, use as few words as possible. Have a professional voice speaking about your firm's abilities. Be careful not to state the obvious. People can recognize that it's a living room or kitchen, so use your words to describe a special feature you've incorporated into the design.

Today, Websites have replaced Yellow Pages ads, although it's still advisable to keep a listing under your subject in the Yellow Pages. But instead of investing in large Yellow Pages ads, designers refer prospective clients to their Websites in these ads.

Websites today are very changeable. Have your technical consultant design your Website in a way that you can make minimal changes in your studio, or have that person on a monthly retainer to change it often. Designers find it necessary to change and update their Websites frequently. Some do it every month, some every quarter, and some even every week.

Many design firms are establishing an area on their Websites where clients can go anytime to check their projects and determine their exact status. This feature is often suitable for new construction or contract projects that have a lot of detail. Many builders are using this feature, but it's quickly becoming a tool for interior designers as well. Designers suggest this feature needs to be controlled, in that the design firm may want to keep some of this information as inner-office communication or as direct communication with other design consultants. Passwords permit individuals to access the information that is appropriate to each user.

There are many specialists who set up Websites, including some college students who do it with great skill. Setup and service charges may be calculated on a monthly basis. Or in some cases, Web designers charge a yearly fee for setup and service for that first year, and then a continuing fee for updating as needed. Or, the updating can be done within the design studio itself. Webpage companies often furnish designers with a picture frame and software, so if designers want to add to or change their Websites, they can do so themselves in their own offices, rather than always having to go to the companies for service.

Magazines often use Websites to find or qualify references for their publications.

Most Websites are a work-in-progress. The number of hits varies, depending on keywords. If a designer has featured a published article or a client who is well-renowned or a star, this will often bring many hits. One designer said the firm gets almost 40,000 hits per month, but that is often due to certain references, rather than clients looking for a designer's particular portfolio. But it does bring the firm in front of a large number of people.

Many designers today are linking their Websites to ASID for added credibility, so clients researching these pages will know that the designers work according to the practices and standards of the professional organizations they belong to.

Designers are concerned about the quality of their Websites and are putting tremendous energy, time, and investment into coming up with appropriate sites.

Points to consider:

- Make sure your site is user-friendly. You need to avoid confusion at all costs.
- Make sure graphics and photographs can be downloaded quickly and easily.
- Make sure the colors are appropriate on your photographs and general layout. Distortion can ruin a wonderful photograph.
- Make sure your links function properly so there's no breakdown.
- Make visiting your Website an enjoyable experience for clients so they come back again and again.
- Know your audience. Design the site according to what you think your audience is, then monitor it. Use Webmetrics, which will tell

you when people enter your site, how much time they spend there, how many hits you have, and the key words they've used to find you.

- Look at the sites you most enjoy and the ones you feel fit the design field best. What can you learn from them?
- Your Webmaster will place search terms—the keyword Metatags, words that best describe the site's content—into your site so your clients can find you easily when using search engines. It's important that these words relate best to your particular style of work and your overall Website.

Blogs

Blogs are becoming increasingly important. They often position designers as experts in particular areas.

Here's the definition of "blogs" offered by Webopedia, an online encyclopedia about computer technology: "Short for Web log, a blog is a Web page that serves as a publicly accessible personal journal for an individual. Typically updated daily, blogs often reflect the personality of the author."

Blogs are a way that people can interact and discuss a particular subject. They also help clarify whether the person blogging might be a reference or a professional you want to work with. Blogs can also explore a particular topic or issue further.

Designers find that by having blogs they stimulate the interest of clients. The designers can develop rapport with the clients that might turn into future relationships.

Blogs are a very inexpensive tool—something anyone can do. It was surprising to hear a recent Book Channel discussion regarding publication editors and blogs. The editors stated that their publications are accepting blog information and often use it on the same level as information from professional journalists. Blogs were once considered amateurish, but they have become much more accepted and a well-researched tool. It's not just what kids do—but what professionals do as well.

In fact, you have to be careful about what you blog, because it represents you as a professional. There's a great deal of discussion about whether blogs should be anonymous. Many people feel this is inappropriate, because you wouldn't know who you're corresponding with. This issue will continue to be debated in the future. At this time the most important point is that you should maintain a high standard in your blog and direct discussions in the way you feel they should be going.

You also may want to link your blog to your Website.

PowerPoint

Many firms today prepare PowerPoint presentations, describing the qualities of their firms and the personalities of their staff as well as illustrating examples of their work. These presentations can be emailed to prospective clients, or made available to real estate agents or other professionals who may be representing the design firms in securing new clients. When we find that the University of Chicago's School of Business and other university business schools are requiring prospective students to present a PowerPoint presentation with their applications, we realize how common this form of communication has become.

Portable Video Projector

There's a tiny laser in development that will allow you to turn your cell phone or MP3 player into a portable video projector. You'll be able to point your phone to a wall and project an image the size of a sixty-inch TV screen. New things are happening every day. All these new technologies are changing the way we present ourselves. We're in a field that's supposed to be new and high-tech; therefore, we need to keep up to date with everything that's available.

Voicemail

Make sure your voicemail recording message is friendly and short. Also, respond to your voicemail messages quickly, or have someone else respond to them if you're not available. People aren't pleased with waiting today. Shorten the waiting time. Make your replies as efficient as possible, but also pleasant.

CHAPTER 10

Techniques That Develop and Nurture Relationships

It's cheaper to keep one old customer than it is to get a new one.
—Pepper and Rogers, *The One to One Future*

After you've established the clients you want to develop—your new list of prospective clients—decide how you want to build a bridge between your firm and this "best" client. It takes five to ten contacts and many different techniques to develop an appropriate relationship with a client. You may wish to use a combination of several techniques discussed in this section.

These techniques include public relations and publicity; your logo and Webpage; CDs and videos; and promotional mailings and advertising. Also included are networking, entering design contests, entertaining, community service, and participating in show houses. If you have a message to bring to the public, you could write articles or do public speaking. There are as many methods as there are designers.

- Select methods compatible with your style of business.
- Choose the person or persons best able to accomplish these goals.
- Allow a budget for the tools needed to carry out your plan.
- Arrange your schedule to support the program.
- Commit yourself.

In addition to specific techniques of developing relationships, most designers have many wonderful ways of extending hospitality. In today's world, bringing people together face to face is the most valuable thing we can do. There are so many ways to do this that are not particularly expensive and yet can support and nurture beautifully the relationships we need for our type of business.

Public Relations

Public relations has three goals—to make you known to your resources, your peers, and to your potential clients. Any public relations person you hire will tell you that those first two are easy to accomplish, but the third is much more difficult.

The success of a public relations program is reflected in the firm's ability to win the right types of business, or in the resulting sales. If you have targeted your market and developed a good definition of your firm's specialty, your chances for success are better.

There are two basic methods of obtaining sales. One is direct. The indirect method consists of creating a desire, which is part of marketing. This can be achieved by advertising, public relations, and other types of business development.

Advertising is a direct method of saying you have something specific to sell. With advertising, you take aim at your specific target audience. Direct mail allows the same control. Publicity, an aspect of public relations, is more indirect. You depend on a publicist or an editor to write appropriately about your firm.

In its broadest sense, public relations is any interaction between you or your representatives and your market. How do you sound when you answer the telephone? Each person on your staff who comes into contact with clients should present him- or herself in a way that reflects well on your firm.

Public relations includes customer service, and doing the best work you can possibly do. Encourage clients to think of you as part of their team. The hours and the energy that you spend working with those clients will be rewarded manyfold.

Keep in touch with your clients. You should talk to your current clients on a weekly basis and your past clients preferably on a monthly or quarterly basis, if you want to keep them as clients. This is also one of your best sources of referrals. Remember: It costs ten times as much to develop a new client as to keep an existing one.

Where Do you Spend Your Time?

The way we spend our time and where we spend our time can greatly contribute to our marketing efforts. Are you spending time where your potential clients are? If you're a dedicated designer, you're happy to show off your design prowess and to share experiences with your clients. Find a way to use your downtime, either in contributing to a project in the community or being around your potential clients. Designers who are able to do this often are able to build close relationships with clients, relationships that support them in long-term client relationships. This is what we all want. The question is: How can we develop these relationships?

One way is to share part of our clients' lifestyles, charities, social events, or simple everyday activities. So look at where you are spending your time. Is there a place or a way that allows you to accomplish some of the things that you enjoy or need to do, while establishing communication with potential clients?

Public relations includes participating in community activities, going to Chamber of Commerce meetings, the historical society, and other community projects, especially those that relate to our potential business. Even where you do your grocery shopping or where you exercise can turn into a public relations effort. A group of male designers gets most of their business by going to the YMCA at noontime. They meet other businesspeople on an informal basis, some of whom develop into clients.

Find some common interests with your potential clients: play tennis, do aerobics, jog. . . . Clearly, if you aren't interested in an activity or if it isn't appropriate, don't do it. For example, it will be hard to appear actively interested in the PTA if you don't have children! Find an activity that complements you.

Remember, developing a client takes a minimum of seven to ten meetings. If you can do it informally at the country club or during another activity, you are likely to build rapport and a structure on which you can base that large sale.

Make it a point to meet people. Leave your studio for lunch. Go to dinner with people. Be seen. Donate your services to a charity function, so you can share a client's special interest.

Creating Publicity with Special Events

One of the most successful methods of publicizing your work to the right potential client is to have a party at the just-completed project of an existing client. Our clients love to celebrate with us. It gives them the opportunity to show off the space they're so proud of and also introduces the designer to many new potential clients.

While working on the project, suggest to the clients that they give a party when the job is complete. This gives the client something to look forward to while things are confused and out of synch, and it encourages craftspeople to finish the project by a specific date.

Ask your clients to think about their prospective guest lists, and offer to help with the party's arrangements by furnishing the champagne, food, or flowers, or any number of these things. Share the overall expense with clients. You might also suggest that you will show them how to present this space—how to "dress it in party clothes." If they agree, you can set it up, creating the format for their future parties.

This method is very successful for our firm, and several other designers have had tremendous success with it, too. Very often we train our staff to explain special details of the job as they take guests on a tour of the finished project. It's an effective way to use that just-completed design as a promotional tool.

Hold a Student Career Day

Holding a career day for high school students and their parents can be good public relations for a design firm. Use a display of your work to demonstrate and explain the interior design field. Students benefit from contact with a professional interior designer. You are seen as the exposed and, in effect, a career counselor.

You benefit in many ways. The career day presentation creates good will; you are contributing to the community. It brings in the parents, giving them firsthand knowledge of the quality of your work. They see you investing in their children. Therefore, you are part of their team. Participating in career days can also aid in future recruiting of student assistants to work in your studio.

Use Your Studio

When your studio meets your standards and fits your image as a design professional, use it. Use it as a place to make some of those seven to ten contacts required to make a sale. Your studio is an excellent place in which to demonstrate your work efficiency. Find ways to bring people in to see your studio—not just your clients, but people you would like to meet.

You may also offer your studio as a meeting place for a community group of which you're a member. Place examples of your work strategically so that they are noticed by people who walk into your conference room. This allows you to introduce your services casually to people who may have no idea what designers are about.

Sometimes its easier to get and keep the full attention of your client when you schedule a meeting during a mealtime. If possible, set it up in your studio presentation area or conference room, and have it catered. This allows you to devote the entire meeting to the subject of design.

Establish a time schedule, and stick to it. Let the client know that lunch will be served at noon and that he or she will be finished by 1:30. Because so many people have special diets, check your client's preferences in advance.

Keep the materials needed for the presentation separate from the food. Either make your presentation first and serve the meal later, or serve first and present later. Even the most beautiful samples lose their effectiveness when smeared with food.

There should be at least one small design touch that sets this meal apart from the average business meal—the tablesetting, placement of food, napkins—any small but interesting touch.

Seminars or Clinics

Very often, design studios will present seminars to their clients and the community on subjects ranging from historic preservation and Victorian decor to environmental issues and more. If your firm sponsors a program on an appropriate subject, it boosts your credibility. It shows your audience that you understand what makes up a quality presentation on that specific subject. Don't hesitate to use outside consultants; a good presentation adds to your firm's prestige.

A successful seminar—one that builds goodwill—has several key elements. The first element is planning. Decide on the size of your target audience, whether you will present a single program or a series, and whether you will charge. It is usually wise to charge for these programs in some way. If people pay a fee, they are inclined to be sure that they don't miss any of the programs. People tend not to value what is given freely.

The topic must be appropriate to your firm's style of work. If your clientele loves historic restoration, and has inherited antiques, a seminar on the correct use of battered cement pedestals and chicken wire as decorative elements probably won't go over too well. Likewise, a seminar dedicated to do-it-yourselfers isn't appropriate if you're trying to develop clients for your firm. If the audience is composed of facilities managers, the topic can be technical. It's best to look at your potential clients and to gear the subjects to their particular interests.

Choose the right setting. If you plan the talk as an informal gathering, your studio conference room may be large enough. If you open the talk to the public, it may be necessary to rent a space. Hold the seminar in an appropriate facility, so that the people attending are comfortable. We are designers; therefore, people attending a program of ours expect to come to a reasonably good space. They expect comfortable chairs. They expect controlled temperatures and a well-designed presentation. They know that as designers we understand the difference between so-so and just-right; anything less will only cause problems.

If your program is suitable, you may use it as a fundraiser for a charity. This not only gives you a new potential list of clients, but shows that you are very committed to a local charity. This helps build that network of people that encourages the development of our practices.

Present the programs professionally. Depending on the subject, you may want to bring in an expert. When you bring in an expert, audiences recognize that you have associations with other qualified people and can therefore cover a wide range of subjects.

For a seminar, you need a group of good professional speakers. Few speakers can handle a long seminar themselves unless they have been highly trained. Breaking the seminar into teams can ease the pressure. Find a star. Find people who are experts in their fields, and let them talk about their specialties. If you're a well-trained public speaker, maybe you should handle the presentation. If not, find somebody else who is qualified and appropriately trained.

People who attend your seminar will have the opportunity to meet many of your staff people and the members of your team. If you bring in an expert speaker, that leaves you and your staff free to chat with the individuals who attend. It gives you a chance to meet them and to interact around a subject in which both of you are very interested.

If you're the expert speaker, consider what your message is when designing your speech. What point do you want to make? What thought do you want your audience to take away with them? Use this as your beginning, because you want to leave that audience with a clear idea of the purpose of the speech. Then build on it.

(For more on public speaking, see Part 2.)

Networking

The process of networking is most often used for business development. It is not so much what you know, but who you know, and how you use those contacts that counts. Through networking, you can learn information about jobs, people, and situations that credit reports don't cover. A good networking system is of great value in finding the right type of client.

Each of us has been involved in at least one networking group. Some have been productive and worthwhile, while others just don't make it. Effective networking must have a goal, a strategy, and a direction. The basis for a networking system is your list of friends, a telephone book, your correspondence files, and your address book.

First of all, for a networking system to work, you must make regular contact. You may meet every Tuesday morning for breakfast, and at that breakfast, each of you should bring at least one lead. This is a requirement: You don't go to the meeting unless you can suggest a lead for one of the other people at the table. Exchanging updates on every member's activities paves the way for more useful conversation.

Don't be afraid to make the first contact. If specific people would be good contacts, be assertive. Make a phone call; say hello; talk to them at a meeting. Explain your position and the ways you could work together. Make a referral, and bring them a client. Then they owe you one.

Ask the right questions. You're there to find out what is happening in the field: what's new, what's terrific, and who's doing something—who could use you. You can probably acquire some information about anything just by contacting four or five people and asking where you can find a particular craft or item. People like to be considered authorities. So ask the right questions. This is not just a social visit; it's an opportunity to develop business.

It's also valuable to network with your competitors. Understanding their trends helps us know how to compete with them. If they've added twenty-four people to pursue business with doctors, maybe we should consider another arena. There are many ways to share information without jeopardizing your business. Good relationships with your fellow designers can save you a lot of aggravation and money by simply sharing tips.

Stay in touch. Meet regularly. Sometimes it's better not to start a relationship if you can't keep it up on a four-to-six-week basis. Send articles out of the newspaper to members of your group. Do anything you can to let the people in your group know you're still interested in them.

Send birthday and anniversary cards. If you can learn these dates for your contacts, keep them in a book and organize your mailings by month.

Send thank-you notes when someone does you a favor. A hand-written note makes more of an impact than a verbal thank you, but that is important too.

Promote other people. You accumulate goodwill by introducing people to each other and recommending them for projects. When I meet people who are good in their disciplines, I try to introduce them to the right people in the right situations.

Work at enlarging that network. Usually introducing people to a network makes it stronger; however, if it gets too large, it's not as effective.

Finally, evaluate the results. Have you received any business from being in this network? What type of referrals are you getting, and how much time are you spending on this program? Is it worth your investment in time? If you find that you've made eight or ten visits and come up empty-handed, perhaps you are in the wrong networking group.

Evaluate the people. The most valuable people understand your practice and may have worked with you. A good network contains people who are exposed to potential projects at the right time in order to be valuable to you. Which time is right depends on your specialty. If the project has progressed too far for your services to be needed or there is already a designer involved, there is no point in asking for leads. If you have made changes in your firm in the last year, or key people in the network have changed their positions and no longer have access to information you can use, you may need a different network.

Who are the people with access to information at the right time? Real estate agents know of clients looking for property; developers know of companies considering a move to a new building. Financial specialists look for money resources for new projects. Headhunters and employment agencies know of companies planning to grow. We need clients who are making changes, and our network team needs to be involved in and understand these changes.

Start a "good lead" club made up of people who are targeting the same type of client. This might include interior designers, architects, engineers, landscape architects, contractors, and suppliers. The type of design work you all do should be for similar clients. You may even work as a team on some projects.

Formal networking is not for everyone. You can derive some of the same benefits by asking the consultants you work with to introduce you to their clients, and offering to do the same for them. Having lunch with, or keeping in close contact with, an industry person who "knows it all" can keep you abreast of new projects and directions that could help you in your marketing.

Show Houses

The right show houses give you an opportunity to present your talents and expose your work to people who want to see quality furnishing or are interested in retaining a designer. Participating in a show house can be a strong marketing move if it's appropriate for your practice and if show houses present well in your area.

Designers have been doing show houses for years. These have been excellent fundraisers for many charities and community projects. They've also been an excellent way for designers to demonstrate their abilities. There are still some show houses that are very worthwhile. Certain designers are gaining great profits from them. One of the designers in our group has been so successful in doing show houses that not only has she gained a tremendous group of clients, but she's also been able to sell almost everything she has put in her room, and, in some cases, in multiples. At one show house, she sold twenty-three of a particular type of screen, eighteen of a certain type of lamp, and so on. Fortunately, the rooms were of such quality that they were very well publicized, and the designer has the personality to engage people as they go through her space. It has been nothing but a positive experience for her.

Other designers have found show houses very expensive and unrewarding. Today, you must be very cautious in deciding whether or not to participate in a show house. It depends on the level of design you're doing. Many show houses, which at one time had only top-name designers and extremely high-quality rooms, now have a lot of inexperienced designers not working at the level we would like to be associated with professionally. Before you decide whether a show house is for you, consider the type of client you want to gain and exactly how the show house is being managed. Certain groups have the ability to bring in large numbers of the public and the right people; others do not. I saw a reasonably well-done show house that brought in fewer than a hundred people a day. The designers had invested quite a bit of money. Unfortunately, the house just wasn't what it needed to be. There are so many elements that should be considered when running a show house. Experience is a major one. The following are factors you need to consider before you make the decision to put an investment in a show house.

Check on the coordinators. Have they run a show house before? What are their responsibilities? Some show houses ask you to staff the rooms; others insist your work speak for itself. Before you commit your firm to participating in a show house, find out what rules and regulations apply.

If you choose to participate in a show house, take the time to do it well so that it's representative of your work. One of the advantages is that you control the project and can design anything you like: a barrier-free room for use by the physically challenged, an office, playroom, or home exercise center. You have an opportunity to educate the public, to show that designers can understand its particular needs. The resulting room may be something you want to photograph for your portfolio.

The personal interaction is valuable. There may be several hundred or more volunteers working with designers in the house. They are potential clients or may lead you to potential clients. Often, a design group shares sponsorship with a charity. This adds an emotional appeal to the project, making it seem community-oriented, rather than just a commercial venture to showcase design talent.

Designers who participate in show houses are usually selected by a board, people who often hold social positions within the community. It takes a great deal of effort and time to do a show house. Usually this is about a year, from planning to completion. Check your schedule, and be sure you have the time and stamina.

Room allocation is often determined by a selection board or by chance. If you have a choice, consider both the room's accessibility to visitors and its photographic qualities. Take note of the condition of the room. It may need repairs before it can be used. Take these factors into consideration before you commit to doing a show house room. Be sure you know exactly what you're getting into before you start.

There should be a contract between you or your association and the charity. The coordination structure should be in place. The committee of a show house customarily has a general chair who organizes the entire project and the volunteer structure. This person heads and controls all other committees. Real estate matters—procuring the house and determining what agreements are required between the owner, design team, and charity—are handled by another person. A third person handles financial aspects, ensuring that all monies coming into the project are dedicated appropriately for prespecified expenses or that they go directly to the charity. Any mismanagement of funding can cast a bad light on all the participants.

You should check legal issues. Will you be held liable for events beyond your control? A lawyer should be involved to ensure that appropriate permits and liability issues are covered. You may be responsible for restoring the room to its original condition at the close of the show house. Have your attorney review the contract before signing it.

Normally, the show house will provide you with liability insurance, but it's up to you to talk to your insurance agent to see that the materials used in your room are insured properly for the time they are there. It is less expensive to add this onto your existing policy.

When you participate in a charity show house, it's usually at no expense to the organization: you're responsible for all expenses for your room.

In metropolitan areas, many wholesale sources will supply designers with products for use in their room in order to reduce the cost. The show house staff will have a list of sources willing to supply paint, carpeting, furnishings, electrical fixtures, and even services such as paperhanging and carpentry. This list should be made available to you when you're negotiating to design a room within a show house. In cities away from design centers, these arrangements are generally not available.

A good show house provides an easy traffic flow to accommodate the circulation of a thousand or more people per day. Parking is critical. If people can't park their cars and access isn't easy, they're discouraged from coming.

Is the house properly prepared and heated, if necessary? Are there public toilets, and are the electricity and plumbing appropriate? Usually, the house will be open during some evening hours, so lighting is important. Designers are responsible for cleaning and maintaining their own rooms, but make sure you know in advance what's expected of you.

Twenty-four-hour security should be provided. One or more guards should be available at all hours before the show house is open. Often, these are off-duty police officers.

Publicity is one of the main reasons designers participate in show houses. Before committing yourself and your staff to the project, ask what publicity structure is in place. Sometimes a celebrity is brought in for publicity value. Perhaps a local advertising agency has donated its services, or an experienced publicity committee is involved. Ask when press releases will be mailed and who is to receive them. You may be able to add key names or publications to the list. Close ties to local magazines and newspapers enhance the value of the project.

How will photography be handled? Some show houses designate a preferred photographer who offers a special rate. Sometimes magazines and newspapers send their own photographers. Can you arrange to share the cost of photography with one of the major resources for your room?

All press releases should include a telephone number and contact person the media can call for further information. The person or committee who handles publicity often contacts national magazines, inviting them to see the house. The resources who donated the furnishings will often alert individual editors.

With today's technology, photographs and press releases can be seen immediately by prospective magazines, publications, and television media. When a program is organized appropriately, the large amount of PR that can be gained from a show house is wonderful. This is one of the major benefits designers want from a show house. It can prove to be immeasurably valuable.

A good publicity program is one that encourages everyone who's been involved in the show house—including the person who donated it, as well as the charity or social organizations sponsoring it.

To encourage visitors, special rates for groups should be listed in promotional materials; the committee can also encourage group visitations by offering transportation and lunches. Investigate what other activities are offered in the region while the show house will be open. Perhaps the show house organizers can arrange a tie-in promotion with them.

The printed program should be of good quality. Look at past program books for the quality of their graphic design and their intended use. People keep these books and refer to them to remember the rooms and designers, as well as products and sources. The program can acquaint prospective clients with a good resource list useful for many years to come. If you design a room, invest in an ad. If you decide against doing a room, the show house program is still a good place to address potential clients through advertising.

A show house is usually open six or seven days a week. Ideally, you or a member of your firm should be allowed to staff the room. This way you have the opportunity of greeting the visitors and hearing what they have to say about your room. Some show houses won't permit designers to be present after the show house opens (except to clean the room); this is a drawback.

There will often be a sales office on site where people can purchase items from the rooms. The charity involved is customarily given a commission on the items sold. They also may accept donated items and present them for sale.

Show houses open with a preview party. The party may feature guest speaks or seminars that charge a fee. The proceeds go directly to the charity. Money is also raised through auctions and raffles of furniture and furnishings items. The renowned Kips Bay Decorator Show House in New York City auctions a completely furnished doll house each year.

To get the most out of your show house experience, keep a list of the people you worked with, and keep in touch with them. You've developed some strong relationships, and they can become a part of the networking and marketing plan for your firm.

Designers who do a show house one year should probably skip the following one. It's unusual to be as fortunate as the designer I described earlier who gets immediate work out of a show house. It may not have immediate return.

How to Get Published

You don't have to be a celebrity to get your name in the newspaper. All it takes is an email or fax to the local newspaper when an appropriate situation comes along. Perhaps you've just completed a remodeling project for a retail store client. Articles that mention your firm, that are written about your firm, or that are written by individuals in your firm, can reach more than one potential market. Reprints can be mailed to your list of prospective clients or become part of presentations for appropriate projects.

Try to get your work published where it will be seen first by potential clients. Local newspapers and consumer-oriented magazines are more likely to present you to the right audience than professional design journals, which are read primarily by your peers. There are magazines for every interest: lighting, bathrooms, kitchens, Victoriana, country decor. ... Don't forget trade journals covering your client's business. Whether the subject is accounting, nursing, or zookeeping, you'll find a magazine that covers it. Publishing directories in the library and on the Internet have extensive listings of magazines by type.

Research which magazines are appropriate for your special project and what their publication requirements are. ASID's pamphlet, "How to Get Your Work Published," lists major shelter magazines in the United States and Canada, including their editorial focus, contact information, Website address, design submission criteria, publication rights, and photographic requirements. Double-check the editor's name on the magazine's Website, since each of the magazines lists their detailed criteria online as well, and this information is likely to be the most up to date.

Read three to six issues of the magazine in which you would like your work to appear. This gives you a good idea of the range of what is acceptable to the editors. Write and ask for the publication's editorial schedule for the year.

When interior designers talk about being published, what we usually mean is photography and an article about that project. Check with the magazine to see what special requirements they may have regarding artwork. Most publications want digitized photographs. But check their individual requirements and specifications.

When investing in photography, normally we want to get more than one use out of it. Our Website may be the first thing that comes to mind, but also consider how photographs can be used for publication. The angles and orientation of the photographs determine their placement within a publication. A knowledgeable photographer can assist you in obtaining appropriate shots, whether you're aiming for the cover or another part of the publication.

Also, what we put on our Websites or other types of portfolios may require different types of photographs. Publications have calendars stating the subjects they intend to cover within each individual issue. It is important to understand their calendars so that what you submit is done at the appropriate time.

If any of your work or articles about it are published locally or nationally, have reprints made. Even though so much of our communication is done online, it's still valuable to have certain articles in print you can share with a potential client.

Often, editors will suggest two or three photographers if you ask for recommendations. Don't be surprised if an editor tells you the magazine will consider work only by a specific photographer. The magazine may be using a photographer's judgment to screen projects that don't fit its needs.

If you think a project may interest an editor, it's permissible to send photo image snapshots to determine his or her level of interest before you invest thousands of dollars in professional photography. You need written permission from the client if you intend to publish photography of a project. Most magazines will not consider publishing a project without this written release. You also need a release from the photographer.

Once you have the photography in the proper format, prepare a list of resources and technical details for the project. Include your own well-written description of the project: its goals and challenges, and what was achieved by your design. Include the name of the photographer in your write-up; it could get you noticed. Editors may know the photographer's work, even if they're unfamiliar with yours.

If you plan to write an article, the topic you choose should be one you have researched and with which you are comfortable. (For more on this, see Public Speaking in Part 2.) Consider the publication. Most of us work within a limited geographic range and would not benefit that much from national circulation. Design trade publications, which may be easy to break into, simply expose details of your working arrangements to your competition. This is not the vehicle in which to meet clients. It's usually better to be published in a small local magazine or newspaper your clients read than in a national publication beyond their scope of interest.

When your article is published in a national magazine, have reprints made to use as promotional material for your design studios. People save articles to use the author as an authority to support their own positions.

There are many ways in which you can use material written by other people for your own benefit.

An article cut from a newspaper can be sent to a client with a comment added. This may reinforce your particular theories more effectively than something you wrote yourself.

Publicity

Make a point of meeting the editors and writers of your local newspapers and area magazines. Volunteer your expertise in design matters; the next time they need a design term clarified, they may call you. This builds a relationship that may lead to your being quoted as a source within articles or eventually to an article about your firm or your clients. But don't expect quick results. Magazines work on a lead time of one to nine months, and people rarely act immediately on what they read. They may carry around a clipping for years before they're ready to hire a designer.

When you see an article by a writer you feel is of value and interest, let him or her know that. Let writers be aware that you're reading what they write and what your feelings are on their subjects, so your name will become familiar to them.

News Releases

Also known as "press releases," these are probably the most frequently used tools for getting out publicity about your design firm. However, news releases are often rejected by the media—either because they're written poorly, are incomplete or inaccurate, or have little or no local interest. Newspapers don't have the space to print all the releases they receive; certainly, magazines don't. To increase the chances that your releases will be used, first you have to understand what "news" means.

One practical definition is that "news" is what newspapers, magazines, or Webzines print—and what radio and TV stations air. "News" is not what your design firm or public relations consultant necessarily thinks it is. To write news, prepare the material as if you were a reporter working for a newspaper—using the same format and following the same punctuation and spelling rules.

Most releases begin with a heading "For Immediate Release," or else a date after which it's all right for the publication or medium to use the news you're sending. List your company's address, phone number, and other contact information—including a Website address—at the top of the page. This is followed by a subject headline and lead paragraph—including the main point of the story.

One good way to get your main point across is to use the traditional "5Ws and H" of journalism, answering the questions What, When,

Who, Where, and Why as well as How. Communicating the main point is important, because the editor may choose to print nothing but the first paragraph.

It's helpful to have direct quotations from someone in the company to liven up releases. But they must be accurate.

Keep releases brief. In most cases, one page is sufficient. If you think the story calls for additional background, you might want to attach a fact sheet as an addendum with the basic information about your design firm or special event.

Always fact-check your releases. Verify spelling, grammar, and punctuation. An otherwise valuable release might be rejected for language errors, let alone factual ones. You might want to consult the Associated Press (AP) Stylebook, which is commonly used by newspapers.

It's a good idea to include a good photograph; editors need these to design the newspaper or magazine pages.

To find news and get it used, you have to be familiar with the publication or other medium to which you're sending releases. What kind of articles do they publish? What interests their readers? It's also helpful to know the right editor or news director at radio and TV stations receiving the release.

More important, though, you have to know your own firm intimately so you know how to find news.

What is news?

- Announcements of a new office, new service, new product or production process, your latest financial results, or a new company policy.
- Bringing in a prominent speaker to a company function or holding a special event—such as a charity fundraiser.
- A spot release in order to announce a crisis.
- Response releases, such as replying to a report critical of your firm in the news or by a government agency.
- Hiring or departure of key personnel.
- A "guest column" that might highlight an unusual person or trend in your firm.

How do you send releases? There are many different ways—from snail mail to email or fax. Computer transmission is becoming the rule. You might be tempted to follow up releases with a phone call, but remember that an editor's time is valuable. The best way to get your release used is to find something with genuine news value—and write it well.

Media Interviews

When you have a media interview, make sure you know ahead of time what you want to say. During the interview, be careful to give concise, simple answers so you can be quoted easily. Media people are always aiming for a twenty-second sound bite.

Keep your comments very positive, but nonpromotional. Provide your interviewer with a media kit that has reproductions, not originals, of photographs. Make sure the kit includes information you can leave with the interviewer to help him or her understand the type of work you do. Follow up your interview with a thank you. It may be a small gift, or simply a thank-you note. Don't ever give media people information you don't want put "out there." Say only what you want known. There's no such thing as "off the record" in these situations.

Public Relations Professional

A professional public relations person develops relationships with editors in the same way a designer might but on a broader scale—and usually for more than one interior designer at a time. Professional publicists network constantly to keep up on what editors want and can use. They function as go-betweens to smooth the flow of information from those who have it to those who need it or might use it.

What should be publicized? Anything that is news: a new client, a completed project, a new direction for the firm—some kind of growth or change. Sometimes you initiate the flow with a press release about a project or a client. Sometimes the publicist calls you with a specific request from an editor. In either case, you have no control over the end use of your material. Once it leaves your office, it's out of your hands. If you need control, advertise.

Should you hire a publicist? It's a great idea, if you can afford it. Today it costs a minimum of $5000 a month for a good person; plan on sticking with a publicist for at least a three-year period, or don't begin. It's possible to hire publicists for shorter spans of time, or on a per-project basis, but it doesn't always pay to do so; ordinarily, they don't know very much about your firm, interior design, or how to present a designer. Hiring a publicist is an investment in time as well as money.

Publicists are most useful when you consistently do spectacular work or have new products and ideas to communicate throughout the year. When you receive so many requests for information and photography that it interferes with your ability to run your studio, you need a publicist to sort out which requests deserve your personal attention.

It's much easier for publicists to work with products than with individuals: Public relations for interior designers can be quite expensive, and it takes just the right person. But you don't have to do it alone. Several chapters of ASID, the American Society of Interior Designers, have hired a publicist to cover than. As their members complete projects, the publicist tries to place stories about their work with editors.

High-Impact Public Relations at Low Cost

Most large or national product manufacturers have public relations programs, for which they need photography of products in use. Manufacturers of carpeting, laminates, wallcovering, and tile usually have such a program. Manufacturer associations, such as the National Association of Mirror Manufacturers, the Marble Institute of America, and the Wool Bureau, all have public relations programs. By working with your resources, it's possible to achieve the kind of exposure that no interior design firm could afford.

When a product manufacturer photographs a design project, it is usually because his or her product is predominant, if not used exclusively. Some designers specify projects with this in mind. If your project meets the manufacturer's standards and fills a need, the manufacturer may offer photographs of it to a magazine or include your work in publicity packets for newspapers and news syndicates. These publications will often contact you for further information.

If specific product manufacturers do not choose to publicize your work, and if it does not fit into any of the categories of available design competitions, this does not mean your work cannot be publicized. However, you may have to hire a photographer and contact editors yourself.

Consider entering contests. Often, organizations that promote specific products also sponsor design contests for installations using those products. You don't even need to win to attract the attention of editors, because many ask to see every entry, not just the top five. Entering design contests offers a chance to see photographs of your projects in every magazine throughout the nation. Most clients love the exposure, and you get tremendous exposure, too. There is no way most of us could pay for this type of exposure, but there is a cost in the time and effort it takes to prepare professional contest entries.

Awards are also valuable. If you've received an award recently from any source, make sure that your clients know about it. It doesn't matter whether the award is from a local Chamber of Commerce or a major national competition. Your clients are happy to hear of it because it validates their faith in you. Work with the award sponsor by providing him or her with names and addresses of publications that should hear about the award. This is good for both you and the sponsor.

Specialty Shops

Specialty shops make buying easy and fun for clients. They can select a store based on their distinctive needs or style preferences. There is such a wide market that clients become confused. In specialty shops, they find what they want easily. The trend toward specialty shops is also true in the design field. It is just as hard for you to find the client who likes your particular style as it is for the client to find you. By having a specialty shop, you have identified your firm as a specialist.

There's so much to choose from. Clients' tastes are educated by magazines, television, other peoples' homes and offices, show houses, and more. A specialty shop presents a design style in infinite detail, right down to the accessories. Shopping in specialty stores is easy and fun, and that is what buying from designers should be.

Some specialty shops are franchised. If you open a franchised shop today, you have about a ninety-five percent chance of success. If you start an individual shop and style it yourself, you stand about a five to ten percent chance of succeeding. Franchise lines are styled and made in bulk. There's an opportunity for lower prices and rapid delivery, even for exclusive items not available through regular sources. The lines are usually broad enough to allow for creativity.

Direct Mail

Direct mail is the most selective method of advertising and promotion. It consists of any advertising or promotional materials that a firm sends to a prospective client. Some firms produce newsletters; others use a newsy business letter. Even today with all the junk mail, people still like to receive a well-written business letter. Direct mail, as well as any other type of advertising, is most effective when done on a continuing basis.

Mailings keep your name in front of both prospective and past clients. Tell people of your design activities; you could even send photographs. Send a simple letter or even a postcard, alerting the client to publicity you might have received. Or send a reprint of a recent newspaper article about your work. Plan a year-long program. It need not be expensive, as long as you are consistent.

Screen those candidates, however, because it is a rare designer who can afford to do mass mailings. Mailing list houses say that any response over three percent is excellent. Use a list of potential clients developed through referrals, past clients, and personal contacts. Then design a mail program; you will be sending six to ten pieces to the same person. For best results, send a series of related pieces, and follow them up with personal contact by phone or in person.

Direct mail can still be a valuable method of advertising and promotion, although most people feel Websites have taken over. It depends on the type of clients you're dealing with and the way they use the Internet. In some cases, a good piece of written material is still valuable. One of the most effective tools is a postcard featuring a designer's work. Many designers make up many portfolios using groups of photographs. It's a wonderful way to get multiple uses out of your photography expenses.

When publishing a newsletter, be careful that you have enough material to do a series of at least six. Many people start a newsletter and then don't have sufficient material to continue. Many newsletters that were faxed are now being sent strictly by email, although some fax letters are still popular. Even though it's quite expensive, a newsletter is still a valuable way of keeping in touch with clients, especially if they know it's something personal from you. It's amazing to see the difference between a letter with a little note on it or some personal comment versus a communication that appears to be photocopied. Most mailings today are very selectively positioned. The idea of doing mass mailing is almost out of date.

Very little of our advertising really pays. With selectivity, however, it can be a valuable tool. The key is, the right pieces are workable. Just sending something is a waste of money and not valuable, unless that "something" is outstanding.

How well does direct mail work? A firm in California developed its client list from scratch after moving there from New York. Within three years the firm become very successful, just as a result of direct mail. Several firms have increased their share of the market by sending out promotional mailings.

Mailing lists targeting a special interest group by profession, neighborhood, or income level are available for a fee through a number of sources. Dun & Bradstreet offers such a service. (The section in this book on tools of market research gives more detail about mailing lists.)

Advertising

Advertising and public relations often work together. Some experts view any promotional effort as advertising, whether it's a brochure, your stationery and business cards, or a direct mail campaign to your prospective client list. The graphic presentation for all advertising should reflect the design standards of your firm.

Should you advertise? Advertising is a direct way of presenting your company to your clients. If you use a publicist and you're interviewed by a magazine or newspaper reporter or editor, there is always a chance that individual will represent you inappropriately. Advertising allows you to present only what you believe people should know about your firm.

Advertising is not as effective as it once was. Even television shows have dropped back on commercials, because advertising hasn't proven to bring results.

Often people are so busy they just don't have the time to absorb the material being put in front of them.

Consider the money you invest very carefully. If it's selectively placed, advertising can be very worthwhile. Everyone has a Webpage, which has become part of every designer's vocabulary, as well. But we still have to be careful about investments we make. Person-to-person contact is really the most successful form of communication. People want to get to know you; they want to know why you're involved in this profession and what you bring to it.

We do need reminders as we go along, whether it's in advertising or public relations. We need to let people know that we're still actively involved in the interior design profession and what we're doing. They're curious. Find ways of presenting yourself that are appropriate and not terribly expensive. Keep the program as an ongoing thing. Make sure something goes out on a regular basis. Don't wait until you have a need for business and say, "Now it is time; I must do some promotion or advertising." Work at building your company on a day-in-day-out basis.

If you do decide to advertise, do so with great discretion and use professional assistance, especially if large dollars are involved. It's advisable to use good professional help. Moreover, since we're designers, it's expected that we do everything in a well-designed manner. Therefore, all our advertising and promotional materials need to be well presented.

If your firm is new or if you're changing your specialty, advertise. Advertising is a way to keep your name in front of potential clients. Physicians are doing it, attorneys are doing it, and there is a professional way to handle it. Hire a professional to design your ad. Your advertisement should be in keeping with the tone of your firm and your particular segment of the market.

Where should the ads run? You obtain the greatest advertising impact from publications with the appropriate audiences. A publication's audience is made up of those individuals who are interested in, and responsive to, a particular advertising vehicle. Your ads should run in the trade publications of the professionals you want to reach, in local newspapers, and in the programs of show houses if these are popular in your area.

How frequently you advertise is up to you, but professionals suggest that advertising is most effective when it's consistent. If you will be advertising frequently, find an agent who will work with you. "Frequency," the number of times you advertise during a specific period, and "circulation," the number of copies of a publication sold or distributed during a specific period, are terms agencies use. A firm that advertises infrequently and only in low-circulation publications is probably a small account.

Even though you may be a small account, there are small agencies that will work with you to develop your public relations and advertising objectives. Ad agencies will sometimes make suggestions about ad placement, bringing to your attention publications you might not have known existed.

A good advertising agency for a design firm has handled similar accounts in other fields, or at least firms of similar size. A firm that handles only large accounts will not find your firm very interesting. There is no point in interviewing fifty agencies, but try to see three or four so you have a basis for comparison. Schedule a session with the agencies. Let them come into your studio, meet your staff, and see what you're all about. Before making your final choice of advertising agencies, speak with other companies that have used a specific agency.

Give your agency an outline of your company history, as well as copies of any other advertisements you may have run and of articles written about your firm. Provide any information that demonstrates how you relate to your clients and to the public. Anything on paper is valuable. It acquaints the agency with the kind of information you want to disseminate, and how you would like to look to the media.

Designate one person on your staff to be responsible for working with the advertising agency. The ideal person has an in-depth knowledge of your firm, so he or she can comfortably discuss it. This person will act as the liaison, gathering information and forwarding it to the agency as needed.

Once the agency has all this information, ask the representative how he or she would handle your account. Ask for a budget recommendation. Most agencies want to work on a yearly basis. A well-coordinated advertising program deserves at least a year-long plan.

Normally, the advertising agent will need to return to his or her office to put together some suggestions. These suggestions should be reviewed by the CEO, your advertising liaison, and one or two other primary people. Visit the agency's office and see how it works. Review the budget and establish priorities.

You may wish to start with a small project and see the results, rather than committing to a long-term relationship. Create a general plan and budget for the year, then make a more precise plan and budget for six months. At my firm, planning a complete format of advertising and public relations programs and coordinating them with staff activities has worked best. Decide what you want to promote in the next six-month period and how you want your money spent, then put it into a format you can discuss with your advertising agent or consultant.

Advertising and public relations are investments that don't carry a guaranteed response. In the end, however, investing in a well-planned program often proves worthwhile. When a company that had run continual advertisements stopped, eventually the work slowed down. In order to keep your name in front of your public and to reinforce your image, some form of public relations and advertising is necessary.

CHAPTER 11

Who Will Lead?

Who will lead? In a small company, of course, it's the owner or principal; in a larger company, it's probably a team. Nevertheless, in most instances, the CEO or president is the leader of the marketing program. But no one can be left out; marketing must be a cooperative effort of everyone in the firm.

Someone needs to maintain records and see that we keep on schedule. That doesn't necessarily have to be the principal. In small firms, it can even be a consultant you bring in periodically or consult with by telephone. This consultant keeps you on target and makes sure you've accomplished all the necessary social interactions and technological tasks.

Technology plays a large part in our program. A lot of things we would have mailed in the past to clients and prospective clients are now emailed. This is a marvelous way for us to keep in touch visually in a way we could not do in paper form. Our program has to be a constant effort; therefore, it takes leadership and direction. It takes someone who understands the ability and goals of a company and is willing to review the market from that perspective. It takes someone who can determine the best design system for developing your firm and for creating the right connections to do so.

Design firms must have a committed client focus at all times in order to stay profitable. We need to do more than entice or educate. We have to try, really exert an effort to find out what our clients are thinking and then base our presentations on their wants and desires.

The Japanese have been very successful at this. They deliver, and they deliver fast. Nordstrom's is known for its high-quality customer service. Its goals are in line with its customers': value, a great shopping experience, and great customer service. Every staff member is invested in this mission.

A design company must be seen as a friend or a team member. There must be trust, an understanding relationship that can weather all types of trials . . . an honest relationship built on respect. Each tries to do the best for the other.

Do everything you can to help your clients see your relationship as dedicated to their best interests. Keep excitement levels high. Keep your studio attractive, fresh, and looking new.

Use your creativity to design ways to continue to promote your image. Select a person to take the responsibility to manage your marketing program, and someone to provide leadership. These roles could be performed by two people, but who is best suited to do so? If no one on your staff fits the role, perhaps your next investment should be in someone who does.

The leader must see his or her role as a special opportunity and should believe it is the *most important* mission of the leader's career.

The leader must have a vision about the future of the field and the firm's position in it. The vision must be in market development. What will this program do for the firm, and how will it complement the working process? The leader must understand the business environment and be able to see how your firm fits into this environment.

> The leader must be a team builder; a good plan is a product of the team.
> The leader must have great communication skills.
> The leader must lead by example. It's easy to do something new when you have seen it done before.
> The leader must be able to keep everyone motivated.
> The leader must be able to keep the program focused.
> The leader must measure results.
> The leader must find appropriate ways of acknowledging and rewarding achievement.

> "Marketing should be the concern of the entire business, not just the marketing department." In his book *The Marketing Mavens*, author Noel Capon explains how we must put customers at the center of our businesses. It isn't a question of what we want, but of what clients want. We should make that the guiding philosophy of our firms. Capon, a professor at Columbia University Business School, takes a very scientific approach to marketing. His aim is the differential advantage of your firm over any others—and using that advantage to create long-term winners, not just short-term ones.

While the leader supplies the vision and fire, a manager's role is equally important. Plans and fervor aren't enough. The manager makes the program work and adjusts it when necessary. If one staff person cannot make a phone call, the manager decides who the next best person to do it is. The manager sees to it that day-to-day goals are met and that the program stays on target. If your program entails more paperwork or a different paperflow, the manager makes it happen. When a public relations firm or an advertising agency is involved, the manager is usually the liaison to it.

The manager keeps the program on schedule and makes sure people and supplies are ready so the firm stays on target.

Extended Team

One of today's key directions is the extended team. The team effort doesn't stop at the design services level. It must include the client, consultants, craftspeople, and perhaps the manufacturer. No single discipline can produce the perfect product alone. Interior design is a sophisticated, technological, and scientific discipline. Only the well-coordinated efforts of the design production staff and the corporate management of the design team can bring the end product to the high level needed to meet the progressive demands of the 21st century.

To understand the future directions of the firm's clients, the design team must have information from the client company's strategic man-agement group. The consulting designers need to extend the resources of in-house designers and facility management staff to meet the many changing demands, even after the project is finished.

Computer technology can speed interaction between clients and all design consultants, whether they are large multiservice firms or single-person specialists. Some large firms with facility management departments will only work with interior designers and architects who use a specific CAD program. This may affect your decision about what kind of computer to purchase.

You have to allow for ongoing changes when you structure your relationship with a client. Whether the client is buying products from your firm or not, purchasing needs to be addressed. For routine replacement of furnishings, it can be less effective for a facility manager to write a furnishing contract with a vendor he or she has never worked with before than to do so through the designer who has used that vendor on a regular basis. Obviously, this affects what you specify.

Even product manufacturers are adopting a team approach. Some resources offer to coordinate their products with other materials that will be used in that project. Mergers and acquisitions within the office furniture industry mean that we can go to a single firm for seating, workstations, and freestanding desks.

Many people come into the design field because they want to work alone, but this is not the best time for one-man bands. The economic climate suggests that the best and most profitable way to run a firm, and to give the client the best project, is with a good working team.

Working in a team is one of the leadership directions of the design field in the 21st century. When you have people working with you, you can't just tell them what to do. It's a question of setting an example. During a project, it isn't what you say, but the way the client sees the project unfolding, the way it's managed, the way they see you coordinating it—and the responsibility and position you take from an administrative viewpoint. How is the job working? Can you design this project in a way that it really looks well managed and professionally run? This will do more to bring you new clients than any action you take.

Scheduling Marketing Efforts

You should do something that relates to business promotion, marketing, and communicating with clients every day. These are not functions you can just perform occasionally. If you do, your mindset isn't ready for the business of marketing. Also, your practice is less likely to be effective and profitable.

You must devote time each day to certain marketing and sales issues. This is very hard for designers. We get totally involved in a project, and when we've finished, we say, "I guess I'd better do some marketing."

No marketing and client development plan works that way. You need to make these activities part of your everyday life. Spend part of every day keeping in touch with your clients, reviewing your projects, seeing how you can stay up to date, and keeping those projects coordinated. Telephone ten or more past clients every week; call ten prospective clients each week.

As you work on your business development program—and this is a progressive process—you need to hold meetings regularly and renew that commitment. Make sure that everyone has agreed to buy into it. Ask your staff members to sign up for their parts of the program; let them decide what parts they will play during that next block of time and how they're going to do it. At the next meeting, review and evaluate their success.

12

Preparing Marketing Materials

To appeal to your chosen market, you will need to update graphics for your stationery, collect letters of commendation, write brochures and sales letters, and arrange for photography or a video for your portfolio. You will want to arrange for a photographic portfolio for your Website or for your traditional portfolio. You should also prepare resumes of your major staff members, a history of your projects, and a list of the firm's capabilities. Every item that leaves your office should present your firm in a professional way.

Graphics

Look critically at your business cards and stationery. Do the graphics project the right image for your firm today? Graphics have style and date, just as design does. A good logo is part of your branding. It must be distinctive and memorable and have some relationship to your corporate style. Ask someone experienced in corporate images to review your logo to make sure it conveys the right message about your firm. This isn't something that you should do yourself.

Your logo is an important part of your brand and must work in a variety of venues, from your Website, to your business cards and stationery, to ads, and even product labels. Your logo should reproduce on a photocopy. Embossing and white-on-white don't copy; this can be a problem, because clients often make additional copies of presentations.

If your graphics are in several colors, they should still be readable when converted to black and white. The typeface should be legible and an appropriate style and weight.

One of the first things each client sees is your business or calling card. Cards should be a standard size and include all the basics: your name, title, and telephone number; your email address or Website; the company name and type of business; and your logo, if you have one. Your business card represents you when you and your staff cannot be there. The information should be complete and the graphics appropriate for your style of business. A novelties salesperson may need a card that has fold-out gimmicks; most designers do not.

Your stationery should be of a standard quality and color to accept a correction fluid if you need it. Do not use erasable bond; the typing can smudge. Most of the newer computer printers can use both fan-fold and single sheets of paper and offer draft and letter-quality printing. Use reasonably well-designed stationery; it is attractive if stationery and business cards coordinate.

Letters of Interest

Once you have appropriate stationery, you can send out letters of interest. When you see a project happening down the street, you simply drop the firm a note. An effective letter of interest includes four main points.

1. You noticed the project and would like to acquaint the firm with your firm.
2. Your company is prepared to handle some of the details of this project.
3. You have materials and answers to some of the firm's problems.
4. Ask to meet with firm representatives to compare your company's abilities with their needs.

(Please see sample letters on pages 114–116. Letters of interest can be forerunners for sales letters, which are covered in the section on preselling in Part 2.)

Ask for Referrals

When you finish an outstanding project and your clients are very proud of the job, it's good marketing to ask your clients if they know other people who might benefit from your types of services. Since they have worked with you throughout the project, these clients understand exactly how your firm works and what you have to offer. Do they know other people who might be able to use your services? In most instances, clients are very happy to recommend you.

Ask for a Letter of Commendation

A client who is pleased with your work may be willing to write a letter of commendation. Ask clients to explain in this letter how your services have been valuable to them. Some designers ask for several sheets of the client's letterhead, write the letter, and then ask the client to sign it. It's much better, however, if the client agrees to write it in his or her own style and, of course, on his or her own letterhead.

Then take your group of letters from bank presidents, corporation heads, residential clients, or whomever, to show to potential clients. Or you may wish to have them photocopied to use in mailings to prospective clients. Many times these letters explain how you fit within their system, and this is very valuable to the potential client.

A letter of commendation for an architectural firm stated: "We chose your design firm because we had seen some of your other projects. We feel we made an excellent choice. Your solutions were extraordinary, imaginative, beautiful, and practical. Our new atmosphere makes working here a pleasure, and we are more productive." This letter was on corporate stationery, signed by the chief executive officer.

Another letter of commendation said simply: "We enjoyed working with your firm. You kept on schedule and displayed pride and professionalism in your efforts to bring us a well-designed project. We are so impressed with your firm that we will recommend you whenever we can."

Using letters of commendation instead of having the new client calling the previous client directly can help you position yourself with a new client. Some designers have a portfolio of these letters to show to new clients. Comments from the letters, and in some cases the complete letters, are featured on their Webpages. Some even feel this kind of portfolio is more valuable than a portfolio of photographs.

Portfolios

Whether you are a beginning designer or an established professional, your portfolio is an important part of your professional presentation and must be updated constantly. This doesn't mean older designs can't be included. The important thing is that everything you include is representative of the work you're doing or want to be doing.

"Befores" and "afters" are exceptionally good. People love to see how you solved a problem. Examples of details are also very worthwhile. When we see the photo of a complete room, we often miss the details. And yet, as each of us knows, it's the details that take professionalism and a considerable amount of design time and care.

It's desirable to create your portfolio in such a way that it can be changed easily, according to the type of client who will be interviewing you. That way, if you're designing medical facilities, you can show the prospective clients projects that relate to medical facilities. If you're doing a certain type of residential work, you're able to present examples of this type of residential work.

The major issue today is not to confuse our clients. So it's usually best to have a portfolio that can be styled to represent the situation you're currently dealing with. Your design specialty will influence the style and presentation of that portfolio.

Some designers use portfolios a great deal; others don't even have them. More clients are asking to see a designer's Website—and not just corporate clients.

An effective portfolio must be representative of your work, which means it can't be something you compiled way back in school; it has to be current. It has to be tailored to the type of work for which you are marketing, so a flexible format is a must. Clients don't want to see projects that don't relate to their business. Vary the portfolio according to the client's needs. If you are going to see a banker, don't take country club projects, because this isn't what he or she is interested in. Take only examples of financially related institutions that you have designed.

Since good photography is expensive and only certain projects photograph well, you may want to design a project or two each year specifically for your portfolio. When designers are starting out or moving into a different specialty, they often take a project on a very low markup basis or even for the cost of merchandise—with the understanding that the client will permit the designer to have total control of the design. That could include photographing the project to show the designer's skills in the way he or she would like them presented.

Often we work on projects that would be just perfect for photography, but one must consider whether the clients are comfortable having their projects presented in different publications. There's a great deal of emphasis on privacy today, so don't be surprised if a client doesn't permit a project to be photographed. This is unfortunate, but becoming more common.

Your portfolio can be effective in many different forms of presentation. Whether you select an online version, a CD, or a traditional portfolio, it has to be representative of your work.

Brochures

What about brochures? Brochures are not as popular as they once were. Websites have taken over. They seem to be where most people are putting their energies. Many designers feel they need something to leave with a client, so they create a nice folder or some form of brochure that usually can be altered to fit each situation. They can insert articles written about them or photographs to make the brochure more customized. Or, they may have a very simple brochure, explaining their general qualifications and a list of services.

The type of brochure you choose will vary considerably, depending on the specialties you're working in. Regardless of the type, it shouldn't look homemade. Have a graphic designer work with you on the brochure. He or she will show you how you can alter and develop some of the details of the brochure to suit different situations and clients.

The brochure text should state your general objectives, your values, and some information about your firm. It might also have a blank page on which notes can be written while discussing a particular issue with a potential client. Design the brochure so that you can replace it every six months, because this type of marketing piece dates quickly.

Photography

Why should you photograph your work? For a number of reasons: insurance records, a memory aid while you're working on a project or later, a tool for your marketing program, or possible use in a public relations or advertising campaign. The question should be how, not why. If all you need is a visual record while you're working on a project or for your long-term memory file, you can take some excellent shots. There's wonderful and convenient equipment available today. Every month they're coming out with something newer and better.

Fortunately, we're now able to save photos on the computer and flash cards so we can have thousands of shots. Previously, the cost of having that many photos would have been prohibitive, and storage would have been inconvenient. However, when you're considering photography for your portfolio, and especially for your Website, professional shots can make a tremendous difference.

If you plan to use photographs for publicity or advertising, hire the best photographer you can afford. The better the quality of the photography, the better your work appears to be. Take the time to look at photography in national and regional design magazines, and try to see the differences between professional photography and snapshots.

Good photography has an arresting quality. It takes hold of you and elicits a reaction on an elemental level. Excellent photography can manipulate the way you feel about a subject by changing the way you see it. The magic of photography is achieved with angles, lights, and the photographer's skill. Space looks different through a camera lens. Don't be surprised if you have to move furniture or alter your design just for the photograph. An excellent source of information on interior design photography is Norman McGrath's book *Photographing Buildings Inside and Out*. There are also a number of other sources worth referencing: *Photographing Architecture and Interiors* by Julius Shulman, *Professional Interior Photography* by Michael G. Harris, and *Interior Photography: Lighting and Other Professional Techniques with Style* by Eric Roth.

The photography in national design magazines and advertisements represents serious financial investment. Not all of your work merits, or even requires, such an elaborate and precise visual record. You might try to get your client to agree to pay the cost of photography. Clients may be interested in owning these photos for many reasons: for personal records or insurance, or for marketing their property at a future date.

Most design studios hire professional photographers only for projects they feel have some value for publication or make a particular contribution to their portfolios. However, keeping a photographic history of a project from start to finish is worthwhile.

Consider the final use of your photographs in determining whether you need black-and-white or color prints. If you plan to submit photography to a magazine for editorial use or advertising, check the publishing requirements. Don't invest in a form of photography that the publication for which you are aiming cannot use. These days, even a good-quality color print can be acceptable because the technology exists to correct less-than-perfect images.

Interior photography is a specialty and an art form; a skilled amateur may be able to produce arresting photographs that show what you want, but don't count on it.

Interior photographers compensate for unique problems. What you see when you look into a room is not what the camera sees. A camera's distortion of small spaces is so extreme that what you see through the viewfinder as perfectly centered is, in fact, off to one side. This distortion can vary in degree from camera to camera (it is worst with the throw away cameras), and the distance between the subject and the camera. The skilled photographer knows how to compensate.

You don't need to be a photographer yourself to get good results from a photographer, but you must provide some basic information. No matter how brilliant the photographer is, he or she is not a mindreader. If you don't tell him or her what you expect, don't be surprised when you don't get it. Show the photographer the pictures you've taken and some of the key shots you'd like incorporated. It's often helpful for a photographer to see amateur shots when discussing the opportunities for professional ones. On rare occasions, a photographer is so experienced that he or she will be able to tell you what is important about your space, but don't take this knowledge for granted.

When you are considering photographing a space, review the following points with the photographer:

What spaces are important?
Does the room have a focal point?
What qualities do you wish to capture?
Is there a particular mood or style that you want that photograph to present?
Do you need a complete room in order to convey this message? If you don't, shots of certain areas will do.
If you are hoping to be featured in a specific magazine that has special requirements, the photographer needs to know.

If you designed a table to enhance a sculpture, tell the photographer. If you want to emphasize efficient use of space, tell the photographer. Otherwise, you may get photographs that do not help communicate the qualities of your work.

Schedule the photography right away. Interiors change with use; they weather and acquire marks of wear. For example, a carefully placed display of collectibles may be shoved aside to make room for a stack of work brought home from the office.

Interiors are at their best during the first month of the installation. Not all marks of wear can be camouflaged successfully. Be sure that your work is photographed correctly the first time; you probably will not get a second chance. If the work is being photographed for possible publication, bear in mind that it may take several days for the photographer to fine-tune the lighting and the angles.

Videos

Videotaping can be an effective way to document projects from beginning to end. With the help of a reasonably good photographer you can create a dramatic and enjoyable presentation, especially if you add color and music. Even though most designers put some of their work on their Websites, it's often beneficial to create a video explaining the process of design. It should show how you really work but be no more than eight minutes long.

Make this video available to prospective clients. They often enjoy popping a DVD into their computer or DVD player to get a feel of how you work and what you're about.

Videotaped presentations don't have to be costly, although some design firms have invested heavily in this area. Fortunately, videotapes are much less expensive to produce today than they were at one time. Video presentations date so quickly; don't put so much money into one that you can't afford to change it with minimal effort. Videotapes can be altered and updated easily.

A collection of your photos can be worked into a presentation. Clients like to see before-and-after shots. You can take photographs of new products in furniture showrooms or at market and have them built into a simple, short videotape. Leave the tape with potential clients for a day, and then pick it up in person. This will familiarize the clients with your work on their own schedules.

You know your own community. Obviously your letters of interest or commendation need to appeal to the type of people you're writing to. Here are a few examples other designers have used. Keep in mind that you want to, in some way, personalize these letters, to show that you understand your prospective clients' issues and how you can bring value to them.

Dear Mr. Cross:

We understand that you will be interviewing design firms to help you renovate your health care facility. Our firm is interested in being retained for this project.

We have had a general interior design and space planning practice in Home City since 1982. During this time we have been responsible for a number of projects similar to yours, including the space planning and specification of furnishings for over 200 patient rooms and adjacent lobbies in two area hospitals, dental and optometric offices, and dormitories for 2000 students at a residential college.

On most of these projects, in addition to providing the traditional design services, we also analyzed the space, developed the project jointly with the client, and supervised the contractors as well as the installations.

You will be particularly interested to know that on the hospital projects we worked with Stevenson Bros., a highly skilled general contracting firm with an excellent record in this state. We and Stevenson Bros. are prepared to collaborate again on your project.

Our staff includes specialists in planning and design, both of spaces and of furniture. In addition, we also have longstanding working relationships with several local structural and electrical engineering firms and the well-known architectural firm of Tower & Stone.

To tell you more about our firm we have enclosed a brochure, project fact sheets, and a magazine article about one of our past projects. Also, please look at our Website for examples of our work.

We look forward to meeting with you to discuss our qualifications in more detail.

Sincerely,

James Doe
President
Doe Design, Inc.

Sample letter of interest.

Professional Administrative Service
123 North Broadway
Stamford, CT 06900

Prospective Clients:

We chose the architectural and interior design firm of I. B. Designer
and Associates for our office space and all public areas, as well as for
the entrance to our new corporate storage facilities in Connecticut.

Our choice, we feel, was excellent. Mr. Designer's unique solutions to
the almost overwhelmingly large spaces are pleasing to everyone who
is working in these areas—a factor most important to me and my firm.

We are all very proud of our various new facilities, as is Mr. Designer.
We would definitely recommend this firm to others for any project
whatsoever.

Sincerely,

J. A. Smith
President

Commendation Letter—Sample 1.

John and Elizabeth Jones
112 Country Club Road
Cincinnati, OH 19475

Professional Interior Design, Inc.
123 Front Street
Cincinnati, OH 19475

Dear Designer:

Elizabeth and I have been meaning to formally write and thank you for the wonderful contribution you have made to our family over the last three years.

Your talent, incorporated with your guidance and support, has provided us with two wonderful residences. Both are very different. Our city home, more formal, is easy and satisfying for our many activities, which include a considerable amount of entertaining. It's hard to believe, but we had more than 900 people here during the month of December. After all that "wear and tear," things still look great.

We love our mountain house as well. It is warm and so relaxing! We always feel equally at home here in the country. The personal touches you suggested give us the comfort we desire.

We both want to thank you particularly for the education we gained and the pleasure we experienced during the work process. We came to appreciate many of the skills and beautiful products you brought to us, since we understand their value.

You and your staff were very dependable, and their assistance was greatly appreciated. It was exciting and fun, and we now have two lovely residences we are happy to call "our homes."

We look forward to your continuing with us when we have needs for updates and changes.

With pleasure,

John P. Jones

Commendation Letter—Sample 2.

CHAPTER 13

Becoming a Major Force in Interior Design

It's important to select an area in which you really fit and are comfortable. Often this involves a cultural and educational background. Who are the clients you'll be working with? Are they the people you're accustomed to communicating with successfully? Find an area where you really belong.

One of the things designers tend to forget is that they need a strong infrastructure to support all of the details of their specialties. Without this, you can't do an excellent job or position yourself properly. Review what it takes to perform at the highest level in your specialty, and be sure you have the team and resources in place before you begin. The following issues need to be considered.

Becoming a force in the interior design field takes a very clear definition of your strategic objectives.

First review your mission statement, the objectives and goals of your firm:

- Consider your present position, then decide where you want to be and how you're going to get there.
- You must understand your firm's abilities and the competitive market so you can define your objectives clearly.

Analyze your segment of the market:

- How do they make decisions?
- You must know how they think, and how and when they're likely to use your design specialty.

Analyze your competition:

- Know their strengths and weaknesses.
- How do these strengths and weaknesses compare with those of your firm?

Identify any elements that will influence your success:

- What does it take to make you successful?
- Come up with a list, and draw up a plan to make it happen.
- Decide what's most important and set your priorities.
- Identify the cost in time, money, and effort it will take to accomplish each element in your success plan.
- Make sure you know what it takes to do accomplish each goal and what you can expect in return.

This is really a lot to cover. As you go through this book, you'll find that most of these strategic objectives are discussed in greater detail. The important thing to remember is that design is a serious commitment.

Act on your plan. There is no point in having a plan unless you are committed to making it happen! Don't let your plan for success be an abstract concept. Decide what action to take, and how to keep the plan in constant motion.

PRPPQ-Relative Perceived Product Value. This marketing term means public opinion. Check on the PRPPQ of design services.

Commitment

When you work for a design firm, you know the excitement of commitment. We are very deeply committed to our design work; we must be as deeply committed to marketing and selling and to client interaction. Otherwise, we won't be able to put in the energy needed to succeed.

In-depth commitment must radiate throughout the firm. As you work on your business development program, and this is a progressive process, you need to hold regular meetings to renew that resolution. Make sure that everyone has agreed to buy into the program. Don't just assign roles. If your staff really understand the mission, let them try to decide for themselves what they will be doing in the next block of time. You may need to assist them with this, but it's wonderful when they buy in and are dedicated to what they can contribute.

There is no space in the program for negative people. The leader and all players must be invested and deeply *committed* to the program.

They must enjoy the excitement of being part of the team. Leadership is key—this may be the role of the president. If this person is not the right type, find someone who is.

You won't enjoy the process if you don't have that in-depth commitment, and dissatisfaction can radiate throughout the firm. We must all have this commitment as one of our key objectives.

Enthusiasm

Are you passionate and enthusiastic about what you do? Do you really exude your enthusiasm in every interaction you have with people—not just your design clients, but everywhere you go and everything you do?

During a recent trip to Paris, the members of our Designers' Business Forum were fortunate enough to visit a wonderful florist, one of the most outstanding in Paris. Marc, owner of Hysope & cie, is very active in doing work for couture designers. When we notice the florist's work in magazines featuring flowers, in most instances it is his work.

When Marc explained to us how he works and the energy and effort he puts into his business, we were amazed. He said that he buys his flowers at 3:00 A.M. and is in the shop by 6:00 A.M., which gives him and his staff time to prepare their flowers. The shop opens at 11:00 A.M. and closes at 8:00 P.M. Twice a week Marc goes to Amsterdam for the market, which is 1000 kilometers away. The market opens at 2:00 A.M. Marc makes sure he and his staff are there when it opens to get the best selections.

Marc went on to explain that he's very particular about the flowers he uses and every fine detail. Listening to him, you realize this is a living florist. He exudes his passion and enthusiasm for his field. This was a tremendous attraction, contrasting with other people we met who work because they have to and have "only a job."

Our clients are resources. Everyone we meet knows how we feel about our profession. Be sure that you're able to radiate this enthusiasm. If you find yourself getting tired or burned out or don't feel well, go home and do something different to renew your energy. You can't let your market see you in any other way but as really dedicated to your profession.

Stick to It

In his book *The Dip*, Seth Godin describes the difference between successful and unsuccessful firms. It's easy to start something, but the important question is how to keep it going. Only businesspeople willing to persevere will become successful. The goal is to keep going and really stick to it. Don't quit.

Selling as Communication

14

An Introduction to Selling

I wish I could eliminate the word "selling" from this book; for many of us, "sell" and "selling" have so many negative connotations. The process of selling is an opportunity to build a long-term relationship. I'm not a salesperson; I'm the person who entices through creating a vision and a buying opportunity.

It's really critical to understand that "selling" means communication. It's not forcing or tricking someone. It's helping potential clients understand what we have to offer, helping them realize we have something they may not be aware of and need to know about. This something can enhance their lifestyle. We have to help our clients understand the benefits interior design brings to them.

Design is an investment, not a casual purchase. Both client and designers must invest in the project; therefore, it is important for both parties to spend sufficient time and research to be sure that it is the right investment for both. The right selection can affect and enhance many areas of our lifestyles.

Selling interior design services requires finding a prospect with a need, want, or desire; demonstrating to that prospect that you have the ability and experience to meet the need; and converting that prospect into a client. Your portfolio can be designed to support your communication effort; however, what sells a job is your skill at communicating your firm's ability to do the job. People buy from people, not from pictures.

Selling is a skill that can be acquired and mastered. It depends on your ability to both understand the particular client and to build a relationship with the client that supports the structure needed to do the job. Most successful professionals can sell. We are all salespeople from the day we were born. The question is: Do we sell the right things, at the right time, to the right people, to accomplish our goals?

> Jeffrey Giffamer begins his book, *The Little Red Book on Selling*, by saying, "If they like you, and they believe you, and trust you, and they have confidence in you, then they *may* buy from you." He also illustrates the point, "People don't like to be sold, but they love to buy."

Designers receive little training in communication, yet in almost every instance we must communicate well. There is no design if there is no one to pay for it. Sales are where the money comes from. To work on the kind of projects you want, someone must first promote design services. We must sell and build supportive relationships throughout the project. Who is better able to present this than the professionals who understand what they are designing?

Some interior designers are excellent communicators. A salesperson has to be positive, enthusiastic, and proud to work for his or her firm. A salesperson knows and respects the competition, but believes his or her firm will do a better job for the client. Most good salespeople have a lot of drive. They are willing to do whatever it takes to get a job. They have to keep their enthusiasm high; they cannot allow themselves to be discouraged. Even after they've lost a project or a sale, they are challenged to go on to the next.

Most effective salespeople operate under the K.I.S.S. principle, which means Keep It Short and Simple. Good presentations are prepared with precision, but they are delivered in a short, simple, and direct fashion.

There should be no surprises when you are trying to sell to a client. Make it easy and comfortable. Encourage them to ask questions. The more clients talk, the less you talk and the more you learn about their wants and needs and the way they think. In a sales conversation, the client should talk seventy to eighty percent of the time and the salesperson, twenty to thirty percent. This is the perfect balance.

Learn to listen. Very often, clients know what they want or at least have strong feelings they would like to express. Try to encourage your clients to give information and to tell you what they think is important. During a sales development conversation, your ability and willingness to listen is crucial. So are your skills of observation. You often pick up visual cues from surroundings or body language.

A good salesperson has developed judgment. When an executive is involved in nine or ten matters simultaneously in his or her office, it isn't a good time to press for a major decision.

Learn to direct a conversation. In trying to develop rapport, show interest in the clients, but try to keep the conversation related to the issue at hand. Good interviewing techniques build close relationships. Our interactions with clients show whether we have been working on a wavelength that they understand.

To succeed at selling, you must do it every day. You need to set up a schedule of interactions, whether by phone, in person, or through the mail. If you do so only once in awhile, you get out of practice. If there is one thing you need, it's practice. The client should see the designer as a competent professional and someone whom he or she can trust with design problems.

Be proactive: be the first person to call. Schedule your week and your day to allow for a standard time for getting in touch with clients. Of course, our business is to respond to needs, but it's more impressive if you can say that you have recognized a potential problem and suggested the issues the client should consider.

The Process for Selling

Market Plan:
> Know your firm.
> Know your client.
> Know how to reach client—bridge methods.
> Build confidence—position the firm.

Contacts:
> Meeting them—on your Website, by phone, in person, or by other direct methods.
> Building the confidence, trust, relationship (two-way contacts are the best way to do this).

Observation and Documentation of Needs:
> Combination of knowing your clients and research and development required to present an appropriate solution to their needs.

Design Work:
> With information supplied, prepare solution that will fit all of the clients' needs—design, budget, time, etc.

Presentation:
> You present your solutions to clients' problems; show them how your firm can solve their needs.

Approval:
> The client approves the solution presented by signing the proposal, confirming changes, or doing whatever is needed for next step.

Confirmation:

An ongoing effort to be sure the client's needs are met—that they are satisfied. This is constant reinforcement early in the job as well as follow-up. Keep in touch after the job is finished. (This is also a good way to promote yourself for recommendation to another client.)

Referrals

Sales Force

Sales is a highly skilled, organized profession dedicated to bringing a needed product to a buyer—an interested person able to afford and buy it. The sales process can vary substantially, depending on the firm's specialty and extent of services.

Many designers don't like to sell. If you are one of these, team up with a partner who *lives* to sell. To succeed at selling, you must find it rewarding. Otherwise, you won't be willing to go that extra mile necessary to win the job.

If selling goes against the grain for you, you ought to find someone who is really excited about it, who enjoys doing it, and who would like to partner with you and work with you to develop your opportunities. I don't necessarily mean a partner in the company structure sense; you could partner within a corporate structure, under a business structure, or simply work with a team member. It is so easy to sell someone else, but often difficult to sell yourself.

There was a day when the marketing or sales department of a design firm was considered lower class, not quite professional. It often occupied the last office down the hall. Today, the "Rainmakers," the people who bring in the projects, are the highest earners in most firms; they usually dictate their firm's direction. Many firms will not employ anyone who does not bring in work. Even the lowest level of support staff is expected to be out there generating business.

In many leading firms, the Rainmaker is the CEO or another top executive. This person determines the direction and the success of the firm. After all, without work, we don't have the opportunity to design.

Who should handle sales? Consider what is most comfortable for you, but recognize that part of the process of presenting your firm requires you to have a sales force ready. All key performers should be ready to play their parts. Once you find potential clients and know where your firm is going and what services are appropriate for you to render, decide who will carry out the sales effort. Have your system ready.

Each person in your firm should play some position on your sales force or marketing team. Each person has abilities and areas of strength. Although they may not be marketing director material, they still are part of the team. Marketing requires a total team investment.

Team or Partner Selling

Selling can often be more effective and more fun when you work as part of a team. Yes, it may take a lot of effort to get used to working with a partner, but once you develop a rapport, you'll practically know what they'll be saying next. You'll know what move they will make next, and you'll know exactly how to develop your presentation so it really bonds the client to your firm.

Look at your organization and see if you would perform better as a team member rather than alone. Then decide which members relate best to the client, and which members know each other's ways well enough to develop mutually complementary styles. This takes experience and practice.

Buckminster Fuller talked about synergistic issues in which two or more people working together can do the work of five or six. Sometimes two people produce less work than one. In a good situation, teamwork can lead to more exciting selling and presentation formats. Teamwork helps sell your services, because it's generally more interesting to the client.

Creating the New, Exciting, and Different

Today, focus groups are not considered the answer. If you ask people what they want, they often don't know. They don't know what to ask for, but they want something different, better, and exciting. They want to see something new and innovative. They want something that will change the way they live or work. As designers, this is our life—creating the new, different, and exciting. Therefore, we need to consider the clients' wishes as part of our presentation. What is your firm offering that no one else is? What can we bring to clients' lifestyles they've never even considered?

Problem Solving

Problem solving is one of the strongest sales tools in today's market. Clients are looking for firms that can take care of their problems, and most clients believe that their problem is totally unique or exclusive to them. Clients tend to believe that no one else in the world could ever have imagined their particular problem.

In fact, most of the problems we encounter are typical for certain situations, and we can almost guess in advance what the problems will be. But to the clients, a particular problem is unique. This is the first time it has happened to them. Allow them this feeling. But also bring them to realize that you understand their problem and that you are accustomed to dealing with situations of this sort because your job is to solve their problems.

You have to bring clients slowly to the realization that you are equipped and prepared to handle all sorts of problems. This means taking care to explain in detail how just one change in their businesses or lifestyles may mean that what worked fine before may no longer work as well. For example, ten people cannot work in a space meant for six, nor can six work as effectively in a space designed for ten. There are too many wasted movements.

Attitude

Attitude and approach are essential elements of selling. Be able to relate your product to something the client understands. A good example of this is how a particular furniture manufacturer addressed businesspeople through a magazine article. When asked the purpose of office furniture by *Success* magazine, Richard "Dick" G. Haworth, president of Haworth Inc., said, "It's a management tool. It helps people do their jobs. It transmits a culture of a company." His statement makes people think differently about furniture, makes office furniture a management tool instead of a bland necessity. Thus, office furniture becomes more desirable. Remember, selling is educating the customer so that he or she wants what you are selling, then turning that want into a need. Haworth's statement brings life and activity into furniture; it's part of the company's management system.

Spending time with clients is invaluable. Haworth also suggests that salespeople see clients in person as often as possible. Although technology in the form of telephones, faxes, and emails is wonderful, it does not replace personal interaction. Haworth feels it is important to stay stimulated by the customer.

The way we feel about design and our firm radiates from every movement we make. Clients speak to us with their body language; we project our feelings and attitudes in the same way. If you are not up and ready, it's best to stay away from that "special" client. We schedule these personal visits to enrich our opportunities. So spend time and effort to be sure you are really in the right, positive frame of mind.

Design is valuable. Keep this firmly in mind.

A very successful designer told me that a prospective client said she had a resale number or card that enabled her to buy the same things as he could buy in the design centers—so why did she need him?

In his gentlemanly Southern style the designer replied, "Honey, you don't have any idea of what to buy, and you don't have any idea of what to do with what you buy."

Today, clients can buy almost anything we can. They have access to most design centers and to many other resources through the Internet and other direct sources. But the key is, they sometimes spend a lot of money and receive no value.

Good design and great project management add great value to a project. With the right designer, clients don't waste money on wrong selections or mistakes. They *invest* money carefully, resulting in projects that function well and bring them joy.

CHAPTER 15

The Client Comes First

"Customers use our time up until their decision to buy. After that we are using *their* time. Therefore, we must deliver immediately," Stanley M. David wrote in his book *Future Perfect*. The objective is to shorten the time between their decision to buy and completion of the job.

Clients are the most important part of any business. We like to think they depend on us, and they do, but without them we have no business. Clients are the core of any business. They come to us with needs and hopes, and it is our job to help them accomplish them.

When clients call, you cannot think of it as an interruption. Clients give us an opportunity to work. This is the reason your business exists.

Nordstrom has built its retail stores on the creed: "Existing customers are our most valuable asset. The staff who serve them are their most valuable players." Anyone who has shopped at Nordstrom knows that the policy is strongly felt. It is the people who represent Nordstrom on the sales floor who exemplify store policies.

Keep in mind that your staff represents the company as the clients see it; the CEO isn't the most visible person. Yes, the customer comes first. This attitude starts at the top. Everyone on the staff must believe that customers are the reason the firm exists. Too often, the CEO has been burned out by too many experiences over the years and isn't quite as happy as he or she should be in dealing with clients. When this happens, the CEO should not be the leader. Set a clear policy for your firm. You all relate to clients. Dedicate time and effort to reinforcing the policy.

Acknowledge all types of staff behavior that demonstrate positive actions. Reinforcement is the best way to make them actions a habit.

In every staff meeting, mention good examples of positive attitudes; they require constant positive reinforcement.

Customers see themselves as important. They don't like to be treated as second-class citizens. Find out their needs, and make sure that they are treated well.

- Customers like to buy from people they like.
- If you or your staff are not nice to them, they'll use another firm.
- Customers want what they want when they want it. Often their wants are based on emotion rather than fact. If they feel they need something, they will establish a reason for wanting it.
- They feel that because it's their money, they want to set the rules. You must find a way to tailor your services to their systems.
- Customers will stay with you if they believe they are important in your eyes. You can't forget them if you want to keep them as ongoing clients.
- If they are unhappy, they will tell everyone, so exert every effort to keep them happy.

Dale Carnegie wrote in *How to Win Friends and Influence People*, "People are what they are because they can't possibly be anything else." We need to remind ourselves constantly that they have the right to do things their own way in their environments. We can't change them. Either we must learn to work with them or we should find other clients.

Know Your Clients

1. Spend time with them. Talk to them. Ask questions. Learn their ways, what they feel is important, their problems, and their joys. Record clients' personal information to build rapport in your future communication. Make note of the personal information they give you with pencil and paper, or your PDA, but don't spend the precious time you have with them keying in all the details.
2. Be sure your firm's telephone manners are what they should be. Check on this regularly. Are the people who answer the phone properly representing you? Consider everything from quality of voice (some voices do not project well over the phone) to volume (be sure it's at a comfortable level that can be understood). Does the person representing you know about the company? Are your employees giving out the correct information in an appropriate style?

3. Find out which system of communication was the best for your clients. Some people prefer emails or faxes rather than the telephone. Understand which system is best for the client, and then design a system that fits appropriately.

4. Establish an appropriate style and monitor your emails. Be sure they really sound the way you want them to. There have been so many shortcuts taken in email. Some of them are not very professional, nor do they extend the courtesies a company should be demonstrating.

5. Make client service a team process. Be sure that everyone involved in your company is aware of his or her position on the team.

6. Keep in mind that client relations is a lifetime project. You are never off-duty. What you do on your personal time can either build or erode your client base.

7. Find a way to conduct surveys regularly. Ask clients what they want, and what they like and don't like about your firm. Measure their preferences, desires, and objectives. Keep an ongoing record of results.

Courtesy and Respect

There was a day when "snob appeal" was in style in many galleries and design studios throughout the country, but it's surely not considered appropriate today. It's amazing to hear stories about how clients have been turned off by a ridiculing comment by a salesperson in a showroom or design studio. When such situations occur, it's an automatic turnoff. Wherever you take your clients, be sure everyone treats them respectfully. When a client hears a salesperson in a showroom say something about another person who has just been there, he or she automatically thinks, "What are they going to be saying about me when I leave?"

In any case, we have to be careful about what we say. I was appalled to hear someone say something extremely inappropriate in an office. It turned out the ugly comment was heard by a person on the other end of a phone, who in turn threatened the company with a lawsuit. Fortunately, I was able to talk the caller out of it for the moment, but it's really sad when great relationships, which have been built in so many ways, are totally destroyed when some foolish person makes one inappropriate statement.

Building Client Loyalty

• Know who the client is—not just the owner, but the staff, their sources, and clients. If the client is a hospital, know the staff, patients, visitors and suppliers. The client is not the building, but the people who use it.

- The client must become a team member. He or she must play a part in the design process.
- Your entire staff—not just you, the principal—must know the clients, not just by name but well enough to understand their goals and philosophies.
- Create a standard method of communication and an appointed communication schedule. Relationships need constant reinforcement.
- Save your time and that of the clients by using communication methods that are comfortable and compatible with the way they work and live. Consider paperflow styles. Do they prefer verbal or written communication? Do they prefer emails or faxes? What is the best time of day for them for personal visits, phone calls?
- Keep your promises. Be realistic in setting response dates—and meet them. Don't promise something you can't deliver.
- Record the personal information they give you—this is easy to do on a computer. Use this to build rapport. Send gifts or congratulations, birthday cards, and so on. We all like to be acknowledged and celebrated.
- Treat clients as if they're lifelong friends. Make every task and interaction suggest that you will be working with them forever.
- Personalize. The art of putting pen to paper has definitely been revived. Personalization is enormously important. "It's seen as a revolt against the impersonal nature of electronic communication," according to Patty Stracher, manager of the National Stationery Show. It's amazing how clients respond to a personal note, even if it's only a few lines. It shows that you really care.

Find Out What's Important to the Client

When approaching a client, find out what's important to him or her. A few weeks ago, a contractor told me, "I make sure that I treat all my clients the way I would like to be treated." I said, "Wrong. Treat your clients the way *they* want to be treated."

He looked at me with a very strange expression, so I explained, "You're really into cars. You've always had very unusual European automobiles and you understand cars. I don't understand cars at all. When I take my car to the garage, I want the mechanic to drive it, check what needs to be fixed, and deliver it to my driveway. That's all I want from him. I don't want all the technical information, because I don't understand it. I do want to know that he drove the car and he's sure that it will work for me. I need that reassurance. You don't. You know cars. You will want to know exactly what he found and a detailed description of all the problems."

Consider what is important to the client, not what is important to you. Spend time in the very beginning interviewing that client. Be sure you understand just what his or her needs are. Then, after outlining the client's needs, go back to your team and see what you can do to meet them.

Be Proactive

Don't just react to clients. Be proactive. You be the one to make the call. Respect their time, and create a system that also respects yours. Recognize clients' needs by taking the time to call them with a well-organized agenda. Schedule a convenient time each day for getting in touch with them, and advise the clients so that they know they can expect to hear from you. Doing this allows you to be well prepared with information and updates. You maintain your image of a professional; you are in control, and the clients feel that you're really on top of the job.

Yes, we do need to respond to clients' demands, but this proactive approach is much easier to control than fielding phone calls at the client's whim. If a client does make a request, explain that you and your staff are working on the project now, and that you need to discuss this issue with the appropriate people and then get back to him or her. You recognize the problem the client presents, but you also need time to present other issues that require consideration. Finally, ask, "Does this meet your needs?"

Email has helped us in many respects, but it also has created a standard of speed. Clients believe they can email you and you can immediately email them back the exact information they need. But we all know that a question often demands a lot of review not only by yourself, but sometimes by many others before you can give clients the correct answer.

It is not good in any relationship for one side to always be on the defensive. Try to put your firm in a position in which it can control the process.

16

Rapport

B uilding rapport with a client is an essential part of developing a good relationship in any project. Take every opportunity you can to meet with the client face to face. Yes, we need to use telephones and other modern technology to communicate with clients; however, nothing can ever replace personal interaction.

Interview clients to elicit their opinions and attitudes toward the project. Learn to listen carefully. You must understand just where they are coming from. Learning to develop their interest through conversation is integral to your success in this project. If the client's main interest in a space is to hold large parties, ask how many parties he or she will have in a year. Then, ask what else the space will be used for. Lead the conversation, framing your questions to obtain the information you need, but always refer to the client's main interest.

Having an interest in common with a client often solidifies the relationship. Sometimes you have to work to build rapport. At other times, it just happens; it's serendipity. Several years ago, a young designer was hired by an older couple whose previous interior designer was a design superstar and whose reputation preceded him wherever he went. The young designer got along famously with the wife, but despite the designer's good background, the husband seemed unwilling to begin the project. Then the young designer happened to comment on the outstanding collection of rifles in the man's study. Surprised that a young girl would recognize the guns, the man questioned her. Her father had taught her about guns, still targets, and clay pigeons when she was a child, and that sealed the relationship. A few days later, the wife called and told the young designer that her husband felt she was capable of handling the project because she can shoot.

I like to meet with a new client in person, both to see the project and to have some interaction to lay the groundwork for mutual respect. At this time, you might want to bring your portfolio with histories and examples of other projects that are similar to that of the client's. It is usually best to keep those illustrations as close to the client's type of project as possible. So in your initial phone call, ask what the client has in mind. Then carefully select the materials you will take to show him or her. During this initial phone call, many designers will refer clients to their Websites. Others will select particular illustrations they think are appropriate and email them to the clients to review before the meeting.

Define your firm. Explain exactly what you do and what the capabilities of your practice are, and enumerate the types of work for which your firm brings in specialists. (In the Design Service Outline, there is a space for other consultants who are involved in the project. Is there a code specialist, an architect or engineer?) Make sure the client understands who's involved.

As you discuss the proposed project, think about what the client wants before you make definitive statements. It is not your job to meet with a client and, within an hour, define exactly what you would do on the entire project. The client feels that because you are being paid a fee, coming up with a project concept will take some effort. So if you have ideas, hold onto them. Listen to the client, develop the project, and take a week or a little longer (depending on the project) to come up with your solutions. Coming up with the answers too fast takes away from your professional credibility.

Speak in terms your clients will understand. It is important to be direct and honest. This is not the time to bring out your best list of professional terms and design jargon—these are professional shorthand and can confuse the client. Don't embarrass your clients. Make them feel comfortable with your firm and your terminology, so they see you as part of their support team.

As you discuss aspects of the proposed project, keep the clients' comments in the forefront. Restate to them what they have given as priorities, and discuss what you will do based on those priorities. You might say, "Based on the selection that you have made, we recommend these items."

Bring the clients' preferences into the project as often as possible. Show them that their priorities are also your priorities, and that you are constantly aware of them. It's a good idea, once they give you priorities, to review those priorities and make sure that they are clearly defined—both in your mind and in the way the client has stated them. Very often, clients lack the ability to communicate well in design terms. If you need to interpret these priorities, take the time to make sure that you and the clients both understand what you're supposed to be doing.

Individual clients like to make some decisions. Corporate clients expect you to do a study and to suggest the best options or courses of action. Most clients like to feel that they have made the selections, so present the project with options and choices. Explain your selections and why you feel that certain possibilities may be better than others, but still let the client understand why these decisions are made and give him or her two or three selections from which to choose. Especially in working with corporate clients, you will find that clients like the responsibility of making their own decisions.

One of the major problems in presenting design services today is confusion. We lose a lot of projects because the clients are confused by the massive amount of products and information out there. We must be so careful to present what's appropriate to the clients' specific situations and help them understand that one of the major roles of a designer is discrimination—being able to distinguish between appropriate items and those that should be eliminated.

If you give a client a choice of twelve options in an unfamiliar area, he or she probably will not be able to give you the best decision. When you narrow down these options to the two best and allow clients to choose between them, they feel they are in control. You perform professionally in sorting out the issues and bringing matters down to the point that making a decision is easy. Be very realistic in talking about how much things are going to cost, construction issues, and also the time that will be involved. If the project involves a great deal of remodeling, completely changing or altering the use of the facility, and possibly making it unusable for awhile, tell the clients so that they are ready for it.

No client likes to be surprised with a final budget that is two-and-a-half times the original; nor does a client like it when a three-week project turns into a four-month project. Clients need to understand exactly what they are committing to in order for you to maintain a good relationship with them. So don't surprise them.

Early in the interview (again, see the Design Service Outline), speak about the client's expectations regarding scheduling and budget. Sometimes, clients feel a project can be done in just a few weeks and that it's very simple; yet you know that it will be quite complex. Now, in the early stages of your relationship, is the time to clarify these matters so that the client's expectations are within the realm of your firm's capabilities. From the first time you meet the client, and throughout the project management phase, schedule weekly phone calls. These scheduled contacts, initiated by you, keep clients up to date and will save you a tremendous amount of time in fielding later phone calls from the clients. Keep them informed; let them feel that they're part of the job and are very important. Try to make it a point to initiate the call rather than wait for them to call you.

You need to identify the person you will be working for. There should be one person on the job that all information goes through. This will keep the lines of communication clean and clear. The contact person can relay your progress reports to others in their firm and keep everyone informed. This is the best method of retaining rapport with the client.

Who is really responsible for the job? How many people will be involved? What decision-making process is there? Put this type of information on your first page of notes in the client's file, even if you don't use our Design Service Outline. Understanding how your clients make decisions, who they are responsible for or to, and what kind of information they must have to keep their superiors informed is critical. They may need certain types of information; you must decide the most effective ways to furnish it.

How do you discuss a problem with a client? At many points in a project, there may be problems you cannot fix or cover. There are times when a client must make a decision about a problem issue, an issue he or she is not going to be happy about. Don't tell the client about the problem until you have a solution or two. If you tell clients about the problem too soon, they may make it larger than it is because they probably don't understand that they have options. Explain the problem and present your recommendations at the same time, always giving options and explaining your own choice. When you do so, say, "We understand that there may be information that we don't have, which may affect the solution you choose."

Then clients go home feeling they have an answer—a choice, and not a problem. You must consider your legal liabilities, but it is still best to use this approach.

We know that the many ups and downs of the economy affect our practices. When the economy has a negative influence, the designers who stay very close to their clients have a better chance of maintaining their client base. Very often the firms that stay close to their clients are small design studios. Staying close means their clients see them as part of their team. People buy from people . . . they don't buy from organizations.

Interior design is based on personal relationships. Develop that rapport with your clients using these procedures and others you may have discovered on your own. If you want to keep a client and stay out of court, you need to maintain a relationship that constantly supports the client. Clients need to feel that you are part of their team. As long as they feel that they are important, they are not likely to sue you and they are more likely to refer that next project to you.

Treat your contractors and your suppliers the way you would treat your clients, and they will become team members in selling projects to your clients. This can do a great deal to build rapport. One of the main things that designers need in order to complete jobs properly today is the right quality of vendors and contractors behind them. With good vendors, designers can supply their clients with many things that would not otherwise be available. Building this team, and this rapport, is critical for a good marketing practice.

Give recognition for jobs well done. When a contractor or member of your staff is working well on a project, take a minute to give that positive reinforcement, as Spencer Johnson and Ken Blanchard suggest in *The One-Minute Manager*. Go out of your way to compliment the deserving person, but find a specific task that has been done and praise it specifically. This means more than general compliments.

CHAPTER 17

Organization

O rganizing is a necessary part of selling, just as it is part of every other thing we do. The interior design discipline is based on organization. The NCIDQ test, which evaluates interior designers and qualifies them, is based strongly on our ability to organize. The important thing is that designers must be able to follow instructions and realize they get only so many points for doing the plumbing. Therefore, they have to consider how they're going to spend their time and make sure they organize the project properly. A designer must complete an accredited design program before being qualified for the exam.

A selling presentation, or any other type of marketing program, must be organized. It must have structure. Large corporations invest a great deal of time training their salespeople in the organizational process of selling to ensure that the total process, step by step, is adequately covered. Some programs feature nine steps; others have ten or twelve. This varies, but there is a consistent order to the presentation structure.

Prepare a list with an organizational format of every topic that needs to be covered in the meeting with your client. Without it, you're more likely to miss things. You'll come back without certain information because you have not reviewed the client's thinking thoroughly. You have not checked with the client to make sure that the foundation is secure before going on to the next level.

Before you schedule a meeting, make sure you have your checklist ready. With that checklist, you'll not only make sure that every item is covered, but you'll appear far more professional. You'll also be sure that the meeting will be very successfully presented.

Sometimes we work on a design for weeks or months; of course, we understand it and are comfortable with it. But the client may not have such a clear understanding. We owe clients a carefully planned orientation if we expect them to buy into our plan.

Take the preparation time not only to review objectives but to consider all personal information previously gathered, such as the decision-making process, areas of comfort and experience, and the clients approach. The more you can tie together a client's preferences with your decisions and plan, the easier it is for the client to understand and accept.

Too often, meetings are arranged to meet the expected schedule without allowing for the proper preparation time—not only for generating and reviewing design materials but also for considering the many different demands for styles of communication. This client is different. In fact, he or she may be *very* different from the client you met at the previous meeting. You must shift gears and be ready for the client's style.

Communication is the key to a client buying your design. So design your approach to clients as carefully as you do any part of your design project.

The forms are a suggested way of organizing a meeting. You may want to make some changes based on your own style. The important thing is to have a guide you can follow to make sure you keep the meeting on target and come out with appropriate results.

You will find that if you use a Meeting Planning Guide (Figure 17-1) as a basis for your meetings, you will think and act in a more directed manner.

For the meeting, make yourself a list that covers items to be discussed, with space where you can note the results as the meeting progresses.

Set Priorities

The purpose of this documentation is to force us to see priorities. Sometimes our priorities are different from our clients'. Many of us have spent endless hours developing part of a project that has no value or interest to the clients, even though we think it is the most important part.

Decide what's important to you and spend your time on that; otherwise, you can end up wasting too much project time on something that is really not relevant to the project. Look at that time schedule. How does this fit with the priorities? Is it really worth it?

When you take on a client, one of the first things you need to do is to find out how the client will handle a given problem. How does he or she deal with problems? It's a good idea to review different issues with clients to see what is important and what they are willing to invest in. This is part of your interviewing technique, and it's worth repeating throughout the job. Be sure you know what your client's value system is.

MEETING PLANNING GUIDE

Client Name: Date:

Current Situation:

Problems or Needs:

Goals and Objectives:

    Overall:

    This Meeting:

Questions That Need to Be Answered:

    Client's:
    Designer's:

What information, etc., will client need in order to make a decision?

What *values* are we offering?

How can our firm provide the best *benefits* to this client?

What *questions* can we expect the client to ask?

What are the best *answers* to these questions?

What are the *commitments* the client needs to make at this time?

Considering the situation, how will I measure the *accomplishments* of this meeting?

Figure 17-1

Investment

A client isn't spending; he or she is investing. The challenge to the designer is to present what we're doing in a way that explains the value of and reason for this investment. When clients realize the value and understand the reason, they're more than willing to give us their approval.

It isn't just about a client's physical requirement. Consider the client's requirements. He or she may need a certain size conference table with a hidden microphone and a very durable finish. But clients are environmentally concerned today, they may want wood from a managed forest, so documentation of sources and the system of handling must be included.

Use this form to define qualities and sources of information. You should have the sources of the quality statements to support your recommendations.

Synopsis

Before going to any client meeting—either in person or on the phone:

- Review previous and existing knowledge of the project.
- Be sure there is a reason for this appointment. Yes, it's good to spend time with clients to get to know them, but as professionals we need to be sure we use every minute effectively.
- Outline the goals and objectives for the meeting, including questions the clients generated in a past meeting or by phone. Include the answers to the client's questions.
- Review the questions generated by your work or research.
- Review information that you or others need to progress with the project.
- Schedule the next meeting.

						Date Sched.:	
MEETING AGENDA							
					Time:		
Client/Subject:			Location:				
Purpose:							
Results Desired:							
Scheduled:			Actual:			Meeting Cost:	
Start:	Stop:	Total Hours:	Start:	Stop:	Total Hours:	Billing Rate:	Value per Hr.:	Total:
Persons Attending:							

Agenda:

Items Required for Meeting: Person Responsible:

Meeting Notes: Decisions:

Figure 17-2

Results of Client Meeting

Client Name:_____ Date:_____

Items Incomplete:

Needs:

Research and Information Required:

Date and Method of Next Contact:

Source © Design Business Monthly

Figure 17-3

Value Worksheet

Proposed Design Features	Purpose or Benefit	Support Information

Source © Design Business Monthly

Figure 17-4

Client Meeting Debriefing Summary

1. Specific Interest:

2. Communication methods that resulted in positive response:

3. Techniques used: Results:

4. My feelings:

5a. Decision style:

5b. What's important:

6. Client's knowledge, thoughts, feelings about our firm, our approach:

7. Is this client similar to other clients?

8. What other things have I learned?

9. In which ways did I perform well?

10. Which areas deserve improvement?

Figure 17-5

CHAPTER 18

The Art of the Interview

The art of listening makes the difference between a good relationship with clients and one full of problems and misunderstandings. To be a good listener, show that you are committed to the conversation. If you are interested in what your clients are saying, look at them. Maintaining eye contact is essential, because some people feel that when you aren't looking at them you aren't paying attention. At the very least, your looking away is distracting. Do not participate in any other kind of activity during the conversation, but dedicate your interest to them.

On the other hand, in some cultures, people feel uncomfortable when someone looks directly at them. If people come from different social backgrounds, we need to understand their social mores and incorporate them into our interactions. The important thing is to demonstrate that we're engaged with clients and concentrating on their issues—that we're not distracted by anything else.

Give clients feedback. Let the speakers know that you are concentrating as you listen. Say, "Yes, I understand." If you interrupt, do it politely to bring out points of interest or ask questions that might clarify the issue.

Handle distractions and interruptions discreetly. If something happens to distract you, deal with it, but come back as quickly as possible. Clients must know that you are dedicated to their conversation and to what they have to say.

Take notes. They can be short and abbreviated, but write down enough so that you understand what has been said when you reread them. After the conversation, review the notes with the client. Say, "This is a summary of what I think we covered here. I'd like to go over it with you to make sure it's correct, so that when I go back to my office I'll know where to start." (Figure 17.2 shows an outline that you might use.)

Sometimes you may want to tape a conversation. Even if you do so, you should still summarize the conversation with the client at the end to make sure all points are covered. Whoever types up these notes should work only from that end portion of the tape, which clarifies your discussions. You have listed all the issues, you've reviewed them with the client, and you have gone through the decision-making process. Making a printed transcript of a total conversation is really time-consuming, and it is much more difficult to locate any information you need in a bulky transcript. Often, things change during a conversation. It is much better to have just the summarized format.

It's most effective to make a list of all the issues covered during a meeting. Then, at the end, I pull out a tape recorder and dictate a summary of the meeting from my notes in front of the client to confirm the decisions we've made and the ways to move forward. This dictation is then typed and becomes our official meeting notes. This is generally a much better and more efficient system than taping the entire discussion, although there may be some situations in which it's important to have a backup tape of everything that was said during the meeting.

Emotion can be confusing, and clients do get emotional over their spaces. Sometimes when they are very angry, clients will say things that are almost impossible to understand and may be taken incorrectly. This is another time when it is very good to say, "Now let me summarize exactly what you said." At that point, you may even ask the client if you can tape a summary of the clarification. This also works well with phone calls.

When you walk into a client's house, go with the attitude that you are there to learn and to listen. Even though you are trying to evaluate the situation, be careful not to go in with a judgmental attitude. Listen first. Let the clients tell you what they want to say. After you've absorbed their information, you can deal with your own opinion. But listen with the attitude of "I am here to understand what you are saying" or "I'm evaluating the situation carefully before I consider passing judgment."

Evaluating a situation too quickly can be dangerous. Some situations take years to develop. Often the easy-to-see situations can be evaluated quickly. After all, you've been doing this for years. You know how things work. But the client thinks his or her situation is unique and serious; after all, it is not worth paying a consultant for a common problem.

Do not assume that the client really wants your advice. After you have summarized the situation with the client, ask, "Exactly which issues did you want us to help you with?" It may be that clients really are not interested in your working on certain issues, even though they may appear to be disturbed about them. They may not be ready to handle those situations.

It is best to let them explain the project to you. Afterward, review it with them. You may wish to say, "The way you've explained it, these are the issues that I think you want addressed. Is this correct? Let's go over them carefully and decide whether this really is what you want to address first." Allow the client to set the priorities.

Watch for visual clues. Very often, the posture of clients, the way they move or the way they appear to be uncomfortable about certain issues, may tell you something about what they really feel but are afraid to share with you. Sometimes we use very different words to describe our thoughts, but body language gives us a clue about their real meaning.

As we listen to our clients, often we don't understand what they're saying, or maybe it doesn't relate to what we're doing. Ask them to explain.

- Could you explain more about _____?
- That's very interesting. Tell me a bit more about it.
- What do you feel is the most important part of this space?
- Could you explain more about how you use this space?
- What type of space would be more comfortable for your situation?
- What would make this room work better in view of your changed situation?

Listen carefully. Before going on to the next question, restate to the client what you think was said. Then explain how this may influence the design direction. Very often in hearing your version and what it will entail, clients realize that what they said may not be what they actually wanted. Rather than saying up front, "You're wrong," it's often better to go back and explain. "Are you sure this is what you want to happen?" is a safe question.

We are constantly communicating, but the question is how adequately, how effectively, and how articulately. One thing most of us learn is that the more time we give clients to talk, the better they feel we are presenting. Some of the best presenters I've seen are those who did really very little talking. They are the ones who let the clients talk; they let the clients explain their objectives and missions. They make the clients feel important. We are not selling; we are building long-term relationships. We are building rapport. Developing relationships and rapport is a positive, pleasurable experience for the client.

Think about past presentations—what went well and what didn't. Try to figure out why some things worked and some failed, because you have to do everything possible to make the designer/client relationship a special one.

1. Be sure you know what the clients really want. What are their real concerns? Ask questions. Sometimes the "calling cards," the reasons the client says he or she is calling a designer, are not the real concern.
2. Take time. This relationship-building experience requires care and time.
3. Don't rush to answer a question. Wait a minute. Leave a few seconds of silence. Take time to consider a client's question seriously before answering.
4. Answer clients' concerns in a caring manner. Show your professionalism. Don't condescend.
5. Review all the points discussed to be sure you are all going in the same direction. It's often necessary to review and consolidate different comments to be sure the parties understand one another. Sometimes these change in the course of the interview. It's best to treat people as very important.

Verbal Finesse

Sometimes it isn't what you say, but how you say it. First of all, let the clients know that you are committed to them. Don't just say you'll see that X gets done; set a date and a time and make a commitment to do it. If you have agreed to have X completed by Tuesday, see that it is done before then.

When you disagree with clients, you can risk alienating them by saying so directly. It is better to say that there are several ways to handle the issue. Tell them you will try your best to understand their viewpoint, but, in return, ask them to consider yours. Perhaps you, the design firm, have misinterpreted their viewpoint. Convey the idea that your plan was not done casually, but you must have missed something.

Because their viewpoints have not been rejected out of hand, clients will be more willing to contemplate an alternative method. You, as the person put in charge of the decision-making process, must make the final decision. Once you have explained your position, perhaps the client will concede graciously. Or the client may explain that because of other aspects of the situation, the decision must change direction. There are priorities that the client's institution considers much greater, and these must take precedence.

The more research you do in advance, the less likely this is to happen.

Do your best to prevent clients from making costly mistakes. If you know their decision is wrong, put off acting on it. Give them more information so that they can make informed decisions.

Don't blame the client for making a wrong decision or handling it incorrectly. It's probably your fault for not presenting the situation properly. It can help to say to the client, "I feel I haven't presented this properly. I believe that we are putting the project in jeopardy if we do not make the decision this way. Here are the reasons." Take the blame yourself rather than saying that a client lacks knowledge or has done something wrong.

When a client asks for something, nothing is impossible. Everything can be done, but can it be done within reason, within price constraints, and without taking excessive amounts of time? You may want to safeguard yourself by telling the client, "Let me get you the estimates on this, because I have a feeling that this may be far more expensive than we expected. When we get the costs, you will be better able to make the decision of whether you want to make the investment."

Ask your clients what they want and need. Make it easy for them to tell you by asking if they would be willing to act as "unpaid consultants" in helping you improve your services. Are there two or three things that they can suggest you do to improve your firm?

Instead of asking clients if they are happy with the project, ask if there is any way you could improve it or give them better service next time. What's important to the clients? Enlist their help in seeing things from a client's perspective.

Be honest with your clients. If time is an issue, tell them you have a time problem now and must leave to work on something else. Let them know that you have a problem, and that you will get back to them when you can.

The best way to learn about a client is through the Socratic method: ask questions. Then listen carefully, speak occasionally, observe, question, and probe. The way you ask questions affects the answers you get. Don't always offer an opinion or make a judgment. Try to be neutral. Don't agree or disagree, but listen carefully to what is being said.

> Use nonverbal probes: smile or nod and watch the body language of your clients.
> Try short verbal probes: Yes, Sure, Right, Of course. How do you feel? What do you think of that?
> Use echo probes: repeat what the client says in order to encourage him or her to expand on the topic.

One of the most difficult things we learn as designers is when to stop talking. When you interview clients, let them talk. There is a way to present your issues professionally while allowing clients to express their thoughts. The format for the Design Service Outline is effective, because you are reviewing the different services of the firm while asking about a client's needs.

See if you can work on developing particular clients and find ways to make them comfortable in presenting to you—not just listening to you presenting to them. Can they reveal their needs, express their problems? Can they do so in a cooperative manner?

The ability to give clients what they want is a big part of selling, and you cannot do it without the help and support of your staff. Enlist their cooperation. Instead of announcing that the firm has a deadline that must be met or you'll all be in trouble, you could say, "We have a challenge here. We have a client who has a need and if we can please this client, I know it will lead to additional work. In your opinion, what can be done to ensure that this job is completed on time?"

Sample Interview

For a business client:

Q. How long have you been in this space?

A. About seven years. We didn't plan to be here this long, but the rent is reasonable and moving seems too complex. The neighborhood is good, and clients know where we are. I know the building isn't perfect, but we have learned to work with the problems. But we must have more space.

(You have learned more than you asked. People generally will give you their reasons for doing or not doing things.)

Q. You mentioned that you were considering adding space across the hall, rather than moving to a new location. Is this a good location for you?

A. Reasonably. It is convenient to where we live and to our clients. Most of our sources are nearby.

Q. How many of your clients visit the office?

A. About eighty percent.

Q. What are the reasons?

A. They come in to consult on how our services are working for their firms and to see our new, state-of-the-art equipment.

Q. And your clients are involved in what types of businesses?

A. Normally businesses with fifty to three thousand employees, directed to sales, marketing, and distribution.

(This indicates the type of business it is. Continue along these lines to learn more about the company and the way it works. You will find that this puts the client at ease. Ask clients more about their clients' needs, how much time they spend in the office, the size of their projects, and the number of years of service. What is their sales approach? Throughout the interview, draw the clients out to learn their backgrounds, artistic styles and detailing that appeal to them, etc.)

For a residential client:

Q. How long have you lived here?

A. Twelve years.

Q. It looks like a great neighborhood.

A. It is great for the kids, and that is one reason we want to stay here. If it were just my husband and me, we'd probably build our dream house on a mountain. Chauffeuring the kids to social activities every day is more than I want to deal with at this point. Besides, this is close to where my husband works. If we were farther away, I'd never see him.

(This answered my unstated question of why they sought interior design services. The house was in a nice neighborhood but not in the exclusive area I would have expected, based on his position and expected income. Some of the client's plans seemed too extravagant for the quality of the house, but he and his wife's reasons for staying there, their desire for personal convenience, and the social activities of their children make the investment worthwhile for them. They can well afford the budget. So why shouldn't they have some of the conveniences that others in the same social position enjoy? They put a high value on family life and want to encourage the family to make its home the base for much of its activity.)

These are simplified short interviews that demonstrate the technique of asking leading questions. The point is that you must see clients' buildings as being *valuable* to them. These are spaces with emotions, memories, and history that are a part of them. A designer must see how these intangibles fit into the rationale of the project.

CHAPTER 19

Your Brand

The only products that have a future are those that are created
by passionate people.

—Tom Peters, *The Pursuit of Wow*

Why Branding Is Important

Branding is an often talked about subject today. This is a topic likely to
become even more significant in an increasingly competitive business
world. Brands command higher prices as well as lower sales and promotion costs. They're likely to give you a greater share of the market
and make both employees and clients feel more satisfied. What's more,
brands can bring you greater recognition—among the media, economic
analysts, and industry leaders as well as your clients.

Brands pave the way for marketing success, because when people
hear the name of your firm or brand, they have memories—which
influence buying decisions.

You don't have to be a large or even medium-size company to have
a brand. Even an individual designer can have one. A brand is really a
promise that customers believe in. Your job is to live up to that promise
in everything you do and every time clients come into contact with
your name, message, business, or employees. People tend to stay loyal to
brands—which is more important than ever, since the market is filled
with more products and services than ever.

We realize that a brand is an important emotional symbol that
relates a company or product to clients. There are many elements to

159

branding—most of which, if we've been running our firms appropriately, we've been doing for years. But there are other key points to keep in mind. The following is an overview of branding and comments by a number of people who work in branding on a regular basis.

In addition to having their own brands, interior designers are often part of a branding team for clients because the environment is definitely part of a company brand. What is involved in branding?

- The Product. What is our product? Exactly what are we presenting? We need to be able to define and clearly present our product.
- Position the firm appropriately. Where do we belong in the market? What differentiates our firm from another firm?
- The Promise. What is our promise? This is part of our reputation and what we deliver to clients. Don't make a promise if you can't keep it.
- Presentation. How do we present our brand so that it appears to be outstanding? It's a "Purple Cow." We don't want to look like every other firm in town. What's different about us, and how do we present it?
- Persistence. Once we have established a brand, what do we do to keep it in front of our clients? How are we making every aspect and every move of our company a part of our brand?
- Perception. How do clients see us? What do they think we are? Do we keep checking and testing and talking with them so we understand just how they're reacting to our efforts?

A good branding program has superior perceived value, which gives the company as much as a ninety percent advantage over the average price of similar products. Clients are willing to pay a lot more for something they perceive as valuable, even it it's not necessarily more valuable. Brands not only bring name awareness but also increase the chances your product—and your business—will survive.

A brand starts with the leader of the company, not with the sales staff or marketing division. How does the leader see the brand of his or her company? Although the day-to-day responsibility of advancing and maintaining your brand may fall on the marketing team, brands really grow from the top down. And you need a total-organization approach—each person in your organization expresses and represents your brand. At times you may also choose to have outside consultants, such as in public relations or logo design, to help maintain your brand. But a brand isn't about the superficial; it should reflect the essence of who you are and what you stand for.

A firm must consider what the market wants and is willing to pay. This changes with time. Previously, mattresses were an inexpensive, common item. Now they've become luxury items—with some mattresses advertised to sell for $50,000 a set.

Clients are the most effective vehicle in promoting your brand. It's unfortunate, but today marketing and advertising are not as effective as they used to be. When consumers consider investing in something, especially something serious or expensive, they ask their friends who they use and what they buy. Very often that's the direction we follow.

Recessions are the best time to build a brand. At this time, your competitors often hold back on the money they're spending. It's a great time to put an effort forward and make your company noticed.

Branding is a major asset to your firm. It's traditional to look at financials and include assets as the properties you own, your inventory and so on. Now we're beginning to look at branding as well as at human assets as a major reflection of what a firm is worth.

Communication is key to branding. Technology permits us to send mass emails and use other systems that help us to do things quickly and effectively. If we know our audience and the way they prefer to receive information, we can make a point of keeping our company in front of them on a regular basis. Good communication also involves eye-to-eye and other personal contact. We should take advantage of many different types of communication in order to do our best job.

People don't buy products; they buy a promise. They invest in interior design because they expect it to do a certain thing. They have an image of what they want to accomplish—and that's what they're buying. They're not necessarily buying furniture.

A great brand connects a firm or product emotionally with its target audience. Once a company knows who it is and has defined that audience, the question is to determine systems that work well in connecting the two. But it's not enough. From time to time you need to monitor it to see if the brand is in line with your business goals and with the wants and needs of your clients.

To evaluate the strength of your brand, ask yourself how aware clients are of it; how deep their emotional connection is to it; how trustworthy it is perceived to be; and how all these elements influence people's purchasing decisions.

Clients expect consistency from a brand. That's why they want to use you. They know there will be an expected outcome and they can rely on your firm.

Brands are evaluated by every action your firm takes: the way a staff member answers the phone, the graphics on your stationery, your logo, your staff attire, your vehicles, your presentation, the way your studio is presented, and the products you present and the way they are delivered. They're all part of what clients see as your brand.

With branding, you try to look at your company through your clients' eyes. How do they see your firm? Branding starts with the leader of the company, but it's really about how we can bond the leader and the customer.

It's important for everyone who's part of the firm to be emotionally connected to it. Clients are very sensitive to this. They know whether the people in your firm are really excited about being part of it. If the staff doesn't feel emotionally attached, the clients sense that. So it's very important to consider the emotional attitude of everyone involved in your firm.

Talk to your clients. Keep in touch with them. Make sure you understand their views and their interests. The catch is: listen, listen, listen. Take time to really understand what clients are telling you, because they're your best partners in developing your brand.

Interior designers are often part of a branding team for other companies. But who is your branding team? It needs to consist of the people in your company, but you often need the help of outside people as well. A professional or marketing consultant can be of great help. Some of your clients can also make major contributions. Organize your team so it includes people with different perspectives who can help you single out the best investments for you in developing your brand.

Consistency is the building block of brands. But that doesn't mean brands remain static. Even if you've been in business a long time and have been successful, at some point you may want to extend or revise your brand. You may want to update the brand as the market changes, and as cultural and aesthetic factors and buying habits change as well. If your business or specialty has changed over time, you may want to market your brand differently.

Each of us has a brand, whether we know it or not. But is it the brand we want to have? Are there ways we can improve it? Everything in this book contributes to what our clients see as our brand. It may be your years of experience, your specialty, the way you finish the details on a room—all of these elements are part of your branding.

It's so critical that we're conscious of this—and that we understand that everything we do day in and out is building a future brand—that this special section has been devoted to the subject of branding. We want to make sure our brand is the one we want it to be.

Differentiation

One of the most difficult things we have to do today is to differentiate our firm from others. Whether it's through our Website or other forms of communication, it's very important that our firm be seen as different from others.

In *The Purple Cow*, Seth Godin—who has written numerous books on marketing—explains differentiation with great clarity. The members of our Designers' Business Forum have really enjoyed this book. It has helped us understand why it's so critical for each design firm to be seen as having a distinctive identity. Two of the "Purple Cow" companies Godin speaks about are Starbucks and JetBlue. One of his noteworthy points is that services worth talking about, get talked about.

Clients come to designers because they want something different. If they wanted the norm, they'd go to other sources. They can go on the Internet and buy standard products that are quite nice, or they can go to stores and find some very interesting products. But they want something different. They're looking for a firm that's different. So the question is: How do you make your firm different from all the other firms in your area? This may not mean your immediate area; we may be talking about the entire state, or even the continent. Clients often go to other parts of the world to look for design talent.

What makes you different? In our Designers' Business Forum, one of the first things we do is look seriously at each designer as an individual and try to determine what is unique about that person, about his or her associates and staff members, and the company and market. Then we work to make each individual designer's firm unique. What has the firm done that's remarkable? What is the firm doing now that's different, exciting, and new? Today it isn't so much what we do that's important; it's how we do it. Many companies are doing the same kind of thing, but they're doing it in different ways. A cup of coffee isn't just a cup of coffee when it's purchased at Starbucks. The question is: What can we do that's new and different?

Target your niche. Who are your clients? Be very specific. A product that's for everyone is not a designer product. Each of our items has to be designed for a certain unique audience. We as designers have the opportunity of creating things people really want—something they'll love as soon as they see it, something they'd never know to ask for but will know it's for them when they see it.

We need to find the clients who are really right for us. They're different, they have a certain situation, and we need to target that market. We can't be everything to everyone.

In his book *The Tipping Point*, Malcolm Gladwell points out that it's often the little things that make the big difference. It's that tiny issue that really shows people the product is different.

Remember that people don't talk about something unless it's truly exciting and they think it's fun. They're not going to talk about something ordinary, which is why we have to be exceptional in order for our firm to be worth conversation, let alone referral.

Mark Schurman of Herman Miller says, "The best design solves problems, but if you can wield that into a cool factor, then you have a home run."

Tiffany's blue box. You don't need to say anything when you hand someone that box. Automatically the person knows it's something special.

Learn more about your factories. How do they produce the different products that are key to your firm? Are there things that can be done to a very simple product to make it better or more suitable to your clients? How can you individualize a product and have something that's your own?

Clients are looking for a designer who's passionate and obsessed about the field. They don't want someone who just has a job. They're not interested in that kind of person. Is design still your passion? If it isn't, you need to do something to excite yourself at a greater level or find another area of the field you can be passionate about.

When I think of designers, some are bold and out there, not afraid to say what they do. Others are very reluctant, because they know they're offbeat. But clients today are looking for the offbeat. Be out there. Don't be afraid to say, "This is what's new; this is what's great, wonderful, and different. This is what makes us special and why we're the best designer for you."

Look at the products you're producing. Is it the best you can do? If it isn't, who do you need to join you? Which resources or products do you need to make everything you do truly outstanding and unique?

When it comes to branding, almost all communication that builds a brand is done by word of mouth instead of advertising or other systems. What can we do to make our product worth talking about?

Presentation

In her book *Sole Proprietor*, author Jane Palace explained that she was a master at designing Ukrainian eggs. Her father had recommended that she be the very best at anything she did, and eventually, Palace became known as the "egg lady."

Palace recalls that at a craft show, she presented her eggs in little nests on a beautifully displayed table. They were marked $35 each. An older woman came up and grabbed three of the eggs quickly. The woman said, "Here's a dollar; I'll take three."

From that point on, Palace realized that it was a question of presentation. She began presenting the Ukrainian eggs under glass domes on velvet and found that people easily understood they cost $35, not 35 cents. So much of what we do involves presentation—whether it's the way we present our company or the way we present our clients. When people recognize we're offering something of considerable value, they're more than willing to make the appropriate investment.

Dress

In design we need to look the part. Clients expect a certain quality of presentation. It is usually advisable to dress in a businesslike fashion, although clients do like to see designers working and they understand that we need clothing that permits us to get into action at times. Don't fall into the trap of thinking you must dress as well as your clients. In most instances their income is considerably higher than ours. However, you still can dress with style. Wear something unusual. Some designers prefer or are associated with a particular color, others carry a marvelous briefcase or handbag, while others wear a particular style of suit. There was a day when we wore gloves, or when we chose hats with a distinctive style. Consider your clients, and make sure your attire says "designer." It shouldn't be just common, everyday dress.

If clothes sense is not one of your strong points, enlist the help of a fashion consultant to show you how to style your wardrobe so that it really projects an appropriate image. There are many books, including *Dress for Success* by John Malloy, that have underscored the importance of the appropriate dress for business.

Even if you are very style-conscious, perhaps you should hire an image consultant to review your style and see if you are projecting the image you want. It's interesting to hear a new point of view, and it's hard to be objective about yourself.

Environment

Your office should give a good first impression of your firm. It should be clean and provide for the client's comfort. It is important to be able to offer clients even a limited menu of refreshments—at least good drinking water—and clean restrooms. After all, if you're going to have a long meeting, the restrooms become a very necessary part of the day. So take the time to be extra sure that these matters meet the standards with which you want your clients to associate you.

Is your studio a good example of your work? You deserve to look well in your space, and you deserve a space that is easy to work in. Some well-published designers live and work in spaces that don't represent their work. A good studio need not be expensive, but it must be well designed.

How can you sell interior design when you don't practice what you preach?

Transparency

Today, everything is transparent. There's very little someone can't find out about us.

Transparency has a strong influence on businesses today. At one time, we had partnerships or joint ventures with others and nobody knew who those individuals were. Today, anyone can find out this information in seconds. There are no secrets. Our businesses have to be prepared for this transparency. We have to make sure all the information about us is out there in a form others can understand and not misinterpret.

Trust is very important. If we don't have a client's trust, we can't work effectively for him or her. Our clients must have confidence in us so that there's no fear in their relationships with us.

We've been living in a period of uncertainty and fear, in which corporations we once thought were outstanding are now seen as corrupt. Technology is an effective system of revealing scandals in the business world, as well as in other sacred areas of trust such as religion, professional sports, and the media. It's critical to create circumstances in which it's okay for everyone to know about how we operate—because they are going to find out anyway.

The emotional components of relationship, such as trust and reputation, are more essential than ever for success in today's transparent world.

Business Etiquette

Good business etiquette contributes to your company's image. Keeping in touch with your clients is an important part of a good marketing program. It's important to acknowledge and respond to all invitations, even if you are not interested in attending. Simply drop a note and say you can't attend and that you will continue to give your personal support—or some nice personal touch.

When you are entertained, send a thank-you note. Send it in writing so that the note stays in the person's files, even though you might make a phone call to thank him or her, too.

Be sensitive to the expectations of others. Be sure to return phone calls or ensure that there is some appropriate response made at the correct time, usually immediately.

Good manners are often taken for granted, but today we see article after article in business magazines about business etiquette. It's very sad to realize that we have a whole generation of executives who need remedial training in etiquette. Among the people we work with, it is crucial to show general courtesies and appropriate manners. It is really important to be basically kind and nice to people.

If you find that you're not able to show these courtesies because you're in a bad mood or have had problems, stay away from the clients. There are some days many people just don't belong near people in general, let alone clients. You can't afford to let this part of your personality show, so keep it hidden and find ways to monitor and moderate your personal style so that you at least seem to be a positive, nice person.

I have met designers who are excellent at their work but who have few social skills. It may be that they lack patience in developing relationships with clients. If this sounds like you, then perhaps you need to find someone who will work with you to deal with the clients on a day-to-day basis, to do the hand-holding and the nurturing that are necessary for developing and nurturing your business.

All of us have times when we are overwrought or burned out because of many of the things that occur in our general practices. Find some form of recreation that restores your good spirits.

Teach your craftspeople, and all of the people who are working around clients, to be really polite and speak with the clients in an appropriate fashion. Teach them to explain to the clients those parts of the job and its processes that are important to them. If, however, there are questions or needed changes, then it is most important that anyone working on the project direct them back to the design office; after all they may not be aware of all the issues involved and therefore may make inappropriate decisions.

So let those clients know how you do things. Help them understand the complexity of the many processes, and then they will become better clients.

How does your voice sound on the telephone? Is it weak and hesitant? Do you sound disorganized? Or are you firm and strong? Do you make a good impression? These are points that you can easily test by taping your phone calls. There's a small device available from almost any telephone supply store for that purpose. Simply attach it to your phone, and you can tape your own telephone conversations. I also use it for taping details of telephone meetings.

George R. Walther is considered one of the leaders in effective telephone procedures. He has many rules; here is a mixture of some of his along with others:

1. Always be the one to make the call.
2. Never just make the call. Plan first. It often takes an hour or more to do this preparation.
3. Clear your desk of other unrelated items and have everything related to the issue ready. Go over the material. Check issues with your staff before starting so that you are ready for any questions.
4. Be sure you will not be interrupted. Walther likes to walk around the room using a handset. I like to work with a regular phone so I am sure the client can hear my best voice.
5. Start by building rapport.
6. Carefully outline the items to be covered. Be sure they are in an easy-to-understand order. Make a list of issues on a pad, so you can be sure all the issues are covered.

Questions   Answers
_____   _____

Telephone

The telephone is a machine that can work for you or against you. Like any other tool, its use requires management skills.

It can save you time, yet still there will be days when you wish it had never been invented because dealing with calls has eaten up your day.

Accept the telephone as a convenience and an opportunity to meet people rather than seeing it as a bother, annoyance, or time-waster. The person on the other end of the phone can tell what your attitude is when you pick up the phone. If you're not in the mood to talk to people, arrange for someone else in your studio to take the calls. You can return them when you're in a better mood.

When you're on the telephone, usually you need to speak more slowly than you do in normal conversations. Normal conversation is around 150 words a minute. If you can reduce this to about 100 words a minute, it really enhances communication. After all, the person is not sitting across from you—you cannot tell through his or her body language whether you are being understood. So try speaking a little slower and, from time to time, ask a question to test whether the listener understands the issues you've been presenting. Just check the facts.

It is important to let other people know that you know who they are; use their names. If you're not sure that they know exactly who you are, give them some references. Tell them where you met; mention people you know in common. Make sure that they can put you in context with the issue under discussion. Otherwise, there is no point in continuing the conversation.

Sometimes you'll get a caller who says only, "This is David." That's terrific! You know about nine hundred Davids, so which one is it? You can end up putting clients on hold while listening to "David" in a fog.

Give the other person the benefit of the doubt. When you call, clearly identify yourself. Say you are calling regarding X, which the two of you discussed previously. Then ask if it is a convenient time to talk about it. Just because the phone rings doesn't mean it's a convenient time for the client. And if it isn't a convenient time, ask when you should call back.

I believe in telephone appointments. If I tell a client or supplier that we will talk again on Thursday, I will also suggest a time, for instance, between 8:30 and 9 o'clock, and ask if that is convenient. Once the time is agreed on, I write it in my appointment book with other appointments for that day.

Before starting a phone call, write out an agenda using the meeting form, just as you would for any other meeting. Make a list of everything that you want to cover in that particular phone call. Let recipients know what the agenda is ahead of time, so that if they need a file or need to refer to another person for information, they will have time to prepare.

At the end of the call, summarize what was discussed. This means that when you pick up the telephone, you must have a notepad in front of you, as well as the client's file and any other information that pertains to the subject. When you're concluding the call, ask if the client minds if you put on your tape recorder and tape the summary as you go through it with him or her. Then, when you reread your notes, it's the perfect time for the client to correct any mistaken impressions or add any other items he or she thinks should be brought out. Very often people do remember additional details they would like covered.

Have the tape transcribed immediately, and send a copy to the client. Keep another copy for your files, and do anything you said you would do. Always follow the call with a letter.

In summary, consider a phone call to be a meeting. Schedule it with equal care and concern for the person you're calling, especially if it is a call early in the relationship. Your professionalism must shine through. Respect the client's time.

Common Courtesies

Focus your attention on the caller. You can't be doing four things—eating breakfast, talking on the telephone, taking notes, and watching television; it doesn't work. Be focused, get to the point, and try not to interrupt.

Have patience. Sometimes people speak so slowly that it seems they go on forever! It may be entirely possible to say in one sentence what it's taken them a half hour to explain. But they think it's important. They want to explain it to you. So you must have patience and listen to them. Don't interrupt people. Understand that when you're speaking on the phone, you must have good posture, you must have a good disposition, and you must be ready for that phone call. Many times I will stand during a phone call because it gives me better posture and I feel that I sound better.

Try to be positive in your phone calls. Eliminate negative phrases from your vocabulary. When you're conversing with a client, speak about a subject that you can be sure of. Don't hedge. It's better to say, "I don't know the scheduling. I'll call you back tomorrow morning and give you the schedule." Allow yourself enough time. Schedule a time for a return call. Promise action, and then make sure that action is carried out.

I know there are many one-upsmanship techniques, but I'm not comfortable in that sort of relationship. I believe we must make every effort to present ourselves as professionals if we are to expect the right outcome in a relationship. I believe in being truthful. I try to tell clients just what the story is, but I don't tell them about a problem until I have a solution. A few years ago, a contractor who was managing a large project for which we were providing interior design services would, together with the person who was managing the project, call the client to explain all the problems. She followed her call to the client with a call to me. I'd ask for a solution; she would say she didn't know but would have answers the next day. Finally, I suggested that she wait to call the client until she had some options.

Who should answer your telephone? It should be the person who knows the most about your company, not the person you hired last week. Properly trained telephone receptionists can save you and your staff more time than anyone on your payroll. They can separate the calls that you must handle from the ones on which they can check information and call the people back.

Try to answer the phone within two or three rings, if possible. Try to answer phones promptly, even if you must say to someone, "Excuse me a moment. I'm on the other line. Would you hold for a moment?"

Voice mail or answering machines are useful. I'm delighted when a person has an answering machine, because it provides a way to leave a message with details I want this person to receive. When I leave messages, I try to be specific about the reason for calling, whether it is about details of carpet selection, or needing prices. I try to give them enough information so that when they return my call, they'll have the answers. I don't have to sit and wait on the phone while they dig up information for the right answers. Leave good messages, whether with a person or on an answering machine. Ask any staffers who take messages to be precise, even to the point of reading back the message to the callers. Make sure that they know how to spell the client's name and they know the correct telephone number. Transposing just one number can cost you time. Or suppose there are forty-seven David Wilsons in the phone book!

Check telephone numbers. Check name spellings. Make sure that you know why the person called.

Do you like playing phone tag? This annoying occurrence can be avoided by scheduling calls. All you have to do is say, "I'm sorry that I can't speak with you at the moment. If you would be kind enough to call again sometime after 4 o'clock today, I expect to be back in my ofice." You can leave the message on an answering machine or with the person who handles the phones.

Remember that the caller has taken time out of his or her schedule and that it's a priority for him or her.

It seems everyone now has a cell phone. Some people have two or three. It's often confusing when my car phone and cell phone ring at the same time. This used to be a joke, but now it's real. Trying to keep up with all this electronic interaction is a challenge. Determine how you want to use your cell phone. Some people are very selective; others give their number to everyone. The difficulty is that when we receive a cell-phone call, we may not have the appropriate information to answer the questions or requests the caller is making. Also, we have to be sure we've documented that information. Sometimes, if we're in our car, we're not able to do this with great efficiency.

Be very careful how you handle your cell-phone interaction. It can be professional or seen as very casual. Determine what works best for you, and manage the process accordingly.

Conference calls can be done easily. Even a cell phone can become a tool for conference calls. These can be very beneficial, but it's important to have someone chairing the call, so it proceeds in order and doesn't become confusing. Be sure everyone is aware of who the participants are before the conference call begins, so the comments are directed appropriately. Sometimes, vendors may not be aware that the client is part of the conference call and may discuss information that would not be understood or appropriately received by the client directly without proper screening.

Systems of communication have become so much more extensive and easier to use. Systems that were once very costly are now inexpensive and readily available. This brings us to another issue—time. It is said that the average person now spends several hours a day on email. When we include our telephone conversations, is there any time left for any other type of work? Manage the time spent on your email and telephone conversations carefully to make sure you're getting value out of your investment. This time is as important as the time you spend working on your designs or with clients.

Our Market

Almost all of the easy problems have been solved. Those remaining are difficult and complex, requiring professionals and extreme effort. The key to marketing today is to create something so remarkable that the right people are drawn to your company. You're not pursuing them; they're seeking you out.

Often this isn't a case of doing things for people so they can go on living the same way. Our clients often choose to make a difference in their lives. They want a new lifestyle. Sometimes designers today call themselves "lifestyle specialists," because they're helping clients develop that new lifestyle. In a residential situation, perhaps the clients' children have grown and they now have the opportunity to live a different type of adult life. Or, perhaps the clients have children for the first time, so what they need is much more of a family house. Each phase of our lives and work situation has many variables. The question is: What can we as designers do to help our clients develop spaces that really work for their new lifestyles and life situations?

Volunteering

One of the most successful systems of getting to meet people is to volunteer for a charity in which potential clients also have an interest. Whether it is Habitat for Humanity, juvenile diabetes, or many of the other charity functions, it is a way of getting to know these people and showing that you have a similar dedication.

Guest Column

For a guest column, it's important to find out what your word count is and stick to it. Or, if you are asked to submit an article, submit it in several lengths. The key point to remember is to look at the column from the perspective of the reader. What value will the reader get from this article? We usually suggest submitting the article in three different lengths. This way, you will be able to determine what is eliminated. So often when you leave it up to the staff at the publication, they may cut out an item you feel is critical or distort it in some way. If you give it to them in three sizes, they have more options.

We've found that if something is well written and pertinent to a readers, it stands a good chance of being published. If, however, it needs a lot of work, the publication's staff are often so overworked that they just don't have time to edit it. It's amazing how often publications need fillers—you hit it on the right day and you'll find that your item may be used.

Make sure your publications understand that if they need technical information on a particular subject, you are the source. I have a very extensive library and have become the resource for many publications. Some of them call me for the beginning line and the summary of their articles. I have calls coming from all parts of the country. It's amazing the questions they ask. They need sources that can provide them with exact details. Sometimes they want a general opinion, but often they are looking for points they can't find in their normal resources.

Become well known to your particular publications. When they realize you are a valuable source—they know you do kitchens or you specialize in a certain type of interior—they'll often reference you. You'll find yourself noted in other types of articles that are often unexpected. The important part is to make sure the publication staff understand who you are and what your company is about.

What Associations Mean to Us

Professional organizations do some advertising, although they admit they don't have enough money to invest in the type of advertising design firms would like. Public relations, however, is an important consideration for these organizations. Many individual chapters have a public relations person or department that sends out press releases and information about the work of their individual design members. The national chapter also has a department that's continually sending out releases and other information about design personalities and events throughout the country.

The American Society of Interior Designers (ASID) hosts a competition in cooperation with the magazine *Southern Accents*. The magazine's

Website has an online link to the organization's Website. Both announce the competition awardees and the new fellows of ASID.

When authors or publications are interested in doing articles about design, they can contact ASID and other professional organizations, which refer them to experts they can approach as sources. The organizations also put information on news wire services.

The International Furnishings and Design Association (IFDA) has, since its founding, incorporated designers, publishers, editors, and members of the media. All these varied professionals have the opportunity to interact. IFDA also gives designers a chance to learn the directions of their market and have their designs and issues presented in publications.

IFDA sponsors seminars and training to help designers with their design work as well as their promotional activities.

The International Interior Design Association (IIDA) does no advertising, but it does conduct programs to teach designers and support people the appropriate presentation of products in the furnishings field.

Each of these professional organizations issues publications, which they distribute primarily to their own members.

Your Business Card

At one show house I attended, the designer didn't bring a brochure or anything outstanding. But she did have her business card, and attached to that card was a small piece of the fabric used in the room. Everyone picked up the card and seemed to remember it because it was different. The card also had a definite association to the room she had designed.

Make sure to state what you do on your business card. Some business names aren't very descriptive. After people collect many cards, they can get confused and forgetful. If your card says you're an interior designer, at least they'll connect it with you and with your profession.

Always have your business card ready to hand to people. Whether you're going to a restaurant, a social setting, a conference, wherever, make sure your card is available so the people you meet remember who you are and what you do.

Lawn Signs

In certain situations, a designer is permitted to place a sign on a property, stating that this project is being designed by his or her studio. This is an excellent form of advertising—probably one of the best we can get. Not all property owners permit these signs, but if they do, it's a wonderful way to be seen by the entire neighborhood.

Gifts

The best-received gifts are those sent to a child or grandchild—especially if it's something the youngster is particularly interested in. It could be a special book on dinosaurs or a doll. Your clients will be so impressed when you remember and think of their children or grandchildren, or maybe, in some cases, even their parents. They often appreciate this gift much more than something you give to them. This is true for both commercial and residential accounts. We're in a people business; letting clients know you care about them is important.

In Seth Godin's book *Free Prize Inside!*, the author recalls standing on line in a grocery store with a large number of purchases that will cost several hundred dollars. Someone with a single item whizzes right through the line, while you have to wait.

Does this make sense? You're the one who's really supporting the store, and the other person is buying very little. What Godin is referring to are the extra things you can do for your clients that bring them back and tie them to you.

Those "extras" are among the things that can make a difference in an organization.

In summary, in developing a brand:

Find your niche
- Who are your best clients?
- Review and define your market.
- What are new opportunities for your firm?

Position your firm
- What differentiates you from other firms?
- What is the available market that needs you?
- Know your competition.
- Test your brand.

Explain your brand
- Start with your mission.
- Create a way of presenting your vision.
- Present your brand.

The power of your brand's name
- Protect it; register it.
- Have a domain site.
- Have a Web name.

Logo
- Which design speaks for you?
- Have a professional design a logo for you.
- If you have a logo, review it; it may need to be updated.

Design statement—tag line
- The statement says who you are, what you believe in, and what you do.

CHAPTER 20

Preselling

In order to have clients, you must first have prospects. You can do beautiful design work. You can offer a great specialty. But if there's no client out there who needs and wants your services, you're not going to have any work. In most cases too much of our education is dedicated to developing great design. It often seems that no one considers the client's needs; we're not even told to consider budgets. In many instances, designers who graduate from design school have never seen a real client. We must find prospects who have a need.

Keep a record of everything you do; make a file for each potential new client. There are many software programs that can assist you with total recordkeeping. These programs can dial the correct telephone number for you or send a fax. Or, you can keep records in paper form—whatever works for you. The important thing is have a system that's easy to use on a regular basis. If a prospect is important enough to approach, you need a good record. In addition to the standard information you need to generate, include a general client contact summary with the client's name, source of the referral, and the contacts you have made. Note each contact by date and type: was it a telephone call, an email, a letter, a personally written letter, a brochure, a visit, or a meeting through a social opportunity? This will be kept in the front of the file.

To generate business, you must first market your firm in a way that defines its positions for potential clients. This is where the process of branding plays a part. Branding creates a desire for what we offer. Then you must, by building a relationship or selling, transform that desire into a transaction. You must provide service to that client in a way that builds an ongoing relationship throughout the project, through the follow-up and everything the design firm does.

If at any point in the project the design firm fails to maintain that strong service relationship, it can destroy everything else the firm has done. That is because we have allowed the client to know us, and people who know us can do us harm. Once you have decided to take on a client, you must be prepared to build that continuing relationship, because that is what makes a designer's career.

Does the client have the ability to buy? In many instances, clients just can't afford what we want to do for them, or they don't hold the company position that would permit them to make decisions about our product. It is important to find the right person and to be sure all efforts are directed toward that person. If the clients don't have the desire and need to buy what we want, the relationship you build will not immediately provide you with the business you desire. It is very difficult to define and find the "best" clients and to support them appropriately.

Today you must learn to be directed and to look for clients who are *right* for your firm. If you have a prospect, how do you get the opportunity to make a presentation?

Emissary Method of Selling

Using an emissary is an excellent way to develop a market. Firms often hire a person to act as an emissary. This person will preinterview prospective clients. He or she will size up the project and its general qualifications. The emissary will present the design firm in glowing detail—telling the potential client about the principals in charge, the design staff, and the management group. Then the emissary will set up a time for a formal presentation, at which he or she is also present.

By the time of the presentation, the emissary will have developed a friendship with the prospective client. An emissary will assist in the communication between the client and the design team and will bring business to a firm. But he or she will continue to look out for the interests of the prospective clients he or she has developed.

Introductory Calls

Introductory calls can work very effectively. One example is a design firm that did wonderful contract work, principally office work. The firm was headed by a woman, but a man who was very familiar with all the businesspeople in the community represented her and the firm's offerings. The beautiful part was, this "emissary" was able to speak about the head of the firm in a very professional way and thereby make potential buyers much more comfortable dealing with her and the firm—even though she worked in a male-dominated industry. The emissary served as a bridge to the community.

At one time, cold calling was very effective. Some professionals were trained in it. They told you that if you made fifty calls, seven people would respond and make an appointment with you. This is no longer true. Cold calling doesn't work. The firms built on this system are now using other processes, or else they're out of business.

We need to find ways of making that introductory call in a much warmer fashion. We need to know more about the client. Fortunately, we have many systems of researching clients today. We need an introduction, and we can do that in many ways. Probably the Internet has replaced a lot of what cold calling used to do. Website introductions work well with certain types of specialties. This may be the wave of the future, but today, most design firms use their Websites as a portfolio or a reference, rather than finding clients who use these sites to seek out designers' firms.

Successful design firms dedicate a considerable amount of time to preselling or marketing efforts. They either have people dedicated to these tasks, or if they're small firms, as much as forty to sixty percent of the principal's time is committed to developing clients.

As design firms, we need to look at the amount of lead time from meeting the prospect to the final sale. This runs, ordinarily, somewhere from four weeks to three years, depending on the type of project. This means that not only do you have to maintain regular contact with your prospective clients, but you must prospect constantly to keep your studio as busy as you want it to be. You also have to realize that if you don't do some prospecting and developing today, you are unlikely to have the business four months from now, or two or three years from now.

So many business publications present selling as if it were a battle, and I'm not sure they are wrong. They tell us that we first need excellent training to go to war. Sales are not made strictly by chance; they are made by people who spend a lot of time training and working and developing their particular expertise, not just in design, but also in their presentation skills. Just as in war, we also have a very strong opponent. Somebody else is after that job; you are not the only firm. Therefore, it is a question of who will win the job. Maybe we need to consider our sales development more like the battles of war.

To build a strong future client list, you need to spend thirty to forty minutes a day prospecting. Then you are likely to have a continuing flow of new clients. Schedule your work so you can meet a few clients each week. Developing clients must be it part of your routine. To develop your list, read the local papers for news of new buildings, weddings, divorces, mergers and acquisitions, and partnership announcements—any type of change.

To be a good salesperson, you must have ability and skill. You need to know how to communicate in the sales field. This means that you need good people skills as well as good sales skills, and an appropriate schedule for carrying them out. Secondly, you must be committed to producing and you must be persistent.

Persistence wins clients. An art specialist from a gallery with a mediocre line has sold many exceptional projects due to persistence. He followed up each appointment with faxed information that day. The next day the prospect received a hand-delivered information packet about the meeting. There was information forthcoming on a constant basis, so there was no way his prospects could forget about him. And, in many respects, that consistency is really what brought forward the sales.

A primary reason for making introductory or development calls is to keep your name in front of the clients. This can be done for any reason at all. If you can think of any reason to call them, do so. Send press releases on completed projects or special events you have planned. Send them birthday cards or congratulations—anything that's appropriate. Just keep your name in front of the client with a special need.

Sales Letters

Sales letters are an inexpensive, personal, and direct way to put your message in front of a prospect. There is a technique to writing good sales letters. You don't have to be a master wordsmith. If you follow these guidelines, you should be able to produce an effective sales letter.

Use the first sentence to entice the prospects. Tests show that people are most likely to read the first sentence and the postscript. Repeat the same point in different ways during the letter in order to reinforce that point.

Keep the letter simple and well written. Your prospects will notice errors or imperfections. Be personable. Write the letter as if you were speaking with them, and be careful to feature facts, not exaggerated exclamations. This letter represents your firm.

This type of writing is different from other types of editorial work. It must be dedicated to four specific issues.

First, you must show how the prospective clients will benefit. Your prospects will be interested in this letter only if they get something out of it. Before you write the letter, you should have done some market research to pinpoint the client. You need to know something about this client's situation so that you can relate your specialty to his or her need.

Second, explain the benefits. Be specific. Don't say you have a great service; show it by specific example.

Client Contact Summary

Client Name: _____

Address: _____

Telephone Number(s): _____

Source of Referral: _____

_____

Date	Form	Result	Follow-Up

Examples: B - Brochure, PC - Phone Call, LI - Letter of Interest, SM - Social Meeting

Source © Design Business Monthly

Figure 20-1

Weekly Sales Sheet

Number of Prospects Called:

Contacts with Decision Makers:

Appointments Set:

            Made:

Presentation Made:

New Clients Obtained:

Referrals:

Leads:

Source © Design Business Monthly

Figure 20-2

For example:

- We offer you a design service that is dedicated to increasing productivity within the office environment.
- Our firm will help you with your space planning. It will also manage the procurement of needed furnishings.

Third, present your credentials: the age of your business, professional affiliations, educational background, and other experiences that would support your credentials.

Finally, encourage the client to take some action. Present the benefit of calling for immediate action. Encourage the client to call you because you have a particular offering that is important to him or her. Or better yet, write that you will call the client at an appointed time.

CHAPTER 21

The Presentation

The best place to make a formal presentation to a client is on your turf, if you can manage it and if you have a well-designed studio. It's always better to make a presentation in your own space because then you're in control.

This isn't always possible, especially when you are interviewing for a large project and you are one of many firms making presentations. In this instance, you either want to be first or last. Last is typically the best, and first is usually the next best. The middle is the weakest position. Check the scheduling in advance. If at all possible, position yourself to advantage.

How many people should you bring to the presentation? It depends on the number of people to whom you will be making the presentation. If there are twelve people, your contingent may number five or six. They should include the principal of the firm, if your firm is large. The principal introduces the project manager and other staff who will work on the project. After the presentation, both the project manager and the principal answer questions. If the presentation is held in the design studio, you may give the prospects a tour of the office or suggest a tour of similar projects.

The amount of time the prospective client allows you for the presentation is your cue to how long and involved your presentation should be. Are they giving you twenty minutes or two hours? Design your presentation to accomplish your goals within that time frame.

A few tips that you will want to keep in mind: Do everything you can to make the potential clients comfortable, and make sure your presentation is complete, well organized, and consistent. Your presentation should seem intelligent and assertive. It should demonstrate that your firm has talent and that your firm is a winner. Explain that this project is of interest to you, and exactly how you and your staff will be involved in this process.

Know your audience; research every possible part of the firm, both corporate and personnel. Do the same for a private client. The more history you have on clients, the easier it is to relate to them. It helps immensely to know what part of the country clients came from, their education, social background, and religious and political affiliations.

The presentation requires first that you define your firm, its abilities, and your position with the firm. Second, you need to relate these definitions to clients' needs in a way that shows you understand them. The next issue is to define the quality of the project. What is their timetable? Involve the clients. Restate their expectations and explain your own. Compare their existing project to similar ones from your files. Cover the issue of the budget. Explain the management processes common to this type of project; state who will work on the project and what their roles will be.

When you write a presentation, select the primary point and build on it. Collect all the appropriate information and review, summarize, and simplify. Weave it together in a way that is easy for clients to absorb and process. Create a logical order. Listen to the client's pace to establish the timing or tempo.

Prepare a personal profile/special life events list of each person you're presenting to. If a husband and wife are included, you need to know about both of them. You also need to know about their children. If it's a corporation, you need to know about the key players. It's so interesting to learn the background of corporate leaders. It's been fascinating to find that rather than coming from the traditional management, accounting, or engineering background, some corporate leaders actually were teachers or came from a discipline unrelated to the services or products of the company they are now managing.

There may be a case when clients you're presenting to have experienced the death of a parent or child or other emotional events that would strongly affect their relationship to almost anything they're doing—including their future design project. This is a time to be particularly sensitive to your clients' needs.

If you're talking about new technology, be very, very careful to keep it simple. Relate that technology specifically to the prospects' situation and don't give them too much technical information at this point. Don't just tell a client that an LED lighting system is the solution; explain the workings of the system to the client and how it would be used on an actual job site. Letting a client see real-life application of a product allows him or her to become comfortable with the technology. Support your

PERSONAL PROFILE/SPECIAL LIFE EVENTS LIST OF EACH PERSON YOU'RE PRESENTING TO:

Sports
Hobbies
Work style
Past work experiences
Who really makes the decisions
What turns them on
What they dislike
Real financial situation
Attitude and method of using money
Who their friends are
What their competition does and what it is
Standards of the field
Education
    Elementary
    Secondary
    College
    Advanced degrees
Residences
    Investment they've made in their residences
Company they work for
Professional association
Personal situations
    Marriage
    Children
    Happenings

information with written or other materials that can be reviewed later, but don't leave more information than can be easily absorbed by someone outside the design field.

Give references. Prospects want to know who you've worked for before on projects similar to their own. The next thing they want to know is how your firm differs from other firms. Keep any important facts on the first page of the agenda, and make it very easy to read. You may be giving prospects a very thick presentation, but take into account that they are going to read the front page and the last; the rest of it they probably will never look at.

Make enough copies of the agenda for each attending member of the client's firm. This prevents their having to write down each detail and keeps their attention focused on the presenter. The agenda should either be bound or presented in a formal, attractive manner with your company's name prominently displayed. Usually, clients see many people during a bidding period; you don't want them to confuse your firm with another.

You may want to include additional information about your group, such as magazine or newspaper articles or brochures.

Once you have your outline and agenda of what must be covered, take an appraising look at your visual aids. They should be designed so that they can be read twenty feet away. Are you using PowerPoint or a video? With PowerPoint, you may want to project it onto a large screen so everyone can see. Be sure that if there's something to read, it can be read from a distance. Many people do PowerPoint presentations that can be read only by someone sitting close to the screen. The National Speakers Association, in fact, has encouraged professional speakers not to use PowerPoint. They recommend that we be able to see our clients, so we can interact with them while we're presenting. You can't do that in a darkened room.

Make sure that you can be heard. If necessary, take a lesson or two in voice projection so that you understand exactly how you are speaking and how you are using your voice. Occasionally, you will find yourself making a presentation to an audience of older people. They're not extremely old, but they are old enough to possibly have hearing deficiencies. Make sure that they hear you. Speak clearly.

Dress in a businesslike manner. This tells prospects that you consider this an important meeting and that you have come to them dressed with respect.

Rehearse your presentation on tape. Listen to it and play it again, repeatedly. Rehearse it in front of your staff and strangers; the more you do it, the better your presentation will be. I still rehearse all my presentations five to twelve times. I have learned that people who write well don't write a paragraph just once—they do it over and over and think nothing of it, just as we go back over our designs to be sure that they are just what they should be. A formal presentation needs rehearsal and review. If you're going to be good at it, invest time and effort in it.

Know your presentation. Have an outline if you need it. Reading from a script is unacceptable unless there is a question about a very technical issue and you want to refer to printed material to add authority to the answer. This printed material should be presented only on request; keep it simple unless the client also has in-depth knowledge of the issue.

Always give your prospects something so that they leave with a positive feeling. It doesn't matter whether you give them a special idea or just put in a little extra effort into the presentation.

Your competitors may spend a great deal of money on presentation. Architectural firms customarily go to great expense to do perfect presentations. Consider the costs of presentation carefully. After all, you don't want to appear extravagant. You do want to appear as if you are professional, that you do care, and that you are willing to put the effort into the project. Generally, interior designers will spend about four to ten percent of their fees to get a job. This includes money spent on general promotion and direct marketing expenses for special projects. Established firms customarily spend four percent of their fees. However, a new firm may spend anywhere from ten to twenty percent. The newer the firm is, the more it costs to win projects.

Negotiating is another part of every presentation. Who is the best person to do this? It is usually best to share this responsibility within your firm and for different people to work together. This is one reason that designers work in teams with other design professionals: they realize the strength in group practices, especially in negotiation. Should a difficult situation arise that you know requires negotiation, let the salesperson stay the good guy. Don't let him or her deal with the problems of a client he or she is attempting to sell to. Appoint someone else to do it.

If you need to negotiate a very serious situation—something that is critical—recognize that the chief executive officer is probably the last person who should do the negotiating. Let me explain why. If I'm negotiating for you and I tell a client that I think the designer will accept certain terms, I still have the privilege of going back to you for approval. I can then return and renegotiate if necessary. When you're the designer on the spot and the final decision is yours, you don't have the option of renegotiating. So be careful in choosing the person to negotiate a particular procedure.

Finally, look at your presentation from the clients' viewpoints. Are you giving them something that they really need, and do they believe in that need? If they believe in the need and see the value, then the relationship is developing well. Keep working at your dealings with your clients to establish that kind of a value relationship.

Public Speaking to Develop Business

Public speaking and presenting a project to prospective clients are somewhat similar in their requirements. The audience in a public speaking situation is generally more diverse. Public speaking is included in this section because doing it well is a personal skill. If you are considering giving a speech, here are a few guidelines.

Speaking on the right subject has a strong marketing value. Make sure you know why you are there and what you want to accomplish, what the audience or organization wants from you, and, in turn, how it will affect your future business. Otherwise, don't do it. Preparing a speech takes a great deal of time and effort. Speaking can be a good marketing opportunity, but only if you are a well-trained presenter. Many professionals do well in presenting to individual clients but are not trained to project to a large group. Even if you excel at presentations, don't accept an invitation to speak if the topic is not your specialty or if you are not well versed in it.

Think about the information you're giving. When you start as a public speaker or write articles that appear in trade magazines, you are educating your competition. All of your competition will know exactly what you have done, rest assured. Educating your competition does not enhance your firm's profitability. Is it something you want everyone to know—or are you giving away trade secrets?

Research the subject; don't depend on just your own knowledge. The Internet is a great source for information, but a lot of it isn't verifiable. Be very careful who you're using as resources. The written word is still one of our major sources. Again, it's important to compare numerous sources and be sure they agree with your own philosophy and way of doing business. Don't present someone else's material. Present material that's appropriate to the way your firm thinks and functions. Check with other sources to refresh your memory and pin down your examples. A good presenter will spend one hundred to three hundred hours of research for every forty-five minutes behind the lectern. Even if you know the subject thoroughly, a minimum of ten to twelve hours of preparation is needed, and a shorter speech takes even longer. People who attend lectures are often quite knowledgeable about the subject, sometimes more so than the design professional, because they have spent their lifetimes studying it as a hobby.

Know your audience. Check carefully into their backgrounds. You want them to understand your material, so talk to them, check and be sure to use a familiar vocabulary, one that they will understand. The time they spend with you is valuable and expensive to them. They want to go home feeling they had a worthwhile experience. How many people will hear the speech or receive the message? Will presenting this information promote a relationship between you and your potential client? Or does it underscore your expertise in an area the client doesn't need? Is there anything in the speech or article that could jeopardize your business in the future?

Make sure you include some way for the reader or audience to reach you. Try to make sure the topics appeal to your potential clients. Consider both the subject and potential audience to decide if it is really worth your efforts.

Appearance is important. Dress in comfortable clothing, but a little better, a little more formal, than your audience. Think about your posture and gestures. Over seventy-five percent of your impact depends on the way you present your material. Only twenty-five percent depends on the material itself. Comfortable shoes and clothing that doesn't restrict your movements are a necessity. You can tell when a speaker is not comfortable.

How do you sound? Professional training teaches people to use their voices as instruments in the same way singers and musicians are trained. Pronunciation, enunciation, breathing, and timing affect the presentation. Monotone voices put an audience to sleep.

What are your speech habits? Overuse of "ums," "uhs," and "you knows" can dilute the effect of your presentation. A coach can help point these out and suggest substitutes. Pausing, keeping silent is better than "uh."

Tape yourself during the course of a normal work day, or tape a presentation to a client. Then listen critically.

Check your equipment. There is a wide variety of audiovisual equipment today. Learn how to use it and which pieces are best for you. Arrive at least 1 1/2 to 2 hours before the program to make sure everything is in position and that the equipment you need is there and working properly. Checking the room the day before is even better. Many speakers still prefer to carry some of their own equipment so that they have control. It's really unfortunate if you start speaking and then find the equipment is not working.

Practice, practice, practice. This is the most valuable tip to improve your communication skills as well as your comfort level. Tape each of your rehearsals. Perform in front of your friends and anyone you can trust to criticize your performance fairly. Each time you listen to a taped rehearsal, you will find areas that can be improved. On your way to the presentation, play the tape again so that all points are fresh in your mind.

Professionals do what they are good at. If there is an area in which you lack polish, get a tutor. Take the time to do things well, or find someone who does it well. Don't degrade your professional standing in the community by doing a poor job.

22

Qualifying the Client

The first meeting with the client usually has a time limit, and you may have only one or two opportunities to convince the prospect that your firm is right for his or her project.

No matter how often you've done it, you still need to think about format. What information do you need before you walk into that meeting, and what should you leave with the prospect? Without an outline, you may miss some issues, and this can lead to later misunderstandings with the client.

Learn as much as you can about prospective clients. You need to know in detail exactly what they want, how they purchase design services, and what they know about interior design. Have they used designers before? Whom did they use? What architect have they worked with or are they working with now? What about other consultants? Who does the buying or the approving? What types of people are they? Can you communicate with them? Are they reasonable people? The way you dress is important; we need to dress according to the type of client and project.

Advance effort pays off a hundredfold later. Taking the time to run a credit report protects you from becoming involved in a bad situation later on. Outlining or listing what you want to cover during your meeting will help you feel at ease, and you'll come out of that interview with the information you need. It's all too easy to become involved in great, yet not totally relevant, conversations. However, if you are not specific in your objectives, you run the risk of failing to obtain the information needed to develop the project.

A standard form will help with this process. One that works for my firm is included for you to look over and adapt to your individual needs. A very simple Prospective Client Report (Figure 22-1) lists whom you are going to see, where, and the directions to get there. It can be very uncomfortable riding around looking for a building, knowing that the client is waiting for you. Include the client's phone number so that if you lose your way or find you must be late, you can warn the prospect. Respect the client by being on time. Time is irrelevant to some people, but most people feel better about working with you if you are careful to be punctual. The clients are evaluating you at the same time you are evaluating them. Being on time is one way you enhance their perception of you as a professional.

The Prospective Client Report lists the type of project and the objective of the appointment. After the meeting, write the outcome of the meeting and what preparation is needed for the next meeting on the form.

PROSPECTIVE CLIENT REPORT	Referred By:
Client:	Contact Person:
	Position:
Address:	Phone Number:
New Address: (if moving)	Directions:
Project:	
Objective:	
Result of Meeting:	
Research or Information Needed for Next Meeting:	
Date of Next Contact:	
Financial Arrangements:	

Source © Design Business Monthly

Figure 22-1

At the bottom of the page there's space for the date of the next contact and an indication of the financial arrangements.

We use the Prospective Client Report to determine whether to develop the client, and when. Is the client at the point that we're ready to send a proposal, or do we need another interview meeting or two? If the project is one you would like to develop or if it is a sophisticated one, try to win the opportunity for additional time with the client or for touring the building. (There are many small projects at low budgets for which this is not practical.) The development process is part of your research. Often we acquire information that assists us in evaluating the project, so that our proposal can be on target. The client can see we have a special interest in his or her firm.

Very rarely is a proposal sent after the first meeting. Usually you need more information before preparing a proposal. The Design Service Questionnaire helps define a project. It takes about forty-five minutes to an hour to review this with the client. It's usually advisable to make a second appointment and sit down with him or her to really go over the details. This will also help you understand the client's investment in doing the project—in terms of both emotional and financial commitment.

How many interviews does it take to develop a project to the point that you can present a proposal and get it signed? This varies, depending on the size of the project. If you're discussing small projects, yes, you need to work out some sort of proposal so that you can make this decision within the first interview. Larger projects may take weeks, many months, or maybe even a year or more. This is normal for large projects, and if you want projects on that scale, you will have to put in the effort.

Research

The more time you spend up front listening to what clients want and defining their needs and their projects, the less time you'll have to spend later designing the project and handling complaints at the end.

Research is the foundation of good client relations. Don't walk into a new project without first calling around to try to learn how prospective clients have worked with other design professionals. Speak with other tenants in the building and neighborhood about what has happened on the site. Talk to anyone who knows the client and also knows your firm. The more information you have, the easier it is to communicate properly.

Run credit reports, not just to find out the firm's credit standing but also the personal histories of the people you will be working with and designing for. Who are the company officers? Are they management people, accountants, engineers, or physicians? What are their professional backgrounds and lifestyles? Do anything you can to anticipate likely attitudes about the project. You want to know what prospects know about the design discipline, as well as the styles and methods they use to manage their company.

When you question prospects, try to relate all design issues to items they have and can see in their individual spaces. This is why a personal visit to the site is so important: it's an opportunity to meet the other people involved, whether it is family or staff. You may want to compare their offices to one of their competitor's offices, then to a similar office elsewhere in town. Although the other office may be attractive, perhaps you heard that it wasn't quite as productive. Did it meet their expectations?

What does the prospect think of the style of his or her competitors' offices? What firms does the prospect compare to his or her own? What do the prospects expect of their clients?

Obviously, this type of information can be extremely important in planning the design direction for the new office the prospect was considering.

You may be surprised by the amount of time clients spend on research. While talking to a client about carpet (there was a particular specification that I didn't agree with, and still don't agree with totally), I learned that three people on the client's staff had spent a year researching carpet backings. They had tested over thirty different samples on the floors of their facility and had worked with chemical research laboratories. I felt at that point that I should not even mention the other issues. It was best to use their work as a base and incorporate my design input.

Who Makes the Decisions?

Very often a client doesn't realize or doesn't want to admit to you that he or she is poor at making decisions. That's why you were hired. When you meet clients, find out how they make decisions. Do they make it themselves? Is it a case in which they must talk to their wives or other members of the board? Sometimes a man will not make any decision unless he has reviewed it with his wife, because he feels that she has great taste.

It is important for the clients to see you as the qualified, concerned consultant. It is your job to narrow down the field of choices. It is important for you to place the client in a position where he or she can easily make decisions. If this has not been done properly, obviously the client is going to have difficulty.

Spend some time with your clients and prospective clients and find out what their decision-making processes are. Try to discover what you can do to make their decision-making process an easier one.

Using the Design Service Outline

Any time you work on a new project, it is important to be clear about exactly what the client wants and expects in terms of service. Most clients today do want, or need, a price. They're not happy to work on strictly open-ended contracts. To give them a price that won't be a source of trouble later, we need to define specifically what they want done. Start defining the project at the initial interview, using an outline of questions to make sure you cover all the issues. This is best done at a planned meeting, where the client knows in advance that it will take a span of forty-five minutes or more and has made that time commitment.

The Design Service Outline (Figure 22-2) is written as a form, so that all you have to do is to write in, using a pencil, the client's responses. These may change during the interview. The Design Service Outline has two functions. Not only does it define what the client expects, it educates the client about the range of design services available.

Many interior design clients believe that we only select colors or develop space plans. Simply reviewing with them the general needs and the services on the Design Service Outline uncovers the extent of services available from the design field. We're not coming in and bragging to the clients about past work and our abilities. We're using questions that demonstrate our knowledge and allow the client to be the expert on his own space.

DESIGN SERVICE OUTLINE	Date:
Client:	Contact Person:
	Position:
Address:	Phone Number:
Project:	
Decision-making Process:	
Presentation Form: Floor plans: Boards: Renderings: Models: CAD:	
Stages of Decisions:	
Client's Representatives:	
Staff Involved:	
Consultants:	
Contractors:	
Scheduled Contact Time:	

Source © Design Business Monthly

Figure 22-2

Determining Requirements: (functional and organizational)
Space Analysis:
Traffic Flow:
Work Flow:
Personnel—Expected Growth:
Individual Space:
Visitors: Flow:
Equipment:

Storage: Records:
                 Supplies:
                 Other:

Lighting:
Acoustical:
Audiovisual:
Security:
Handicapped:

Source © Design Business Monthly

Figure 22-2 (*continued*)

Since there may be changes as I go through the process, I fill in the form in pencil. This becomes part of the client's permanent file. Any designer or any person on the staff who works on the project can refer to this to see exactly what our responsibilities are and what someone else is taking care of.

The first page of the Design Service Outline has a space at the top for the client's name and address, the name and position of the contact person, and the phone number. Who is responsible? Who contacted you? With whom will we be working and what are their phone numbers? On a residential job, it may be the husband, the wife, or another person who takes responsibility for the project. For a contract project, the contact person may be a facility manager, a vice president, or some other senior management person.

Figure 22-2 (*continued*)

Design Concept:		
Architectural:	Changes: Details: Finishes:	
Floor Plans:		
Wall Elevations:		
Special Details:		
Cabinet/Built-in Work:		
Furniture:		
Special Equipment:		
Window Treatments:		
Lighting:		
Acoustical:		
Security:		
Audiovisual:		

Source © Design Business Monthly

Figure 22-2 (*continued*)

Who will we be working with? Whom do they want us to talk with? Are there any other people they believe we should talk with? Are there others who, in their opinion, do not have the appropriate information? Maybe they don't want certain staff members exposed to the many details of this project. What staff are we to be involved with?

What other consultants do they have on board? Is the architect already involved? Is the engineer involved? Is there an acoustical specialist? What other specialists and consultants are already part of the project? Do others need to be brought in?

Have the contractors been predetermined? In some projects, the contractors are established and in place long before the design process is firm. In other cases, they are selected later.

At the bottom of the very first page there's a space for the scheduled contact time, the time when you give the client his or her weekly update.

	Page 6
Project Documentation:	
Floor Plans (areas or rooms involved):	
Furniture Plans:	
Lighting Plan:	
Elevations (areas or rooms involved):	
Finish Schedule (special notes to be included):	
Hardware Schedule:	
Window Treatments:	
Special Conditions:	
Specifications:	
Bidding:	
Purchase Orders:	
Maintenance Manual (companies or products involved):	
Moving Plan:	
Schedule:	

Source © Design Business Monthly

Figure 22-2 (*continued*)

Page two of the form determines the functional and organizational requirements. Whether this is a residential or contract project, there's always a space analysis, traffic flow, and work flow. Are you doing the space analysis? Are you going to determine whether there will be any architectural changes or whether these spaces are appropriate for the functions for which they are intended?

Are you doing the traffic flow? Just how does this company function? Are you going to be responsible for directing the work flow?

What about personnel? How many people work in this department? What is the expected growth?

What about the individual space requirement for each particular person? Sometimes this is determined by equipment use. In some large

Project Management:		
Coordination:	Client:	
	Consultants:	
	Contractors:	
Scheduling:		
Shop Drawing Approval:		
Supervision:		
Revisions:		
Change Orders:		
Negotiations:	Prebid Quotes:	
	Contractors:	
Payment Authorization:		
Occupancy Evaluation:		
Postoccupancy Review:		
Others:		

Source © Design Business Monthly

Figure 22-2 (*continued*)

corporations the space requirement is predetermined by status. What are the company's standards and requirements?

What about visitors? Will they be permitted in all parts of the building or just on certain floors? What is the flow? Which areas do you want to expose them to, and which areas must be considered private? How will you handle these guests?

Every project involves equipment today, from the most technical commercial project, down to the simplest residential work. What type of equipment must be accommodated in this space?

The next issue is storage. What type of storage does the client need, and where is it needed? Storage for recordkeeping and supplies is part of almost every project. What other kinds of storage are important to this project, and what must you supply?

Is the lighting to remain as it is presently, or is there an opportunity for lighting design? If so, who will be responsible for it?

What about acoustics? Every one of our projects has some acoustical detailing to it, because acoustics is a matter of hearing what you want and need to hear and diminishing what you don't want to hear.

Audiovisual equipment is common today. Who well be responsible for the audiovisual planning for the space?

Security is one area in which we ask that the client make a direct contract with the consultant or that the client specifically tell us that we are not responsible for security. This has become such a technical specialty today, and one that involves so much liability, that every design firm should be concerned.

What about access for the handicapped? The Americans with Disabilities Act requires new buildings to meet certain federal and state accessibility standards. What does the client need? A residential client may be wheelchair-bound, may have accident-prone children, or may simply like the idea that people with even temporary physical impairments could move easily in the space. What do the clients see as their needs?

The next page is blank because, as you are talking, there are always unplanned details that must be noted, and this outline is structured so that you write down all the information you need to establish the requirements of the project. You may learn necessary details—ones that don't immediately seem to fit any category—in the course of conversation.

The fourth page is devoted to scheduling. What is the owner's projected goal for completing the project? For instance, the owner may expect to have the project completed in thirty days, while you look at it as a three-year project. You had better determine this right now so that you can make changes, either in the scope of the project or in the completion date. Estimate the design schedule, work schedule, and other issues.

Below the spaces for schedules is an area for notes, where you can document preferences or details regarding the scheduling.

Page five covers the design concept. Will there be any architectural changes? If so, who—architect, engineer, or other specialist—is responsible for the changes? If not, does the building stay exactly as it is; are you merely dealing with the interior spaces, furnishings, and other interior details? Document all changes, details, and finishes.

Under design concepts, you'll see the floor plans listed again: the wall elevations, special details, cabinetry, or built-ins. Will you be designing those details, and are they included in your pricing? If you neglect to allow for this in your estimated budget, then you are responsible for providing all the drawings and the working details. This can really eat up your profit on the job.

What about the furniture? Are you using existing furniture, or does the client plan to purchase new furniture?

Has special equipment been assigned? Today there are few spaces, commercial or residential, that don't have televisions, computers, audio-visual equipment, or other electronic devices. Each has special needs and requirements.

Does the project involve window treatments or lighting, acoustical, security, and audiovisual elements? For which areas are you responsible?

The sixth page is devoted to project documentation and floor plans. Are you responsible for certain rooms, or are all the rooms involved? The outline covers the furniture plan, the lighting plans, elevations, finish schedules (and any special notes you may need), hardware schedule, window treatments, and special conditions.

What about specifications? Will you be writing the bidding documents? Are you responsible for all the detail specifications? How much detail is enough for a preselected vendor? How much will have to be bid? The documents for one are considerably different from the other. Who handles the purchasing, and what is your responsibility?

What about a maintenance manual? Obviously, these items need to be maintained. Who will be responsible for directing how this is to happen?

Is there a move involved? In most cases, whether it's remodeling or a new facility, some type of moving plan is required. Are you developing the moving plan?

Page seven is dedicated to project management. Who coordinates the project? Is it the architect, another one of the consultants, or a contractor? Is the client the coordinator? Who is responsible for the overall coordination?

Who is responsible for scheduling, the shop drawing approval, supervision, and revision? How are these going to be handled? Does the client want you to include them in your regular price, up to a certain dollar figure, or are they to be billed as extras—and on what basis? Determining this right now can save trouble later on.

How will change orders be handled? Who will do the negotiating, prepare the prebid quotations, and handle the vendors and contractors?

What about payment authorization? Are you to approve items before they are paid for, or is someone else taking care of this?

Finally, will you conduct an occupancy evaluation, postoccupancy review, and others? The back page is left empty for your review.

Along with the Design Service Outline, we use an overview page for costing. We put each area from the outline on our cost-calculating sheet.

Suppose you are responsible for suggesting architectural changes that might be worked into the project. You are responsible for writing the specifications for all the required finishes and for preparing the furniture plan. A presentation from the acoustical engineer will be considered, but a separate quotation will be submitted—and on down the line.

The Design Service Outline is your master sheet for determining how to bill the project—whether it will be done on an hourly basis with an estimated amount of time, on an overcontract basis, or by some other method.

You may want to calculate this in several ways. For example, after filling in the Design Service Outline, you can list every service and detail that the client requires.

You also consider the length of time that the project will take to develop and complete. Scheduling affects your pricing. Is it a fast-track job or a long-term job, and how much interaction will the project require? Will you need to send documentation to seven different consultants, or will you supply it to one person who takes care of everything? All of this is general expense and needs to be determined.

Once you have completed this sheet and you've worked out the estimated cost according to hours, then you may want to compare some other methods of evaluating costs, such as by square footage. Or you may even want to consider general estimated costs to complete a project, based on several other projects that you have in your file.

We find that this intensive background is absolutely necessary to give a client an appropriate method of working and an appropriate price. By the time you have finished going through the outline with clients, they understand a lot more about the responsibility of the designer on their projects, and they can figure out more easily exactly what they want you to do.

This protects you. As the project develops, should you find that the client is enlarging the project, you can refer him or her to your original proposal and say, "You will notice that in our initial proposal we did not include the fourth floor. We were doing only the third floor. If you would like us to handle this additional area, then we will send you a proposal to cover it." Or you may have it in your contract that you will agree to do this additional area at an hourly rate, or an additional per-square-foot price. This can then be calculated and handled accordingly.

If we as designers are to manage projects professionally, we need to start with a professional base. I don't see any way of doing it other than by using our experience and records and evaluating what the client expects and wants from us. By balancing the two we should be able to come up with a system of working professionally, because this is what clients need from us. They need that organization, and they need that system.

The Design Service Outline is tailored for the needs of a specific firm. It has changed many times throughout the years. You will undoubtedly find that you need items that aren't listed, but I offer my form as a guide to creating your own. We do ours in a very inexpensive photocopied format. We don't need anything fancy or ornate, just a form complete enough to include the details that we need for a given project.

This form stays with the project the whole way through. The estimating sheet for financial arrangements is kept on a separate page, because that stays within the business office. There may be people working as consultants on the design project who need access to the Design Service Outline, but they should not have access to all the financial details.

Try using a Design Service Outline. I think you'll find it worth your while. You'll probably want to develop your own form, since the issues of your specialty may be considerably different. The point is, through the presentation of this type of questionnaire, you're explaining to your clients the complexity of interior design. By the time you're finished, you will have told them not only what interior design is but how it's part of their particular project needs.

When to Refuse a Project

Everything in this book is intended to help you develop and manage a high-quality, profitable firm. So many projects are interesting and appear to be fun to do, but are they the right projects for your firm? Undertaking the wrong project can hurt your firm, but how do you say no to the wrong job? One of the reasons you go out to see projects is to decide whether they fit your practice. The reality is that some projects don't fit. They're either much too large or too small. Remember the 70/30 ratio. If seventy percent of a job is easy to do and you've done it so many times that you can almost do it with your eyes closed, then this is the job for you.

The challenging part should be no more than thirty percent of the project. If you need to learn more than thirty percent, it's probably too risky for you to take it on. If more than thirty percent of the project is new, it will be difficult to make it unusual and creative. It takes too much learning time and extra effort, and it will be hard to get paid for it.

If during the interview or after your preliminary research you get an uncomfortable feeling, the best thing to do is to find a way to drop out of the project as soon as possible. The same applies when the job is not appropriate for your practice, or the client is not the type with whom you can work easily. Handle it professionally.

You might say, "This project is not our specialty. To do quality work for our clients, we find it best to stay with the type of work we're most familiar with." Suggest that when the client has work in your specialty, he or she should call you. You may even want to recommend two or three other designers they might contact. In fact, if you recommend other designers, it's always best to give them more than one person; it lowers your liability on the situation.

Or you might say, "Unfortunately, our schedule does not allow us to take on another project at this time." The client may decide to wait for you. If this happens, it also gives you time to do more research and see if the client's increased commitment may be worth your consideration.

But handle the situation with care. Sometimes your intuition can be very valid.

How Do You Fire a Client?

No matter how careful you are, you may still have a problem client. Sometimes you think in the beginning the client is great. But as soon as he or she becomes a problem, fire the client as quickly as possible. Tell him or her that the project is developing into something that isn't really working for you, and suggest the client find someone else.

Suppose you are in the early stages of client development with a prospect, just past the Prospective Client Report and perhaps past the Design Service Outline, but not as far as the contract or letter of agreement—and you decide you don't want the client. Not too long ago, our firm heard that a prospective client was very litigious and had instigated lawsuits against several contractors. I was afraid that we were going to be the next to be sued, so I told the client that I was sorry, that we wouldn't be able to handle her project for her.

Unfortunately, as it turns out, the interior designer who took the job was sued and had a very difficult time with the client. She was not paid for her work, incurred heavy legal fees, and lost the major part of two years of her life.

If you are at all concerned about whether a client is right for you, perhaps that client *isn't* right for you. A designer who attended one of my seminars told the group that her partner refused to work for attorneys and asked for our opinion. I asked why she felt this way. The answer was that her partner felt attorneys were impossible. Every time she worked with them, she was sued.

After hearing this, I thought her partner was wise; she was aware that she doesn't work well with attorneys. If she had trouble with them on previous occasions, it's probable she would have difficulty with them on future occasions. She does well with physicians, so perhaps she should stick to working with physicians. The fact that she has found her focus may be one of the most important things that has happened in this designer's career development.

CHAPTER 23

Defining a Project

In design projects as in business, it's necessary to define the priorities of the job. What are the most important things that the *client* wants to accomplish on this job? The Design Service Outline is a form that gives an easy-to-follow list, which defines all the priorities and directions of the project. It is important to understand the limitations of the job. Let the client understand that yes, designers can accomplish almost anything, but that everything has a price. Is service X really worth investing in? If so, it affects the priorities of the project. If not, something else takes precedence.

Not only should you list the priorities of a project, but you should review it with the client several times during the project so that he or she is aware of what priorities you are dealing with. It is possible the clients' priorities may change during the project. If you don't keep checking with them, you could be unaware of the changes. Because developing projects takes time, sometimes clients see other advantages, other things that can be done within this given space—and consequently their priorities often do change.

So clarify priorities carefully. This list will also help ensure that you are paid for what you do. You based your quote on the outline. If there are changes, revising the priority list with the client gives you an opportunity to revise your price quote.

How Much Change Is Comfortable to Clients?

When you meet a new client, one of the first judgments you must make is how much change is comfortable for him or her. If a client is to enjoy a space and accept a space, he or she must feel comfortable in it. Anything we do to a space, any improvement, is change. Change usually produces insecurity and some emotional resistance. When you are working on a project and developing a space, consider the client and the situation; don't change it to the point that the client won't be comfortable with it.

Too much change can make us ill, according to psychologists. A number of years ago, *Reader's Digest* ran a chart that let people evaluate the stress in their lives as caused by various changes. Each change—getting married, loss of a spouse, loss of a child, changing jobs, and the like—was assigned a stress value, and when the total of these stress values reached a cutoff level, psychologists could predict illness.

Similarly, too much change in interior spaces is a mistake. I discovered, after doing projects with several corporations, that a vice president is often in charge of the new building. If that vice president develops a building that is a few steps better than what the firm presently had—one which helps the firm develop within the next two to three years, yet is not necessarily state of the art or the very best in every way—this particular person will very often become the chief executive officer and will go on to lead the firm. But if that vice president creates a state-of-the-art building for the firm, one that will carry it through into the next decade, this person is often not advanced to such a high position but simply left in a lower management position.

In the latter instance, the change was too shocking. There may have been other factors as well. The corporate budget for building may have been overspent, even though in the long run it may have been the best thing to do. The new building may have caused havoc or an uncomfortable feeling within the corporation, and this unease may have cost the firm momentum in other areas. So the vice president in charge of the state-of-the-art building has almost never been promoted, despite the great thing he or she may have done for the company.

Interior space is one of the tools of a corporation, just as it is a tool for a family. We have to design within the parameters of what will be effective for a corporation's given life and work style; therefore, one of the best things a designer can do is visit the prospective client's site to see how the client has been working or living and determine the level of design. An on-site visit also assists greatly when it comes to budgeting. Clients often say to us, "I don't want to spend too much money." But how much *is* too much? It's very difficult to tell without visiting the site, where it is easy to judge whether very expensive art furniture or fine, quality products, like those of Ralph Pucci, Baker, or other quality manufacturers, were used in the previous job. If the site is done in hand-me-downs or "old attic," we know the company's idea of low budget is very different from that of the client accustomed to buying quality items.

One of the things I have learned in my practice is that it is best to work within the range of the client's understanding, to educate him or her slowly to the design process. If we rate our projects on a scale of one to ten—with one or two indicating poor quality and ten very fine quality—and we accept an existing space rated a two or a three, the best thing to do is to make that project a three, a four, or maybe a five if we want to keep the client. Taking it too much beyond that can be really destructive to the relationship.

It's not too shocking to bring a site that rates a seven or an eight to a nine or a ten. But it is better to take the two or the three—bringing them up to a five, and then a few years later developing them into a six or a seven—than to go directly from a two to a seven. In the interim, the client will have been educated by the experience of living in that space and will then want a better design. As you work on the design project, make the client familiar with the changes as they occur so that he or she starts to feel comfortable with the new design. Then when the client moves into the space, he or she knows where each item will be placed, why the items are there, and the purpose of the design. Part of this design orientation is an orientation for how to live in the space—not just selling the design.

When setting up a project, prepare a value worksheet (see Figure 17.4) for the products you recommend. List each design feature or product you selected for this project. There is a reason you selected each product, a reason that you believe this designer product answers the client's need. List the particular problem that you feel the product solves or the benefit you think it has. Conclude this sheet with all the support information and documentation that you may have. This information can come from experience from other installations, manufacturers' specifications or information sheets, laboratory reports, or articles on products from magazines or journals.

Today we need a lot of support materials, both to reinforce our professional position and to lessen the liability of our professional recommendations. Put together all this information so that when you go to a meeting, you have all the backup support data right at hand.

Keep the value sheet handy. When a staff member is researching a product or a sales representative is presenting a product, this information will be needed. You will have excellent support information for your selection.

To present our design specialty as it deserves to be presented, we must constantly keep in mind the client's need to know everything about the project versus the worksheet value. We solve problems. We try to give our clients the best products. Be prepared to show just why and how you make your choices.

What Is Quality?

What a designer sees as quality may not be what our clients see. Quality is the presence of value *as the client sees it*. You can expend a lot of effort to polish a project and still discover that the client wanted something different. Talk with your clients extensively, in a regularly scheduled interaction, to develop an understanding of their value system.

Management consultant W. Edwards Deming says, "There is no such thing as 'getting it right.' There is always a better way." As designers, we tend to think our way is best. We may direct the project and make many decisions, but the client *owns the project and pays the bill*. So from the first interview through all communication, keep classifying and charting the client's values. This awareness is the foundation for good communication and client satisfaction.

What If the Client Wants to Do It Later?

When you're working on a project, very often clients will say, "I'm sorry, but I can't do this now. I would like to do it later." A lot can happen between the time you are first contacted and the time you begin to place the orders. The reasons a client holds up a project can be a change in lifestyle or the fact that the project is simply more expensive than the client expected. It could be economic change: the firm's business has increased and it doesn't have the time to deal with an installation, or business has decreased and the firm no longer has the money.

Sometimes, it may be appropriate to encourage the client to complete a project now, when it fits into your schedule and you have the workpeople available to do it. In situations where the client is just not comfortable with doing the project now, for financial or other reasons, what should you do?

My feeling is that it is better to do a project later than to have no project at all. If the client is not ready to do it today, keep in touch with him or her. Be understanding. Let the clients know that when they're ready, you'll be very happy to work with them. If you never call them, they probably think you've lost interest. If you occasionally check with clients to see if they are still interested or if their needs have changed, it may turn into a sale. A late sale is far better than no sale at all.

Closing the Sale

How do you close a sale?   Well, actually, I hope we never close a sale. Our objective is to build relationships, long-term relationships. That's what pays best for any professional practice. We don't want to start and finish a project—we want to build that sale! So, as you look at projects, don't think, "How do I close the sale?" but, "How do I develop the sale?" As you develop it, think of how you plan your rooms or the way you build a building. You first put in a secure foundation and then make sure that everyone understands that it is secure before you go on to the next course of work. You should be doing the same thing when you build a sale or a project.

So don't talk about closing a sale; talk about building a relationship with a client and developing it into a project. Deal with it just as you would construct a job or a building. This will give you a great basis for ongoing work.

A sale occurs when a need is converted to a want. Closing really means obtaining a decision.

One of the most difficult parts of selling is knowing when and how to close a sale or get a decision. According to "Zig" Ziglar, a best-selling speaker on the art of selling, "If you can't close, you can't sell."

Prepare a list of leading questions, questions that cannot be answered with a yes or a no. This requires the client to give an extended answer.

You might say, "Now that we've examined your plans, what other questions do you need answered before you are prepared to make a decision on the project?"

Or you could say, "Taking into consideration your work schedule, when would you like us to start the project?"

Other good questions are:

- What are your scheduling plans, so that we can alert our studio to reserve time for the appropriate people needed for this job?
- When will you need specifications?
- Shall we start working on the final designs for you?

If you don't get a positive response to these questions, go back over the preliminary part of your presentation, restating clients' decisions to make sure you understand their positions. Attempt to reorient or redefine the project.

It is important to keep an itemized list of every point you discuss on a project, as well as the results you achieved. File this list for reference during future contacts. (See Results of Client Meeting, Figure 17.3.)

Sometimes designers lose a project because they oversell. The client is ready to buy, but the designer talks too much about features of the project he or she considers special—and these may be issues that are irrelevant to the client. But losing a sale can sometimes occur simply because the designer neglected to ask for the job.

It takes an average of seven to ten calls to develop a client, and some designers stop too soon. Each time you meet, you should try to establish a date for calling a client before you leave his or her home or office. Again, build this process on values—first their values, and then the complement of appropriate design and product—to develop these values. This creates and endorses want and need.

Debriefing

Understanding why you didn't get a job is one of the best ways to learn. If you've made a presentation on a project and you suspect or know that it was awarded to someone else, follow up. Call the client, and find out who was selected and why your firm wasn't chosen. Before you call or speak with the prospective client, prepare a list of questions so that you can develop the conversation and learn from it. Let the client know that the call is standard procedure, that it helps you evaluate your position in the field better.

Ask how the decision was made and who was selected for the project. Then ask how your presentation compared to the others and what the client thought of it. Finally, ask whether your firm might be considered for any other project he or she has planned.

Talking with prospective clients who decided against using your firm creates goodwill. Tell them that you enjoyed the opportunity to meet with them and to get to know them, and add that you would like to work with them in the future should they ever have a different need. Encourage them to call you. Be sure they know the door is open. Your goal is to leave the client with a pleasant and positive impression of you and your firm. You are professionally disappointed but not angry that you didn't get the project. You do not want losing this project to stand in the way of your being considered for the next one. (See the debriefing guide in Figure 17.5.)

Client's Duties

Before beginning a project, it is advisable to list in writing what you would like the client to do. Some of these issues may be part of your contract. If you are using a simple letter of agreement, give the client an outline of what you expect from him or her. As one example, the client is expected to supply you with all the information you need to do the job. This means the client should tell you how his or her company operates, or how the family lives, because not everyone performs the same functions or lives the same way within a space. In order for you to be able to do your work correctly, you must be aware of the fine details of the client's particular way of working or living.

The designer must be able to have access to this information from other knowledgeable people within the organization. Who are the right people to interview? This may be information that the chief coordinator does not have. Who will understand the future direction of the company and has the ability to supply the correct, detailed information?

You must have open access to the space. At what hours can you get in, who is responsible for letting you in, and what are your privileges or restrictions in this operation? When can contractors work? Precisely what is convenient and suitable to the client?

Schedule regular meeting times. The client must give you a time each week for regular communication. You need to know to whom you will be responsible. Whether it is a residential or contract project, there must be one person who takes this position. This person will be the one receiving the weekly calls. He or she will be the one within the organization responsible for coordinating all of the issues relating to the design. Is that person also responsible for making sure that the equipment requirements are accurate, so that when furniture is made to fit there is no chance there will be a change? Who handles those details? This is why, on the Design Service Outline, we review the decision-making process.

The Process for Approval

You need to know who's going to *sign the documents*. Who is going to be responsible for all of your contracts, purchase orders, change orders, or other documents involved in the project?

Clients should be open with you about their feelings. If the clients have questions, they must let you know so that you don't continue working on a design that may be inappropriate. The clients must make every effort to make you aware of any problems as they arise.

The client must understand the financial arrangements. It is advisable to review these in the very beginning so that he or she has an opportunity to prepare for these issues. That way, when you send the bill, the client will be prepared to see that you are paid at the appropriate time.

The style of the decision-making process affects the client's time commitment as well as that of the designer. If it is to be a participatory process, the client must understand that he or she will be required to spend a specified number of hours per week with you. Going over this in advance will often help the client determine just what type of design process is best for him or her.

It's necessary to review the purchasing and contracting system so that the client understands how the project will be managed. Is the designer to select the contractors, craftspeople, and resources, or will the services be specified for a bid? Will the bidding list be selective? Or will the project be put out for general bidding and possibly go to the lowest bidder—which might entail certain risks?

It's a good idea to go over the different types of processes of completing a job before beginning the job. That way the clients understand what the process involves and, therefore, are better able to determine whether they want you to obtain several prices on it and select from those preferred vendors, whether they really want to put it on an open bid, or if they want you to arrange for a turnkey project.

The major point of this is that you must take the time to go over the client's obligations with him or her as you plan the project. Usually, the client's questions cover many of your needs. If further explanation is needed, provide it. It is wonderful to say, "We can take care of everything," and, in some instances, this might be the right way. But in other cases, we may be getting ourselves into a situation that is far too risky for a designer to handle.

Go over these issues; let the client understand what it will take to complete the job, and just which method is most appropriate for this particular client and job.

CHAPTER 24

Customer Service

What hours do designers work? What are appropriate working hours?
In the current market, there is no such thing as regular business hours. Many clients are unavailable during the day. If you want their business, you may have to organize your schedule so that you are available when they can see you.

Of course, you can tell clients that it is most advantageous to meet at your studio during normal working hours; however, other designers are adjusting their hours during this intensely service-oriented period, so you must as well.

Check with your clients to determine what is really needed, and make yourself available at a mutually agreed-on time. To attract new clients, you may discover that you need one or two late nights a week. Many designers find that clients are not comfortable spending their productive hours buying design. Some studios find the weekends are their best-paying times. One of my best and largest accounts could only see me early in the morning—at 6:00 A.M. So we were finished with our decisions by 7:30 or 8:00 A.M., when the staff began to arrive.

This gave us a block of uninterrupted time and was very valuable in reaching good decisions. It was well worth it, although I needed to be sure I was up and ready. Everything was ready the day before. I was up at 4:00 A.M., reviewed meeting notes from 4:45 to 5:30 A.M., when I left for the meeting. I tried to be five minutes early. I did this every Tuesday morning for eight-and-a-half years. As a result, I wake up early. Some of my city friends don't understand this.

Should you give your home or cell phone number to clients? Perhaps. There should be some way for clients to reach you in an emergency. On the whole, clients will not take advantage of you if you demonstrate your proactive style of working by calling regularly with information.

On the other hand, if they have your cell phone number, clients can reach you at any time of day or night. Some of today's clients don't hesitate to call you anytime. You need to decide ahead of time just how you want to handle this.

What if a client asks your firm for a service it does not provide? If a client asks for a service your firm does not provide, try to find a firm, or several firms, that handle that type of request. Clients hire designers to make their lives more convenient. Many designers have built their practices by coordinating services for other needs. New people in a community may not know where to find needed services unrelated to design, such as cleaning or markets. Help them if you can. It is better to have them depend on you rather than on someone else. Be careful to whom you refer clients, but try to be helpful. It is usually appreciated.

What do we need to do to keep our clients? A current client is worth more than a new one. Keep in touch with your clients. Support them; relate. It costs us at least five to seven times as much to nurture and develop a new client as it does to maintain an existing one. Existing clients know about you, have bought from you before, and have worked with you. So nurture them, keep them, and develop them.

What do your clients think? Nothing is more valuable than your reputation—what your clients think of you. **And unless you ask, you may never learn what they really think**. After clients have lived in a completed project (job) for two years, our firm asks, "How did you find our services? How did our firm relate to your company? Were we easy to work with? What were the hard parts about dealing with the project? What would you suggest that we change in our process?"

Sometimes the answers cover issues the firm hadn't even considered but are very important to the client. Sometimes these issues will be important to other clients. Interview your clients, and see if their suggestions might help you in designing your program to better suit the next client.

Talk to clients often. Ask what your firm can do to make the project better. In your clients' opinion, do you deliver on time what you promise to deliver? Do you do things right the first time, or do you have to do them over? Other questions you might ask are:

Do we listen to you?
How hard do you think we're working to keep you happy?
How much confidence do you have in our services and our products?
How well do you think we understand you?
How well do you think we understand your special needs and requests?
How do you rate our design studio?
How do you rate our staff and our service?
Is our staff helpful and polite?
Do we speak your language?

Before changing your firm's direction, ask your clients. Before you consider any major changes to your customer service program, check with your clients and find out what they really want. Then review the proposed changes in-house, with your staff and others who know your procedures. Ask your clients if they feel this is a better way. After you find that the change really works, put it into action. There's no point in making major policy changes before you're certain they're what clients really want and need.

Design firms need to organize themselves so they meet the needs and services of the clients. Sometimes the services we offer aren't what clients want. We need the skill and knowledge to be able to evaluate clients' needs and find ways of putting them in place. Interview your clients to learn how your firm measures up.

Keep your promises. Don't promise anything you can't deliver. If you tell a client a project will take six months to complete and you finish it in four, you're a hero. If you say it will take six months and it takes eight, as far as the client is concerned, you're a louse.

If you promise to call a client at a certain time, do it. Honor your telephone appointments in the same way you would honor in-person appointments.

Plan for mistakes. When you set up a project schedule, you expect everything will go according to plan. Twenty, thirty, forty, even fifty percent of the time everything will go as planned, but that doesn't always happen. So have a contingency plan for mistakes, delays, and bad luck. Make a list of what could go wrong, and make sure you have standbys ready.

When part of a project must be assembled in front of the client, test it beforehand so you know that the pieces fit together and how they fit. Take the extra time to check on an item's condition before it is delivered.

Develop resources to obtain what the client wants. If you don't have what a client wants, do you have resources that can supply it? If you're a small design firm, you need to develop ways to fill in some of these gaps. I saw an interesting practice in the South that I believe is worth emulating.

The designers in a North Carolina community worked very closely together; they interacted as friends. Each designer had a key to the other designers' studios and would take items they needed—lamps, accessories, or other small items—and leave a note. There was a constant trading of products. This interaction allowed designers to offer their clients a more total project than they could have offered independently.

Working together does pay. Find someone you would like to work with, and see if you can trade and share both products and staff. This works especially well for large installations. We will often borrow staff from another firm. They understand how to do things, and both staffs enjoy the experience of working together. We get to see things that other studios have done and techniques that we may not have tried, and they in turn can pick up tips from us.

Keep your clients updated. One of the most important things in any practice is keeping our clients informed. This is particularly critical during the "Twilight Zone," the period of time between receiving a commitment to begin a project and the completion of plans and the installation of products. During this time framework, clients can be very worried or insecure. They're concerned about what we're doing and how we're doing it. Are we really paying any attention to their job, or are we working on other projects?

It's much more professional for us to call them than for clients to call us. A weekly standard communication is important, whether it's a face-to-face meeting or a telephone call. Schedule a date when you'll review all the details of the project. At this time you'll have everything pertaining to the project available and in front of you, and therefore you'll be able to sound more professional.

If someone calls you with a question while you're doing something else, your answer may or may not be correct. It may lack details because you don't have all the information front of you. If you have everything you need, you'll be able to tell the client exactly where you are in the project and resolve his or her issues more effectively. That will make the project flow much better.

If the weekly meeting is held by telephone, you might want to make it a conference call with someone from your office, possibly the principal or project manager. At that time, update the client as to exactly what's happening. The early calls during the project, for example, might be to inform the client that you have obtained his or her room measurements and are beginning the layouts of the project. Or, it may be that you're doing research on some of the specific issues of concern to you about the project.

At each meeting, ask clients their concerns and questions, then tell them you'll get back to them next week. The object is to try to have all calls going out of your office rather than coming in. The only calls that should be coming in are those about unusual issues or from new clients.

Client updates have proven to be one of the major marketing tools of many companies we've worked with. In addition to making schedules go much more smoothly, these updates encourage clients to perhaps do the next room or add more to their budgets, because they have great confidence your design firm is really on top of their projects.

Train your clients to work with you.   Train your clients to work with you to obtain the best service from your organization. Most of our clients don't understand the process of interior design. It's often necessary to prepare the client for the types of people and processes that their project involves. Clients need to know how to interact, as well as the kinds of information we need, appropriate time schedules, and when it's best to reach them.

You need to train clients to understand what kind of interaction is really needed from them, and how often. Unless you tell them, they won't know what they can do to build a stronger relationship with your company. They won't know how to react to the various craftspeople, vendors, and other consultants who work on the project.

Sometimes it's best to tell a client, "To reach me, call in the morning between 7:30 and 8:00 A.M., or leave a message at the office. I'm usually able to return calls at around noon or 4:30 P.M. A great deal of my time is spent on job sites or in vendor factories, and I want your file in front of me when we talk. Since there are so many details on your job, I want to be sure all the issues we discuss are correct."

When craftspeople are working in a client's space, it's advisable to keep everyone who isn't directly involved in that aspect of the job away from them. Any kind of distraction can decrease the quality of the project. They are artists too, and it's not good to interfere with their progress. For example, if carpet is to be installed, the space must be kept at a certain temperature, and appropriately cleaned and prepared. The right work environment is critical to the quality of the job.

It's much easier and more professional to make clients aware ahead of time that there are certain actions that improve or complicate the process of design and installation. Clients need to understand the work that will be done and their responsibilities. They need to be aware of the schedules and of the inconveniences that are part of construction.

If clients understand in advance what's expected of them to help make the job work better, it's usually easier to obtain their cooperation.

If, however, clients don't realize the complexities of the process, they sometimes feel put out or not considered. Most clients think interior design is really easy. We know that's not the case. We need to help clients understand the complexities we deal with so they'll permit us to do our jobs with appropriate care and professionalism.

Show appreciation.   Show your appreciation, not just to your clients but to your staff. Demonstrate that they are part of the job and that you value their help in making this design project what it is. Do something occasionally for the staff or your suppliers. Send them lunch, invite them to a special party, or send them theater tickets—do something that makes them feel special. Then the next time someone asks them whom they recommend as a designer—a question contractors are often asked—perhaps they will mention your firm.

We all want some form of acknowledgment. By acknowledging clients and staff, we build a stronger business. We shouldn't just stop at acknowledging the clients, but also let employees, contractors, and consultants know they're important to our firm. If staff members feel important, they will work better and produce a better project for your clients. So be sure your staff members feel good about themselves. Thank them for what they've done.

CHAPTER 25

How to Handle Complaints

When a client calls with a complaint, he or she is often quite emotional, even irate. You can turn a complaining client into a positive one, and perhaps an even better client than before.

Most complaints come in by telephone. This can intensify the problem, because you are not dealing with the client face to face. Attitude is important. The problem can escalate, or you can let the client know you really are concerned and want to hear what he or she has to say.

I've learned to say, "Excuse me a moment. I want to get your file. May I call you back in a few minutes when I have all the details in front of me?"

Another approach is to thank the client for calling you because you want to hear the whole story. You *need* to hear from clients because they are the ones you are trying to please. Then let them explain.

During their explanation, ask for clarification on important points; ask them to review all the fine points. Then ask if there was anything that was done correctly. Is the project totally wrong, or it is just a phase or two that needs correcting? Finally, ask for the client's recommendation on how to handle the problem.

Perhaps the client just can't understand why he or she is being billed for an item. We had a situation with one of our clients who called to object to being billed a particular fee. He was used to paying bills for furnishings and for our design contracts, but these were defined in a different way. It was an add-on project, and our contract had clearly stated our billing procedures, but perhaps he didn't look at it.

I asked him to explain the situation, and when he had finished giving me all the details, I asked him to let me explain our billing procedures. If we're not billing correctly, either through the correct word usage or our presentation, it is important for the client to tell us. It is harmful to any company to have an area of communication that is not presented clearly. I thanked the client for taking the time to call me and told him he had brought up a number of points I hadn't considered.

Our position was that in the case of this add-on contract, we had handled details involving other contractors. The problem contractor's quote had included his supervision, but he had left the job. So in order for the project to be completed, we assumed some of those responsibilities. These emergencies are generally the ones that get us into trouble. You want to keep the job moving. You don't want workpeople standing around doing nothing; you don't want to waste the client's money; you want the job finished by the deadline. So you do one of those *right* things without proper documentation or authorization. (This was before fax machines and email.) Actually our billing was well covered in writing, but the wording we had used was not what the client was accustomed to.

We received no financial compensation for any of the contracts and were not paid in any other way for these efforts. It seemed most effective to bill the client on an hourly basis for time spent. We could have billed on a percentage basis, or as part of the contract, but, this, in our judgment, was the better way.

Then I asked the client to tell me where we had gone wrong. He replied that he thought the billing had been presented correctly, but he just hadn't understood it. Then he thanked me for taking the time to explain it.

It wasn't the time that I spent explaining it to him; it was the time I spent listening to him carefully, making him define each point and writing it all down so I could give direct replies that resolved the situation. He also saw that I had a description, a reason, or an explanation for each issue, so he knew I had paid attention to him.

In almost any court situation, the reason clients are suing is not the actual issue of the suit; it's that they felt they weren't getting enough attention. They didn't feel important! They wanted more attention from the design firm. Good telephone manners can help this.

Any time a client calls with a complaint, ask for all the details. Ask if you can tape the conversation, and explain that you want the entire design group and the factory to hear the details so they can understand the nature of the problem.

It's amazing how the client's attitude changes. Immediately, he or she becomes more specific and less emotional. Instead of an emotional, exaggerated explanation, you receive the particulars of the issue. Your request for details proves that you take the client's problem or complaint seriously. Not only should everyone on the team know about it, but you will also take action. By acknowledging the client's problem, you have acknowledged its importance. This is the best way to handle complaints.

Don't stop there. Make sure the complaint is taken care of promptly. Whatever it takes, see that this is done immediately.

Unfortunately, designers must often wait a long time for the resource companies to respond to the complaint. This means the designer must step in and handle the problem itself—and then deal with the supplier. Every design firm should have a budget dedicated to handling complaints.

Often design firms are asked to handle problems that have nothing to do with the part of the job we were responsible for. It doesn't matter. If the client perceives the problem as your fault, *you* have to find a way to fix it, because it is your credibility and reputation that are on the line.

Turn complaints into positive opportunities to build future sales by fixing the problems immediately. Maintain a budget to handle problems. If you have a great year and the problem fund is unused, divide it among your employees who worked hard that year to prevent complaints. This is a good way to reward excellence.

26

Contracts and Letters of Agreement

lmost every designer can tell you a sad story about the time he or she didn't have a contract or forgot to get an issue in writing. Protect your relationship. Have your documents signed and keep them in your file. This ensures that the client has seen the contracts.

Major disagreements between a client and a designer usually arise from a breakdown in communication and can, unfortunately, lead to lawsuits. To avoid being sued, assume nothing, and document everything in contracts or letters of agreement. These should be written as clearly as possible.

Will contracts and letters of agreement protect you? To a certain degree, yes. But there is probably no contract that can be written that someone else can't get out of. Use a contract or letter of agreement to state your way of working and your expected compensation. Contracts define and make the client aware of potential problems. They acquaint clients with trade terms and familiarize them with the ways that designers charge and calculate their fees.

Many designers prefer to use contract documents prepared by the American Society of Interior Designers (ASID). The American Institute of Architects (AIA) has prepared similar contracts for use only by architects.

These have become a standard and are generally accepted by clients. Legal advisors who work with design firms suggest that this standard form stands a better chance of being upheld in court than documents specific to a practice or client.

The purpose of a contract or letter of agreement is to minimize your legal and financial exposure. Consider your situation. Some very large firms still use a one-page letter of agreement. Others use contracts containing seventeen or more pages. Be sure you understand the contract, or don't use it. If you are an interior designer and decide to develop your own documents, the ASID contract is your best source of information. Take the standard ASID contracts from *The Interior Design Business Handbook* (as well as any standard documents you can borrow from other design firms) to your attorney and ask him or her to review the contract provisions, taking into account the types of jobs you do and the issues that have caused you problems in the past. Ask your attorney to prepare or review an appropriate letter of agreement or contract for you to use. Read it carefully, and be sure you understand it before you send it out.

You need some form of a letter of agreement or a contract to cover every project on which you work, small or large. In fact, any billing for more than $500 must be in writing as a letter of agreement or contract. Otherwise, it's not collectible.

Some of the issues you should include are specific to your locale and type of practice. Some very large projects are done with simple letters of agreement. In more litigious areas, accepting even a small project without an extensive contract can be risky.

How to Use a Standard Contract

If you are an interior designer, always use an interior designer's contract (ASID). If you are an architect, use the AIA contract. Legally, an interior designer doesn't have the right to use an architect's agreement; only a registered architect can do so.

Make sure you understand the contract. Don't ask anyone to sign anything you don't thoroughly understand yourself.

Be sure that this contract or letter of agreement applies to the project. Modify the standard language according to the type of project you are working on—such as a medical center, law office, or a residence.

Clients hire you to do a creative job and your very best work. It's important to design your agreement with the client so you can achieve these goals. We know there are often changes, additions, or variables. Plan for changes, and specify ahead of time how you will be compensated for them.

Before you prepare a contract or letter of agreement, you should think about:

1. A definition of the scope of services: What services are to be rendered, and what is the extent of the designer's responsibility? Exactly which areas are to be designed?
2. The schedule: What will happen when, and whether any part is contingent on other parts of the process for which you're not responsible. Are there any time limits or constraints?
3. Who is involved: Have a list of the people who will be working on the project and what their responsibilities are.
4. Quality of job: Efforts and time required to produce this quality of project.
5. Risk: Client history, firm experiences, and other considerations need to be reviewed. Some projects have very heavy risk—high liability.
6. Terms: What do clients expect from us? How are they to work with? What must we do to complete the job in an outstanding fashion in their eyes?
7. Price: What can be charged for this type of project at this time, considering the general business environment, value of project competition, and the client's method of working? Exactly what items will be included in your fee?

What to Put in a Contract

Contracts and letters of agreement should define what services you will perform, state the schedule for performing them, and name the persons who will carry them out. These documents also should give all the details of the way you handle charges, billing, and collection.

1. Describe what design services you will perform, along with your responsibilities. Generally, when a contract document that is ambiguous or incomplete goes to court, the ruling is against the author of the document. So say what you will do, and then do it. Specify what the client will be responsible for. Present yourself as someone who can take charge of a project, yet don't oversell. It's too easy to say, "Don't worry about it; we'll take care of it." Be careful what you commit to, because it is not always possible to do. It is more prudent for a design firm to offer fewer services—just those it can perform securely—than to offer services that may put the firm in jeopardy.

2. State in detail the amount of payment you expect and how it will be computed. Describe the method of billing, whether it is hourly, daily, on a percentage, or a specified total-project-cost basis, and include a payment schedule. It is so much better to say that payments are due when certain phases of a project are completed. This clearly defines when payments are expected. It helps both you and the client to plan ahead.

3. Explain in detail all your billing and collection requirements. You need this for your paper trail. Ask for as much payment in advance as is appropriate. How can you design the cash movement to put you in the best position? Is there a way to be paid more quickly? Define your policy for late payments. How can you outline this so that the client is responsible for any costs that might be incurred?

4. Put a stop-work clause in your document. Legally, you cannot stop work without one, even if you are not being paid. You also will want to include a restart fee for any project that is stopped for thirty days or longer for any reason. That length of time away from a project means you will have to review the project to start it up.

5. Termination fees also need to be discussed. If, for any reason, the client decides to stop the project, what is your policy?

6. An automatic-escalation cost allowing for an increase in fees after twelve months or a specified period of time can prevent your being locked into working at a set fee while your costs escalate.

7. Limit your liability on the project, if at all possible. Your liability should be based on the net fee for the job. If your fee is $30,000, you don't want to be responsible for $3,000,000 worth of merchandise that could have been destroyed in the process.

8. Be careful of the way your contract lists prices to be charged. You cannot control your suppliers' price increases.

9. Your stated schedule should take into account that there may be delays for items over which you have no control. If the project will take six months for design, ordering, and installation, it is safer to say your firm will finish the project three months after the completion of the construction. Also, don't allow your firm to be held accountable for atmospheric conditions. Some things simply cannot be done at certain temperatures, or in extremely wet or extremely dry weather.

10. Spell out the duties and obligations of each party involved in the project. If you need support documents and cannot continue beyond a certain point without them, make their delivery part of the contract. The absence of specifications or engineering and architectural documents could delay the project or add to your liabilities.

11. Note that your design detailing relies on the work of other people. If you are relying on information from a particular source, list it—whether it is architectural prints or client's specifications. If a problem arises from an error based on faulty information, this could give you a legal out.

12. Stipulate who owns the drawings and specifications. You may be liable for design or material failures if your client uses your documents for a different project with different requirements. Copyright these documents. If your client needs to own your specifications, you should retain your ownership of the copyright. Retain the right to use your design and documents; you should be free to adapt the details to other projects, publish them, or use them any other way you see fit. Consider the possibility of licensing the documents. You may want to allow the client nonexclusive rights to copy and reproduce the documents for a specific project. Make sure this license is not transferrable to any other project. Don't stamp the drawings or have them stamped until they are paid for. Be careful to mark on your drawings that the prints are for reference only, for use by the various vendors and the contractor.

13. Spell out exactly how changes will be handled. In the precontract phase, decide how additions or deletions will affect your fee or charges. Require clients to sign and date all drawings and changes so that this does not become an issue at a later date. Often projects grow as the work starts. Tell the client in advance that additions affect the cost of the project, and how they are billed.

14. Disclaim responsibility for changes made by anyone but yourself. Small changes can influence the quality and safety of the design. With this disclaimer, the minute anyone else makes a change, you are relieved of responsibility for the total project.

15. The client liaison should be specifically named. You would like to know the person who is responsible for scheduling and for controlling the job.

16. If the project requires certificates for flame proofing, flame retardants, or other such safety aspects, have the appropriate agencies send them directly to the client's project—that way the agency is responsible, not your firm. Likewise, have any guarantees for the project sent directly to the client so that if problems should occur, the guarantor is responsible.

Considerations

Those are the basics. You also may want an agreement stating that if schedules are met and the budget adhered to, perhaps your firm will be hired for the next project.

Some firms include the client's permission to publicize the project as a standard part of their contracts and letters of agreement. This includes photographing the project.

Look to reduce your liability wherever possible, but also remember that you must offer the client a good project or he or she won't hire you again. Therefore, you must take on certain professional responsibilities. Attorneys suggest that our letters of agreement and our contracts should be designed so that they protect us completely. I'm not sure that this is ever totally possible.

Accept jobs that are appropriate to your firm, projects in which you can satisfy clients. Keep a close rapport with those clients. Keep in mind that you are building this practice first for client satisfaction. If the clients are satisfied, they're likely to hire you again, and they will give you a good reference.

When the client writes the contract for a project, as often happens in a large corporation, ask your attorney to review both your contract and the client's contract to be sure they're in harmony.

When there are overlapping responsibilities, clarify how these will be handled. A contract that involves other architects or contractors should clarify which items are included in your fee. For example, a phrase in your contract could say that since you are involved with the selection and detailing of items involving lighting fixtures, wall coverings and paints, floor coverings and finishes, custom hardware, cabinetwork, other custom woodworking, or doors, these will be covered under the fee for interior design services. A phrase could also say that although these items may be purchased by the contractor, the percentage-of-fee billing does apply to them.

Refer to the *Interior Design Business Handbook* for samples of contracts and letters of agreement and more information on this subject.

If you're receiving compensation related to this project from any source other than the fees you charge the client, clarify this in your proposal to the client. This may include standard fees or commissions that your resources have built into their prices for the specification of their products.

CHAPTER 27

Charging for Your Services

C harging for your services is part of the business relationship you have with clients. You must design it so you feel adequately compensated for your time and efforts, but also make sure the clients are receiving value for their investments.

Determining the appropriate fee structure for a job is of primary importance for your firm's development and profitability. The standard set by the proposal either gives the firm an opportunity for quality design work and profit, or creates a losing situation. If the project is not priced and structured properly, everyone loses. The firm and the staff lose because working on a job that is not a winner is upsetting; the job loses them money, and it could also cost the firm future work. The client is the big loser, since he or she does not receive a first-rate design.

You will not produce the job you want if you see the firm is losing money. Plan for variables. If the client wants an exceptionally high-level job, this may require additional research and development time to determine just what is needed.

When we do things free of charge, clients see no value in what we do.

Pricing, designing, and managing interior design is different than in any other design discipline. Although we can learn from the examples of the other practices, we are not the same. Interior designers expect to spend time doing finely detailed work. Often architects or other design professionals take on interior design and detail it just as they would an architectural project. This can only work for a very architectural project.

Know the job thoroughly and develop it with care. There is no quick sell today. Before you even think about estimating a project, define precisely what it entails, using a checklist similar to the Design Service Outline. A detailed project evaluation, documented at the precontract phase, can also help clients understand just what your design services encompass and the costs involved. They can see that additional items will require an additional contract or fees, depending upon the proposal.

Know the job plan so that you can structure it for a good quality design process. The Design Service Outline helps in defining the job, the services to be rendered, and the scheduling. You should process and complete this form, and then review it with the others who will be involved in the project. It is important to have the project manager, or a person responsible for programming the project, assist in preparing this outline and the costing-out of the project. This enables him or her to understand both the project and its goals.

This effort to define a project will permit you to examine the total project carefully. You will then know how to quote on it and also whether it is an appropriate job for you.

The Art of the Estimate

Estimating is difficult. The ability to prepare good proposals and estimates is an art, but good up-front review and coordination make it achievable. Carefully defining and qualifying a project is the best way to determine the appropriate charging methods. Design firms usually invest large amounts of time on these efforts; a week or more is not unusual for a larger project. It is much better to invest a week's labor to be sure that the job is right for the firm and priced correctly, than it is to take the wrong job and risk losing six months of fees.

Learn as much as you can about the client's past experiences in buying design so that you can present your proposal with references he or she understands. Ask staff members to estimate the time they will need for their parts of the projects, and compare their estimates with past records of similar projects as a safeguard. Some staff members tend to underestimate, while others are more accurate. The person preparing the estimate will have to make adjustments accordingly.

Obviously, the time scheduled can affect the cost of the project. The way your proposal is written strongly dictates the management style for the project. If your proposal catalogs all the processes that are to be done, then your project management list is almost complete. You know exactly who is going to do what when, and approximately how long it will take. Without the project plan in place, it is almost impossible to make an appropriate estimate. As you write your estimates and your proposal, try to do so in a fashion that will make later programming easy.

There are no official sources for standard fee scales for design work. Magazines occasionally publish lists of what has been charged, but these lists are not always accurate or believable.

When creating a quotation, work it out in several different ways and compare them. Use different methods to arrive at these figures; a square-foot price; a dollar volume price of the estimated furnishings and finishing costs, plus a percentage; and an hourly estimate of the professional time that will be needed to handle the project. Then use the method, or combination of methods, that is most suitable.

Compare your estimates with other similar projects you've done. How did you quote those projects? What was the time invested, and what were the end results? This is very helpful, because we can recognize some of the problems and difficulties that can arise in the current project. We'll know how to handle them from similar projects in the past. Do a value judgment on the current project, considering all the issues. Then determine the appropriate fee, based on that judgment.

Before beginning estimations on any project, you need to:

1. Define the scope of the work. What needs to be done? What position will you play? What kind of project is it? Are there any high-liability issues? Is the project one that will require a lot of research, or is it a job you can manage comfortably? How prepared is your firm for this project? If your specialty is banks, and you've done hundreds of jobs for banks, you have all the procedures in place. Therefore, you have standards to pull from. The overall project should move with ease. If banks are not your specialty, you haven't designed one for years, the job will be much more difficult and will require additional time. You'll need to compare the effort you'll have to put into a project you're not experienced with to that of an experienced firm to calculate the fee. You should determine whether this project is right for you altogether, let

alone what the opportunities are for completing it with great skill and compensation.

Check out the job. If it is your type of job, it is worth putting effort into the proposal and into the presentation. If it is not the type of job that is right for your firm, then don't waste your time writing a proposal.

2. Determine the expected quality of the project. Does it require high-quality finishing details, or is it simpler? What kind of quality has the client received on other projects?

3. Evaluate the design team. The architect, design professionals, contractors, and other professionals who have been selected will affect you and your team.

4. Consider the schedule. Is it a fast-track job, or is it one that will take several years to complete? Review your proposal with the design professionals who will work with you on the project, for feedback and time estimates. This personalizes their investment in the project, and they will feel greater responsibility to complete it within the period of time they specify.

5. Investigate the regulations and codes that apply to the project. Are there many city and state codes or corporate standards that must be met?

6. Assess your competition. How does your firm compare with other firms bidding for the job?

7. Predict what you will gain from the project. Can you make a profit on this project? How much risk is involved? Will the time commitments or other restrictions on this project jeopardize your firm's profit opportunities on other projects?

As you consider each job, look at it in terms of the benefits you can expect to accrue from it. Balance your financial expectations and the amount of time you expect to invest in the job. Also consider the marketing value of the job. We have all done jobs that were not overly profitable but later brought us several jobs that were.

Calculate what this job means to your studio. Every now and then it is worth taking a job without much profit if it offers other benefits. It may offer an introduction to a specialty, give you an opportunity to test the waters. When considering entering this type of situation, do so with your eyes open.

If you want to change your specialty, you may find that you need to gain some credentials within the field. This may mean taking a project at a lower fee or even without a fee in order to gain background and experience in this specialty.

8. Evaluate the client. Is he or she accustomed to working with an interior designer? Has he or she had experience either with your firm or with other firms? What kind of decision maker is the client? How many meetings do you expect to have? How many alterations are going to be required? What kind of rapport do you have with the client? Are you going to get along easily, or will it be difficult for you?

Basic Methods of Compensation

There are many ways of charging, and the interior design field varies considerably from the architectural field. Normally, architectural projects have a higher dollar volume than interior design projects, although labor and detailing on interior design projects are far more extensive.

In my experience, the most profitable projects are generally those that have a mixed method of charging. Many interior designers charge a straight hourly rate. Others charge an additional percentage on each item purchased or keep a percentage of the cost of the total purchases. Some discount the retail price; others add to it. There are so many equations for how to charge that it is almost impossible to give a designer a guideline without reviewing his or her own requirements and expenses.

Hourly rates fall within a wide range and vary considerably. Right now the field is more competitive than it has been, and some rates have even decreased. So, while some interior designers charge $100 to $150 an hour, and others, $250 to $500, still others claim to receive much higher rates, such as $1000 to $2500 per hour. But one wonders how many hours they're actually selling.

Some firms believe that charging by the hour is the best and safest way to charge. It's safe because you charge for what you do, and if you can find a client who won't set a limit, this is great. On the other hand, very few firms acquire great wealth by charging by the hour, especially in today's market.

To calculate your cost per hour, look at the costs for each employee, your overhead, and other expenses. How many billable hours do you have per week? Generally, if people are working a normal forty-hour week, they probably are billing about thirty to thirty-five hours. There are design studios that require that if designers are to be paid forty hours per week, they must bill forty hours per week. Either they're cheating or adjusting their time somewhat, or they're working a lot of overtime that doesn't go on their time cards. It's hard to bill forty hours if you're working forty hours. In fact, it's almost impossible. Look at your situation. How many hours per week are you billing out of your studio? Can this be improved realistically? Are you generating income from anything other than hourly rates? It's very difficult to run a studio and to cover all overhead costs strictly on an hourly rate, unless you have a very large studio.

The most profitable studios in our country have fewer than five or more than fifty people. It's very difficult to run mid-sized companies profitably. Creativity requires a lot of coordination, which makes mid-sized companies difficult to manage.

When a company is larger, it can afford a high-quality management person. In larger firms, it's normal for the top person, the CEO or the principal whose job is primarily marketing and managing, to have few or no billable hours. Certain studios structure themselves that way. They feel that it takes a certain number of people to generate the business to keep the others busy.

Review your structure and your staff to fit what is practical for your area. Even if you don't charge by the hour, keep close tabs on exactly how many hours you're putting into a project. Then you will know what you should be charging and what profits are actually being generated by that type of job.

ESTABLISHING YOUR OVERHEAD COSTS

Today, overhead expenses can vary considerably. Have your accountant or business manager calculate your overhead number so that you can determine what multiplier is appropriate to cover your overhead. This usually does not include any direct expenses, which are also billed to the client. Direct expenses normally include blueprints; reproductions; illustrated drawings; models; all of your travel expenses; postage; and freight. Some firms charge a percentage for these direct expenses to minimize the bookkeeping.

Review all overhead costs, or fixed expenses, such as:

- Rent
- Taxes and licenses
- Insurance
- Utilities
- Telephones
- Advertising
- Marketing
- Office expenses
- Automobiles
- Dues and subscriptions
- Loan payments
- Management personnel whose time is devoted to business development or management
- Nonbillable support staff
- Consulting
- Education
- Professional fees
- Resource library

Time-Based Fees

These are structured in several different ways. This is a safe and basic way of charging. However, because the clients may be concerned about overall cost, there are often limits or restrictions put on this fee. If the client is accustomed to working with your firm, then an open-ended contract may be okay with him or her.

To determine your multiplier, add DPE (Direct Personnel Expenses) (refer to the *Interior Design Business Handbook* for details).

$$\text{Hourly rate} + \text{Benefits} = \text{DPE}$$

Add in your overhead expenses (see box for details). Your accountant will help you establish a percentage that must be added to the DPE.

Third, add in your proposed profit.

Time is calculated at: DPE × Multiplier of usually 3 to 3.5 × DPE. Today some firms are working on as low a multiplier as 2.5 to 2.7 percent.

Time and Expenses, Open-Ended

This fee for a project, based on time and expenses, is among the safest and most profitable ways of quoting if you can negotiate it as open-ended with no limits.

Time and Expenses with Upset Limit

This is time and expenses with a "not to exceed" or a guaranteed maximum. This type of fee gives the client a comfortable advantage, but it can be costly to a design firm. Only very experienced firms can be confident of making a profit when using this method of charging. If you use more time, it is your loss. If you use less time, then you are also not paid, so it is your loss again. This contract must be carefully written to demonstrate specifically what work is to be done.

Time and Expenses, Estimated Amount

This is a safer method, charging for your time and expenses within an estimate based on a scheduled estimate of time. The advantage is that this type of fee is more flexible. If the job ends up being more complex than you had anticipated, there is at least a range or a structure for covering some extra charges.

The way you charge can limit or increase your profits. If your rates cover only time and expenses, and you are paid by the hour, you have not risked much. You know that your profit is built into your multiplier and that you will be reimbursed for all expenses. This is an up-front agreement. While this method is safe, though, it offers no change for a great profit. Unless you have your multiplier and your firm structured appropriately, this can be a difficult way to make good money.

Fixed Fee or Straight Design Fee

Many firms that know their area of specialty charge straight design fees. These may or may not include extra costs such as prints, travel, and so on. Today more and more jobs are don on a fixed-fee basis. The designers prepare designs, write specifications, and may or may not oversee the project. They may be responsible for all or only one or two parts of the job. This works well in specialty areas, in which firms know the project and the client very well. It can be very profitable if managed properly. Without great experience there is always a risk.

Per-Square-Foot Charge

Square-footage charges are becoming more popular. At one time they related principally to space planning. Now, many designers who are doing the finishes for new buildings, whether residential or commercial, charge on a square-footage basis. Since square footage is very familiar to clients, they understand this system of charging. Clients have been told by their contractors that their building is going to cost so many dollars per square foot; therefore, they realize that this is a small percentage of their total investment and find this system is very user-friendly.

Rewards of Value-Based Fees

Value-based fees are one of the most popular fees today, especially for those who are very familiar with a specialty. They know exactly how long a project is going to take and how to expedite it efficiently. The person who can complete a project fast deserves to be paid equally, or even more than the person who took much longer to provide a project of lesser or equivalent quality. Your experience in that specialty may mean that you do a better job in forty hours than another firm can do in seventy. I suggest you charge according to the value of the project, rather than an hourly fee.

Retail or Contracted Price

The retail or contracted method of charging means the design firm is responsible for delivering the project and all products for a set fee or a given price. At one time, the term for this was "retail." It meant that designers charged a standard retail markup. Today, the most often used term is "set or contract price," since markups vary considerably. This price may include all materials needed, as well as the delivery charges and any other costs required to complete the project.

The markups on this method of charging vary according to the requirements for the procurement and installation of the furnishings. The responsibilities that the design firm takes on determine the amount charged or the markup.

Design-Concept Fee

This fee is a set amount for developing the initial design concept. The fee is paid for ideas or the development of the conceptual objectives of a project. Compensation is usually on a contracted or a lump-sum basis, because it is the core of the design. Some firms may charge on an hourly or per-diem basis, or include the concept as a phase of the total project.

This fee varies considerably, depending on the design specialty or the firm's style of working.

This method of charging has become very popular. Creativity is something most if not all clients consider very valuable. They can purchase furniture in many different ways, but they want an outstanding and creative design, so they're more than willing to pay a considerable fee for the talent and effort of designers.

Many designers were initially forced to use the design-concept fee but now choose to use it, since they find it more professional and more profitable.

Today, concept development is often easy to sell for a good price, since it is something clients know they can't do themselves. Clients want a great job—something different—and expect to pay high-level fees for that special-quality job.

At one time, firms would use this as a loss leader, keeping the design-concept fee low, to enable them to build a relationship with the client and sell the rest of the project. Today, in this very competitive world, this often backfires. Designers today find that clients are very willing to pay an appropriate fee for a design concept. Many design firms find that this fee is the best profit on the project, since so little profit is generated in selling merchandise.

Designers today are finding that this up-front area, which has sizzle, is what must generate the profit.

We must charge in areas where clients are willing to pay. Even though we know that the project management may be the key to this particular job, we may have to take a lesser fee for this phase because the clients think it's not of great value. So often it's necessary to garner additional fees in the concept or other phase to cover the costs of completing the project appropriately and efficiently.

Design-Concept Fee Plus Percentage—Mixed Fees

Some firms charge a design-study fee plus a percentage of the cost of furnishings, whether purchased directly from the firm or from other sources. This fee will vary according to the size of the project and the various responsibilities the firm handles on the project. For mid-sized to smaller residential or residentially detailed contract work, the percentages usually run somewhere between twenty-five and fifty percent of the cost of merchandise.

On residential work and small contract jobs, many designers charge a design-concept fee plus a percentage of the cost of the items that are part of the design. This percentage may apply to construction, furniture, art work, and accessories.

Percentage of Cost

Charging a percentage based on cost (or a percentage off the list price) was very popular in the contract field, especially with respect to office furnishings. Clients are accustomed to this type of fee. If you mark up an item by twenty-five percent and the client is charged for receiving, warehousing, and so on, the totals are within a few dollars of those charged for offering a typical twenty percent off the list, which is the norm. Sometimes it's not just a question of how you calculate your quotes but what clients are accustomed to seeing. They may think that a discount off retail is much better than a markup based on cost.

Percentage of Total Cost

An interior designer can provide his or her complete services—including furnishings and labor—at cost, adding a fee based on a percentage of the total cost. With this method the design firm makes all purchases and passes all discounts, commissions, and savings onto the client. The client thus obtains merchandise at a wholesale price, plus the designer's fee. This fee will vary considerably, depending on the type of work being performed. Obviously, the larger the job, the smaller the percentage of the fee must be. When firms charge an hourly fee plus a percentage of the cost, the client needs to be clearly informed that project management and follow-up on problems usually represent a large portion of the fee—from one-third to one-half of the total.

Fee Plus Percentage of Savings

This fee may be based on any one of several other methods: straight fee, hourly, and so on plus a percentage of savings. For example: If the project cost is estimated at $500,000, and you are able to bring it in for $440,000, the owner may agree to split the difference with you on a 50/50 basis. More of these incentive programs are being developed because clients can see and understand their value. This method makes it worthwhile for the interior designer to try to plan the project in a price-effective way.

Value-Based Fees

Value-based or straight design fees are based on what this job is worth in a particular market. In a very competitive market, you may have to develop ways of completing projects quickly to stay competitive.

Clients like to know how much a project will cost. Whether we are talking about residential or contract work, I think that a straight, or a value-based, fee is best for the client, and best for the design firm. Of course, it's only good if you know exactly what you're doing, which is why experience and the information gathered from extensive interviews as presented in the Design Service Outline are so important. You must establish exactly what you are doing on this project, and you need experience to determine the appropriate costs.

Value-based fees (or value-oriented fees) are similar to straight design fees but are sold according to value. Some projects have special value, in that they are not routine but have distinctive appeal. For Example: Experts who know the fine points of a particular type of design can do great things because they know the specialty inside and out. They can also do it faster and at lower cost than a general-practice firm. They are due the same fee, or even more, than a general-practice firm. After all, they do a better job. This type of charging should be the aim of a firm that has the ability and the management process to ensure high-level, creative design work in a specialized area.

A value-oriented fee commands a lump sum for a particular project. Lump-sum fees are usually profitable and often the best way of charging when the firm has done a lot of similar projects, knows the client, and has a good idea of the anticipated time expenditures. Designers who deal in specialties generally work on this basis, because they have certain parts predesigned and can therefore complete a job very cost-effectively.

The best way of charging is with value-oriented fees. This has a high risk but also offers excellent opportunities for profit. If you understand the project and you run an efficient design firm, this method can be controllable and profitable. If the project is in an area with which you are unfamiliar, however, it can prove to be a loss.

Today, many design firms combine methods. They may charge a time plus expenses fee for developing a concept, then set a fixed fee for the final phases once the project is determined. Some charge a fixed fee for the concept development plus a percentage of cost of merchandise purchased.

Often when companies miscalculate and are trying to make up for their losses, the job suffers. Look at the project. Determine what it takes to complete the job according to your highest standards, and then calculate your fee accordingly. There are consultants who can help you with this. I help many people to calculate and compare fees in different specialties. Have your fee structure reviewed at least once a year, or at any point when you change the types of jobs you're doing or your specialty. It's always interesting to see what other firms are doing and if they're being appropriately compensated.

Retail or Specialty Companies

Today, traditional furniture stores are gradually being replaced by specialty stores or design galleries. Many clients want to buy a product, and retail organizations respond to that need. With good design service, too, these businesses can be outstanding.

Some designers use a retail shop as a marketing tool; it is a comfortable way for a new client to get to know the designer and still feel in control. The retail method enables a client to think that he or she knows exactly how much the whole project will cost; many residential clients understand product costs rather than fees. To the client who wants to have fun buying, this method will always remain attractive.

Retail or specialty companies usually have better buying methods for a specific group of items. Since they deal with a limited number of resources, they have higher purchasing power. This enables them to provide items at a better price, faster, and with fewer delivery problems than a typical design firm. They have chosen their preferred vendors, given them a large quantity of business, and therefore can expect certain considerations.

Designers as Purchase and Installation Companies

A firm may have one division that designs and then another that purchases, or it may have only one division that purchases or purchases/installs. This is prominent in the hospitality and other contract fields.

> ## KEYS TO SUCCESS
> Keep your methods of charging simple, clear, and easy to calculate. This makes it easy for clients to understand.
> Give yourself a financial base sufficient to allow for quality design development. It takes time to be truly creative—to really do a great job.
> Design a profitable, but fair, structure that allows for flexibility when variables occur. A project changes as it grows.
> Plan and aim to feature this client as a lifelong patron.

No matter how you decide to charge, structure your fees so they're easy for you to manage. Look at your services and what you are offering right now, and take note of the areas in which have problems. Can you reorganize those portions of your fee structure to make it simpler for you to manage and easier for the client to understand?

Billing Process

Review your way of calculating costs to determine how you can structure it to complement your design work. This will give you some profit to reinvest in your practice to ensure that you can maintain your standards.

Mixing fee styles—fee plus percentage or hourly rate plus percentage—often works for higher-level profitability. The design stars can dictate their fees, but most of us must find ways to make our fees palatable.

Your system of charging can make or destroy a job. Consider billing a client as certain parts of projects are completed. Consider the style of installation when arranging billing terms. Will the job be done in parts or all at once? Your structure for payment must be complementary. Look at your costs and your overhead, and also develop an understanding of what your clients are accustomed to seeing within this market. Then try to tailor your fees accordingly. There are consultants who will help independent designers with this process.

Schedule Payments

The way you structure client payments on a project is critical to the ease of managing the job. Have the clients pay for phases rather than by the hour. For example:

PHASE	EXPECTED % of FEE USED	CHARGE FOR
Data collection & evaluation; research and development	15%	20%
Design concept	15%	30%

Although you've invested only thirty percent of your time, you've also contributed your many years of experience and your creative talent. Clients are usually very comfortable with this arrangement, because they consider this part of the design project to be the most important. Building this way will assist with your cash flow. It will also help you cover some of the expenses for areas such as project management, which clients consider easy and therefore object to paying for its true value.

Note: You have fifty percent of the fee, but you have spent only thirty percent of the time. If your clients are comfortable with this, and most firms find that they are, you have a good cash flow. If anything should happen to the project, you can walk away without feeling quite as injured as you would have without this financial cushion.

As you follow through the other phases, you'll see the amount of your percentage reverse:

Project management	35%	25%

Clients think this area is easy and often object to paying for its true value. However, you know that project management is important; therefore, you want to do it in a way that ensures the finished project comes out exactly as planned. So allow for this loss up-front.

Make a list of all areas to be worked on and the appropriate percentage of time to expend. Then create a pricing sheet for the client based on phases completed and fee expected. This pricing sheet makes it easier for the client to understand when you'll be collecting and provides a safeguard.

Be Prepared with Financing Arrangements

Today we don't have to provide as many financial arrangements as we did in the past. If people need financing, most of them use their home-equity accounts. However, there are occasions when it's advisable to have credit cards or other types of financing available for clients. It's amazing how many design firms now accept credit cards. Clients love this. They're now getting credit for their mileage.

Some firms have earned more from their financial arrangements than from any other part of their business. To deal successfully with client finances, you need to establish good relationships with one or more banking institutions. There are many ways to develop financial structures and payment systems, and you must have them available for residential and corporate projects. Sometimes having financing available makes the difference between doing part of a project, or finishing it exactly as you feel it should be done.

In today's market, financing is a changing system, so check with your banks regularly—at least every three months—to be sure you still have those options available. Credit card payments can often help your cash flow. Consider your type of client and which system of payment is appropriate.

Credit cards are accepted by many design firms. This credit system is based on your client's credit; the designer does not have any responsibility to pay if the client fails to pay. These cards allow clients to charge any purchase made in your firm. This ensures immediate payment to both the suppliers and the design firms.

Find a system of financing projects that works for you. Don't take this on yourself unless you are prepared to be in the finance business; most of us do not have the revenue—nor do we want to be in the banking business.

Deposits, Retainers, or Advanced Payment

Traditionally, deposits or retainers were received on all items as well as on design services. Legally we were encouraged to use the term "retainer," because a deposit required us to keep each client's monies in individual escrow accounts.

Today the systems have changed and we can merge the monies. But the term "retainer" still seems more professional. Most designers receive a minimum of a fifty percent retainer on design fees, and from fifty to ninety percent on products. Many design firms are forced to pay for products in advance and therefore want to use the client's money to finance the projects. The amount of the retainers and the system of payment vary a great deal, depending on which part of the country you're working in. Often some smaller communities require greater trust than would ever be expected in larger cities. You need to know your clients and your community's expectations in establishing the format of your payment system.

Adjustments

At times, for various reasons, designers are either forced to, or elect to, adjust billable hours or other items charged to a client. When you adjust your billing, be sure the clients are aware of it. Stamp the invoice in red so they can't help noticing that you gave them consideration. The stamp may say in large print: "Priority Client—No Charge" or "Priority Client—Reduced Fee."

Even your billing system can be used for marketing and sales development. Enclose a reply card with your invoice asking for comments and feedback. This encourages clients' comments but should never replace your personal follow-up program.

Billing Tips

Rewards: Add a client advantage to the fee schedule. State the amount of time you expect client communications will take. If the job is easier because client communication time (not design or staff time) is shorter, you may offer a deduction. For example:

> Design fee will include_____(set fee).
> State all design phases.
> Review and consultation time—20 hours. Any additional time will be charged at the following rates. If the meeting time is less than 20 hours, you will be credited at the same rate.

This is an area clients can control. If they're prepared and make decisions at correct times, you'll find your work is easier. The benefit to the client is a lower consultation charge.

Another way to achieve the same client control is to say, "We expect the design planning phase of your project to take three months. If the support information and decision-making processes permit faster completion (within 60 days), the fee will be reduced by $10,000."

Start-up fee: If a project is delayed or stopped for any reason, a start-up fee or delayed fee may be needed to cover increased costs. (Refer to the chapter on contracts.)

Estimate Within Range

The exact cost of a creative or unusual item is often difficult to estimate. We either have to add considerably to be sure we're covered, or give our clients a range, a to/from price. This is a more professional way of estimating, since we have no guarantee of the quantities or the number of hours that will be required in a project. An estimated range permits us to use our judgment to ensure that we give our clients the quality of product they deserve.

Quote projects on a to/from price basis so they can expect a project to cost in the range of, for instance, $150,000 to $170,000. Make the top range high enough so that you can be sure of bringing in the completed item for less. This gives you a cushion and makes you a hero if the item costs much less.

One year our accountant brought to our attention that the cost of merchandise purchased had increased eleven percent during that year. We had been used to very few increases in the prices of merchandise and had always given our clients a firm quotation on all merchandise they were purchasing from us. We found that we had quoted below our normal markup range while our cost of merchandise and delivery had *increased* eleven percent. This caused us to lose money on many of our projects.

When you buy merchandise, you often don't pay the listed price but the price for the item on the day it is shipped to you. This can vary considerably from the amount you originally estimated. You should try to allow a ten percent variance in your estimates. For example, when you expect something to cost $5000, you should quote $5000 to $5500 so you have some cushion in case there is an increase in price. If an item arrives in need of additional work or repair, you have the monies available to make adjustments and deliver the price just the way you want it. After all, the client *is* paying for your judgment.

Charging for the Initial Interview

Should there be a charge for the initial interview? Whether you charge or not may depend on your geographic area and your type of practice. Many designers want to see the project first to determine if it's appropriate for their studios.

In other situations, designers realize their prospective clients are using an initial interview to gather information to help them with their projects. In such cases, they may charge a minimal fee. A designer in our Designers' Business Forum charges $1250, which includes four hours of time. Another designer charges $750 for an hour-and-a half interview and a summary of suggestions about doing the project, plus the travel required to and from the site.

You need to look at your own experiences and determine just what works best for your studio. If you're going to charge for the initial interview, it's important to have an agreement ahead of time, and be sure your clients understand their commitments. In many instances, designers receive their fees in advance, or they're charged to a credit card.

Stating your policy in advance will save a lot of aggravation. After all, many prospective clients have never purchased design services of any kind before. They don't really know how to buy these services, so help them by giving them the price tag in advance.

Fees

Referral fees may come from many different suppliers. The first question is: Is it right for a designer to accept these additional fees if he or she is already charging a percentage? Designers may accept these fees if they're part of their contracts and are disclosed to the clients from the very beginning.

Profit Issues

The more creative or unusual the design specialty, the higher the profit can be. In today's interior design market, the jobs with the highest profit are usually those that are the most innovative. For firms to brand themselves as doing exceptional work in a particular specialty usually takes development and experience. But with the right branding schedule, design firms can position themselves to be well compensated for their creative efforts. When a firm develops skills in an unusual specialty, the profits increase. When competition enters the field, the profits start to drop until they reach the competitive rebidding stage. Then the firm either changes its specialty or loses its opportunity for good income.

Repackaging Your Services

There are three ways to get to the top of the heap. You can be truly innovative, which is the most difficult way. You can copy someone else at the top of the heap, which is also difficult. Or you can repackage your present types of services and give them a different name. By creating a new category of service, you make the fee scale more flexible. No one knows what the appropriate charge should be.

Find out what designers in your area are charging, and then decide what your rates should be. You need to compare your costs to the market. In some areas you are limited by what the competition charges, unless you provide service that no one else offers. In that case, you can name your own figure based on the value of the project.

No matter how you estimate your projects, the only way to be accurate is to make a comparison to your own past work. If you don't have a similar project for comparison purposes, then you need to speak with several other designers who have done similar jobs. For comparison, it is a good idea to figure the job several different ways and compare them—for example, per square foot versus hourly rate. This method can often pick up an error in your calculations.

When comparing a current project to a similar past one, keep in mind that you should be able to complete the new project faster because you have experience in that area. If you structure your firm properly, you can use this experience to your advantage and therefore have the opportunity to gain even higher fees. It's advisable to bring in a consultant to evaluate your charging system and make sure it's presented appropriately, considering your specialty.

Be sure your clients understand the value of what you're presenting. When we present a fee, and the client questions it, it's usually because he or she doesn't understand the value of what we're doing. If you have properly presented your offerings in a language the clients understand so that they realize the extensive efforts and responsibilities required by the project, they'll also understand the need for a considerable fee.

Negotiation

Negotiation is often part of the pricing. Know what range will, and will not, work for this project. If the fee must be reduced, know what can be modified, eliminated, or adjusted without putting your firm at a disadvantage. Let the client know what he or she will receive: prints, boards, specifications, or real products, for instance. Your client should be made aware of the way you charge and the way you handle finances. When you present a fee schedule or a quotation to clients, it's important to give an outline of all the services you will perform. If the client says the quotation is too high, you can indicate which areas can be eliminated.

Establishing a Designer's Hourly Billing Rate* Example

Salary per year	$35,000
Fringe benefits** (30% of salary)	$10,500
Direct personnel expense (DPE)	$45,500/49
	weeks = $928.507

Using a $2\frac{1}{2}$ to $3\frac{1}{2}$ percent multiplier, you can establish an appropriate billing rate as follows:

$2\frac{1}{2}$: $77.38 per hour
3: $92.85 per hour
$3\frac{1}{2}$: $108.33 per hour

---

* If a designer works an average of 40 hours per week, the usual number of chargeable hours is 30.
** When calculating fringe benefits, include holidays; sick leave; vacation; company-paid payroll taxes, FICA, workers' compensation; any company-paid health, dental, or vision insurance; and company-paid retirement plans.

CHAPTER 28

The Installation

The installation is a special opportunity to build a relationship. It takes place on the client's property. He or she can really see how much—or how little—you care. You resell a project to the client throughout its development. The way the installation is handled is key to obtaining additional work from the client, from his or her friends, and from other referrals. Since referrals make up a major portion of most design practices today, the way the client sees us is critical.

Organizing a polished installation takes time. Although we all prefer to do the complete installation at one time, it may not be your choice whether the installation is completed all at once, phased, or done a little bit at a time. But you can make the process less harrowing for the client in the way you organize and supervise the installers, and by anticipating problems.

Tell your contractors and craftspeople about the project so that they understand their roles and why things must be done in a certain way. To be sure they work well together, you should understand the processes involved in their jobs and program the way they are to work together. Go over the project with each craftsperson or delivery person about three weeks before the installation and again four days ahead.

When you schedule an installation with a contractor, visit his or her warehouse and take inventory of each item needed for the project. Often

249

contractors believe they're ready when in fact they have only ninety percent of what is needed—and that last ten percent can hold up your project. You must decide whether the contractor should go into the space without the necessary materials, hold off, or substitute.

Plan the installation so that each craftsperson and contractor can perform his or her role easily and with the least likelihood of damaging other parts of the project. This can be as simple as preventing a piece from being installed too soon.

If you are on a tight schedule, it can be cost-effective to have a well-paid project manager on site. This person may need to make decisions and adjustments to the project, because a space is rarely exactly what you expect.

Sometimes a client will say that his or her office can handle the installation; try to discourage this. It is a rare client who understands installation procedures, and it takes only one careless installer to mar a project that may have taken months or years of careful effort on your part.

Prepare the Site

Before the day of the installation, tell the building management the date and time you will start work and what your installation team will need. This can range from parking spaces and freight elevators to street closings. Hiring a traffic coordinator to direct people to a lot can be money well spent.

Check the site the day before installation to make sure it is clean and ready. Are the temperatures corect for installing carpet and other items? Is the HVAC system functioning properly? Have the ducts been cleared after construction?

Ask the client to avoid the site during the installation so that the person in charge is responsible and in full control. Specify appropriate times for the client to come and review or approve the process. It is vital for your firm that your representative be visibly in charge. Too often a contractor may point something out to the client, who, not knowing enough about the situation, may seem to approve. This allows the contractor to say, "But the client okayed it," should you object. All too often clients on-site during installations become overconcerned with inappropriate details and increase the cost of the installation.

Tips for a Smooth Installation

Be prepared. Go over the list of everything that is to be installed or done in the client's space. Make sure that it's done in an orderly fashion and that you have everything you need. Try to make your deliveries all at once, so that the client gets the full impact of the design.

For any installation, give the clients an approximate time—morning or afternoon—when the craftspeople will arrive. Don't keep them waiting if you can help it.

The behavior and appearance of the contractors and craftspeople you hire reflect on you. Send only people who have reasonably good personalities, who will show a little interest in the client and will be friendly enough to put them at ease. If the designer in charge cannot be present, be sure that there is at least one person there the client has met before and is comfortable with. This person can introduce the others. When your staff and contractors enter a client's space, they should appear appropriately well groomed and neat. Since they are there to work, a three-piece suit is inappropriate, but so are filthy overalls at the beginning of the day.

Clients believe that their space is important. They want it kept clean and in order. Playing loud music, smoking, eating, and drinking in the installation area are out of the question. Let your installers know your ground rules before they reach the site. On a large project, create an area where they may take breaks, and see that it is cleaned up before you leave. Having coffee or sodas on hand and arranging for delivery of lunches can save you time and money.

Respect the client's space, whether it is a residential or a commercial project. Put down floor mats and floorcoverings when working. Ask the installers to be neat, or at least to try not to make any messes that cannot be cleaned up before they leave the space.

Vacuum cleaners, brooms, dustcloths, garbage bags, materials for touch-ups and minor repairs, and a stain-removal kit should be part of your standard installation equipment. When your installation crew leaves a space, even though they may be back the next day, that space should be clean.

Even if there is a member of your staff on-site, ask each installer to call your office to confirm that he or she is on-site, and take note of the time. Make sure the installer also gives your office a status report on the site, especially if there are any difficulties. You might be told that the paperhanger isn't finished and won't be until the afternoon. Decide what you want the installer to do in the meantime. Adjustments to the installation schedule should be made by your office, not by the individual installers.

As each installer finishes for the day, he or she should call your office so that the time can be noted.

Installation Magic

Make a show out of that installation. Rent a red carpet for furniture delivery when installing a larger project. All too often these are projects under construction and may not be as clean as one would like. Red carpets are available from any of the rent-it-centers at a very moderate cost. Rent enough to run from the van into the building, and roll out the red carpet as you open the truck doors.

White glove delivery includes assigning booties or shoe coverings to the furniture movers so that they do not mar the carpets or other floors in the space. They should also wear white gloves to ensure that no fingermarks or smudges are left on any piece of furniture or fabric.

Cover each piece of furniture with blankets and padding. This not only protects it, but camouflages the shapes. No one sees the furniture until it is in place and the wrapping is removed.

This kind of installation will have a great impact on the neighborhood. Everyone will wonder what is happening at that office building or that residence. Your showmanship calls attention to your firm and sets it apart from any others in the area. Be sure the space is perfectly clean, and that all pieces are perfect and at their best.

Ask your clients to give you the freedom of the property that day, and request that all their staff or family be out of the building during the installation. Schedule a time for their return, say, 4:00 P.M. Depending on the client, you might serve a nice tea, or a bottle of champagne and appropriate refreshments. Whatever you do, make the installation special. Have flowers. Have an extra gift for the clients. Leave something on their desk that shows that your firm cares.

Installation and service during a project really build client rapport.

Include a Maintenance Manual

Years ago there was an ad for Scotchgard showing a woman with a garden hose cleaning her chair. Would you clean an upholstered chair with a garden hose? To ensure that the client understands what constitutes everyday use and that the space maintains its optimum quality, and to safeguard your liability position, it is important to see that the client or end-user receives appropriate instructions on how to use and maintain the installed products.

The budgets we work with are high, and some items we specify are the result of technology so new that perhaps only the manufacturer and furniture designer completely understand them. For instance, very often the instructions to an active ergonomic desk chair are attached by the manufacturer to the chair itself. All too often these instructions are lost, either during installation or by the first user, while the chair remains in the space for many years.

A maintenance manual should provide the central location for documents and instruction booklets. It gives the client a reference, which can lessen the possibility of real problems due to misuse of the furniture. Also include any other information you know about the piece: how it should be handled, moved, or adjusted. For landscape furniture, instructions for future disassembly and reassembly are important.

Cleaning instructions also belong in the maintenance manual. These are furnished by our resources, who may state that specific cleaners are required to maintain flameproof or fire-retardant finishes, especially. Some pieces are sold with guarantees and restrictions. These too belong in the maintenance manual. It's acceptable to clean certain types of lawn furniture by turning loose a chimpanzee with a garden hose, but such treatment could invalidate the warranties and guarantees of most of the furniture and furnishings we specify.

In this manual you will want to list any preferred maintenance people, as well as red-flagging any issue, item, or potential problem. Next to each red-flagged item, tell the clients whether they should check with the design firm, the dealer/distributor, or the manufacturer. For example, we installed a very elaborate stained-glass ceiling that was best cleaned only by someone familiar with the structure. In the maintenance manual we specifically named the person indicated, how the client could get in touch with him or her, and how often we recommended the item be cleaned.

What the Manual Should Contain

The information that goes in to this maintenance manual should come from the manufacturers as much as possible; that way the designer acts as a vehicle for the distribution of information but is not directly responsible for the durability, wearability, or breakdown of any particular part or component. All guarantees and warranties are automatically passed on to the client, as well as certificates for flameproofing or special finishes. This information may save you from being blamed for matters beyond your control.

Whether you present your maintenance manual on a CD or in paper form is up to you. Most clients give much more priority to something they can physically put on a shelf. But you know your clients, and you know what's most comfortable for them. Keep a copy of everything that you send your clients, whether in a computer-generated file or paper form, so you have it for reference in case the clients lose it. Also, if a problem arises, you'll know exactly what information you've given them so you can follow up appropriately.

In some instances, you may want to have the instructions photocopied onto standard pages. When you do this, be sure you also include the original document.

A maintenance manual not only lessens your liability, but is a good public relations and marketing tool. The manual states what can legitimately be expected of certain items in terms of wear and probable length of time before they will need to be replaced. It gives clients a resource and a direction whenever they have additional needs, which means that they will be familiar with your office and prepared to call it when they add, change, or alter their interior space. The client will know that if something happens to a chair after four or five years of use, it is not unusual but expected—and that there is an established maintenance procedure.

You should supply a maintenance manual to the client at installation time or immediately thereafter. It should list each and every piece of furniture, equipment, furnishings, and/or material incorporated in that project—including carpeting, wallcoverings, draperies, window treatments, furnishings, textiles, and lamps. A good manual lists handling precautions and cleaning and maintenance instructions, as well as the correct wattage for the lighting. It also includes the names, addresses and phone numbers of other companies to be called for service or additional instructions for adequate maintenance.

Maintenance Review Service or Updating

Some design firms make a maintenance review service available to their clients. The design firm visits the project every six to twelve months, depending on the type of project, to review the installation. They determine whether any changes are needed and what type of maintenance is necessary. At this time, the design firm can update the accessories and any other elements that need to be improved to keep the space state of the art.

Design is a service business, and we need to be able to give our clients ongoing service. Our clients have invested in their interiors and want the appearance of their interiors to reflect their investment.

Maintenance manuals are a service and a way to encourage an ongoing and profitable relationship. The maintenance manual reminds clients of the designer who worked on their project, and that you take care of their interior spaces. This is, without question, a great marketing tool.

Installing a great job and maintaining it in good condition is the core of the client-designer relationship.

Follow-Up

After the project is finished, if you want the client to continue to be your client and not someone else's, find a way to keep in touch.

During the project you've been in constant touch with the client, sometimes on a daily basis. Don't stop cold when the project is finished. Instead, you need a period of "weaning" during which you may call every week. It is still a scheduled call, and gradually you decrease the frequency to every other week, every three weeks or, four weeks.

PAST CLIENT FOLLOW-UP SUMMARY				
Client:			Contact Person: Position:	
Address:			Phone No.:	
Finish Date:	Job:	Type (room or building):		Size:
Last Contact Date:	Client's Comments:		Follow-through:	

Source © Design Business Monthly

Figure 28-1

Later on, you should be in touch with past clients at least four to six times a year, every single year. Send birthday cards, articles you think they might enjoy, and updates on what your firm is doing. Try to find ways to promote your firm while also making the clients feel they are still important to you.

Use the Past Client Follow-Up Summary (Figure 28-1) to document your contacts. This follow-up process will reap many rewards.

Postoccupancy Reviews

Schedule postoccupancy reviews for thirty days, ninety days, six months, and a year after the project is installed. You may continue the reviews longer, depending on the project. Send a representative to the project to check on how well it is working. Document it. If there are problems, you'll know about them immediately. If everything looks fine and seems to be performing as it should for a year, and then a client calls and says, "This never worked," you know differently. You were there; you reviewed it with them. Everything functioned just beautifully at the time of the reviews.

CHAPTER 29

Learning

B eing a good designer today means continual education. What should you know to make yourself the designer you want to be? There is only one way to find out—and that's to expose yourself to various learning opportunities. According to Peter M. Singe in his book *The Fifth Discipline*, for a company to be successful today, it must be a learning environment; education has to be part of the company structure.

Learning needs to be a part of the whole company's program. Further, to be successful, learning has to start with the top management structure. If the people in management are not ready to learn, if they don't recognize that they need new material, it's very hard to convince the employees they should take their Saturdays or their off-time and dedicate it to education. So it must start with the top.

Everyone needs to be exposed to new material. Everyone within a firm has a role to play in marketing and selling that firm, so marketing and sales training is for everyone. Just as we want and need to learn more about design issues, we also need to be exposed to different methods of building client relationships and doing sales and marketing. Our clients are studying. Our competition is studying. Our clients know when we're doing our job correctly.

257

Learning experiences also help prevent burnout. They refresh and renew the excitement and motivation we felt as students. Schedule regular growth experiences for your staff to get out and learn new material. Promote an environment that encourages learning in your firm; make it an important issue.

How do you get this training? Attend seminars or arrange to have a coach or a consultant come in. The important thing is to make the investment in the type of learning structured to teach your people what they need to know. An outside specialist can say things to your staff that would not be accepted as well if they came from you or other people in the firm with whom they work on an everyday basis. So often, this outside consultant can really cut through to the issues of concern.

To determine what your firm needs to learn, it's a good idea to write down your objectives to see what the needs and problems are. Review your goals. What additional knowledge or abilities do you need to meet them? What is your competition going to be, and how can you best compete? What are the major issues that you need to improve, and how can you acquire this information?

Define the type of information you need to determine the best way to acquire it. Is it something you can learn by attending a local seminar in your community? Your competition may also be at that seminar. You can learn a lot from the questions your competitors ask and the comments they make as to their approach and knowledge base. Or, do you need to go outside of your community to attend a seminar where you have interaction with other firms from other cities? By attending this type of seminar, you are exposed to other companies and other communities. You get a wider view. The networking at seminars is also very valuable.

Encourage your staff to make the most of their seminar experiences by requesting that anyone who is sent to a seminar or a program keep an outline of exactly what he or she learned, and another outline of how that information can be used specifically in your firm. What can be used now, and what applies to future situations? Ask for a priority list.

Schedule a special staff meeting at which the person who attended the seminar can tell the rest of your firm about it. This accomplishes several things. First, it encourages the seminar attendee to listen carefully. Second, reviewing this information for presentation reinforces the learning.

Learn from Others

We can't originate everything ourselves, and sometimes our ways of doing things may be more complex than is necessary. So, look at how other people are doing things and borrow from them. It's faster to polish someone else's method than to invent a new technique. Find the best person you can to emulate. Take what you can from that person's ideas and processes; then polish them and develop them to fit your own way of working.

When you need to develop a special technique, ask other designers if they know anyone who has had a similar problem and how that person handled it. Most of the issues in this book are the result of questions designers asked me, which I later reviewed with many professional consultants. The suggestions have been tested in several design firms and, when they work, recorded so they could be repeated.

Keep studying, researching, and learning. This is how we grow. This is why we have consultants; this is why we go to seminars: We need to know more about our field. Experience can teach us a lot, but it is much less expensive to find a consultant who has done it before and learn from him or her. It can build the speed of your progress considerably. Find people to whom you can relate and you enjoy being around, and learn from them.

> Learn from others. They know how they want to be treated.
>
> Demonstrate sincere caring. This is worth more than anything you can buy.
>
> Help your clients realize their great potential through appropriate interior design. Make them look great.
>
> Realize the excitement of knowledge. Study and learn. Improvement and success start with ability. Today, that takes constant training.
>
> Take the time necessary to build the proper relationships with clients. Only the right relationships will give you the basis for doing a great job.
>
> Our consultants, sources, and craftspeople are what make us. Without them, we cannot do interior design.
>
> Fortunately, you learned enough in school to get a job in design. But keeping that job depends on what you continue to learn from your current teachers, clients, consultants, sources, and craftspeople.

Designers' Business Forum

The Designers' Business Forum is a program developed to help designers, architects, and other creative professionals to establish their best opportunities in today's business environment. These businesses are needed and valued today, but they require a special structure and process to make them successful.

The Forum uses a design process, a system that creative people find familiar and user-friendly. It considers each person's special abilities and works to develop the best opportunities for growth and success for that individual's firm.

The program is highly participatory and interactive. You meet with other designers to share experiences. You benefit from regular personal contact with other creative people. Regular support is available to assist you with daily problems and the process of growing your business. Whenever you have a question or problem, call us first. We will assist you or find support for you. You are not alone.

If you're interested in growing your firm, you'll enjoy the Forum. You'll gain the opportunity to do better work, experience an easier process, earn a better income, and have more time for the pleasures of life.

Our goal is to raise the level of the design profession. Join us. Let's make it happen.

For more information on this program or other issues, contact:

Mary V. Knackstedt
2901 North Front Street
Harrisburg, PA 17110
Phone: 717-238-7548
Fax: 717-233-7374
Email: maryknackstedt@aol.com

Suggested Reading List

Capon, Noel. *The Marketing Mavens*. New York: Crown Business, 2007.

Carnegie, Dale. *How to Win Friends and Influence People*. New York: Pocket Books, 1981.

David, Stanley M. *Future Perfect*. Reading, MA: Addison Wesley Publishing, 1987.

DePree, Hugh. *Business as Usual*. Zeeland, MI: Herman Miller, 1986.

Friedman, Thomas L. *The World Is Flat: A Brief History of the 21st Century*. New York: Farrar, Straus and Giroux, 2006.

Gardner, Howard. *Five Minds for the Future*. Boston: Harvard Business School Press, 2006.

George, Bill, with Peter Sims. *True North: Discover Your Authentic Leadership*. San Francisco: Jossey-Bass, 2007.

Gitomer, Jeffrey. *The Little Red Book of Selling: 12.5 Principles of Sales Greatness*. Austin, TX: Bard Press, 2004.

Godin, Seth. *Free Prize Inside!: The Next Big Marketing Idea*. New York: Portfolio, 2004.

Godin, Seth. *The Purple Cow,*. New York: Portfolio Hardcover, 2003.

Godin, Seth. *The Dip: A Little Book That Teaches You When to Quit (and When to Stick)*. New York: Portfolio Hardcover, 2007.

Hanlon, Patrick. *Primal Branding: Create Zealots for Your Brand, Your Company, and Your Future*. New York: Free Press, 2006.

Harrington, H. James. *The Improvement Process: How America's Leading Companies Improve Quality*. New York: McGraw-Hill, 1988.

Healy, William J. and Marion Gottleib. *Making Deals: No-lose Negotiating—The New Standard*. New York: Simon & Schuster, 1990.

Johnson, Spencer and Ken Blanchard. *The One-Minute Manager*. New York: William Morris & Company, 1982.

Lane, Frank. *Killer Brands: Create and Market a Brand That Will Annihilate the Competition*. Avon, MA: Adams Media, 2007.

Malmo, John. *When on the Mountain There Is No Tiger, Monkey Is King*. Memphis, TN: Archer Malmo Inc., 2003.

Marcus, Stanley. *Minding the Store*. Boston: Little Brown & Company, 1979.

Marcus, Stanley. *Quest for the Best*. New York: The Viking Press, 1979.

Martin, Patricia. *Rengen: The Rise of the Cultural Consumer—And What It Means to Your Business*. Avon, MA: The Platinum Press Inc., 2007.

Naisbitt, John. *Mind Set!: Reset Your Thinking and See the Future*. New York: Collins, 2006.

Naisbitt, John, and Patricia Aburdene. *Megatrends 2000*. New York: William Morrow & Co., 1990.

Peters, Tom. *Leadership.* New York: DK Adult, 2005.

Peters, Tom. *Thriving on Chaos.* New York: Alfred Knopf, 1987.

Peters, Tom A. and Nancy Austin. *A Passion for Excellence.* New York: Random House, 1985.

Pollak, Jane. *Sole Proprietor.* Freedom, CA: The Crossing Press, 2001.

Singe, Peter M. *The Fifth Discipline: The Art & Practice of the Learning Organization.* New York: Doubleday, 1990.

Stanley, Dr. Thomas J. *Selling to the Affluent.* New York: McGraw-Hill, 1997.

Toffler, Alvin. *Powershift.* New York: Random House, 1985.

Toffler, Alvin and Heidi. *Revolutionary Wealth: How It Was Created and How It Will Change Our Lives.* New York: Alfred A. Knopf, 2006.

Wipperfurth, Alex. *Brand Hijack.* New York: Penguin Group, 2006.

Zemke, Ron and Dick Schaff. *101 Companies That Profit from Customer Care.* New York: NAL, Inc, 1989.

Index